BEST OF
Prairie Schooner

FICTION AND POETRY

Edited by Hilda Raz

University of Nebraska Press, Lincoln and London

© 2001 by the University of
Nebraska Press. All rights
reserved. Manufactured in the
United States of America. ⊗
Library of Congress
Cataloging-in-Publication
Data
Best of Prairie Schooner:
fiction and poetry / edited by
Hilda Raz.
p.   cm.
"A Bison original."
ISBN 0-8032-8972-3 (pbk. :
alk. paper)
1. American literature—20th
century.   I. Raz, Hilda.
II. Prairie Schooner.
PS535.5 .B49 2001
810.8'0054—dc21
00-059970
"𝒩„

Contents

Introduction

In 2001 the international literary quarterly *Prairie Schooner* entered its seventy-fifth year of continuous publication. We celebrate this astonishing fact with two volumes, an anthology of fiction and poetry, *Best of* Prairie Schooner: *Fiction and Poetry*, and a collection of essays, *Best of* Prairie Schooner: *Personal Essays*. The present editors inherited a journal whose contributors included Eudora Welty, Truman Capote, Meridel LeSueur, Jessamyn West, Willa Cather, Raymond Carver, Cyrus Colter, Tennessee Williams, Joyce Carol Oates, and many other familiar literary names, and whose early editorial staff included among others the young writers Weldon Kees and Loren Eiseley. The present editors also inherited a tradition of support for new writers as well as a passion for what's new in contemporary writing. The authors in this anthology represent an absent majority of contributors published in fifteen thousand pages over the past twenty years. Boundaries of space stand firm in the practical world of book publishing; we had limits on the number of pages to fill. With a few exceptions, only writers published in the past twenty years were considered for selection because the rights to publish this celebratory anthology have been ours for only twenty years. Before then we could not imagine we would need them, since most journals live and die in a decade and their readers are few. *Prairie Schooner's* success surprised us.

Daily practical concerns, especially funding, often distracted the staff. But early on the editors of *Prairie Schooner* took their lesson from *The Education of Henry Adams*, to consider opportunities rather than difficulties in publishing a literary journal. "The circulation . . . never exceeded three or four hundred copies, and the Review had never paid its reasonable expenses. Yet it stood at the head of American literary periodicals. . . . The difference is slight, to the influence of an author, whether he is read by five hundred readers, or by five hundred thousand;

if he can select the five hundred, he reaches the five hundred thousand." Early readers of the magazine included influential editors in New York where some of our contributors moved to pursue their careers. These editors selected pieces published in *Prairie Schooner* for inclusion in annual prize volumes, which helped increase the circulation. Since then the quarterly circulation of *Prairie Schooner* has grown to exceed twenty-five hundred copies and in the past ten years the size of the magazine has more than doubled. And, *mirabile dictu*, we are still paying our bills.

Generous donors now provide over twelve annual prizes for writers whose influence can best be determined by their contributors' notes in the back of each issue. We've published Nobel and Pulitzer Prize winners, MacArthur grant recipients, Guggenheim, Fulbright, and National Endowment for the Arts Fellows, Whiting Writer's Award winners, National Book Award and Lambda Prize recipients, and some of the best writing on the international literary scene. But for seventy-five years of continuous publication, our primary mission has been to publish the work of writers early in their careers. Our good fortune is that many of these writers have come to triumph and many of them are eager to continue to publish their work in *Prairie Schooner*. Longevity has its benefits. Cynthia Ozick told an interviewer, "It was extraordinary but because all that time I was a failure, I knew it was a mistake. I should have gone out into the world of periodicals. . . . Not to be published as a novelist until you are 37 years old is devastating. . . . Publish, publish whatever you can as early as possible." We are glad to be first on her list of publishers.

What is this thing, a literary magazine? In 1965 the late Karl Shapiro, winner of the Pulitzer Prize in poetry, iconoclast, and second editor of *Prairie Schooner*, described it as "the penultimate form of publication for literary works. A work printed in the literary magazine has only two destinations: the book or oblivion. And while the magazine itself is expendable, the book, no matter how bad, is not." At the Library of Congress conference on the literary magazine, Henry Rago, then editor of *Poetry* magazine, protested. "Hasn't [the literary magazine] also been traditionally, historically, a seedbed for talent? Surely it's damn good for a writer to be published and to be read by serious readers and serious writers whether or not his particular work is going to be put into hard cover. Then also magazine publishing perhaps serves the function of creating a literary audience, creating a literary sensibility or sensitivity. This was the function of little magazines of the twenties . . . and the thirties; they created a literary public, a literary sensibility, whether or not ninety-five percent of the stuff they printed is now remembered." Mr. Rago continued, "I feel that the little magazine is valuable in itself. Even its expendability is a valuable thing. The little magazine is a form of conversation. It is what we have in this country instead of the café. . . . We know each other through the magazines, and we talk to each other through the magazines." Later Bernice Slote, third editor of *Prairie Schooner*, made the same point. Walt Whitman wrote, "To have great poets, there must be great audiences, too." *Prairie Schooner* has aspired for seventy-five years both to develop and satisfy great audiences as well as to provide a seedbed for literary talent.

During my tenure as editor, revolutions in taste, politics, and decorum altered our notions of audience as well as literature, culture, and the responsibilities of a magazine. For example, we may be surprised to know that at the 1965 conference on the literary magazine sponsored by the Modern Language Association of America and the Carnegie Corporation of New York at the Library of Congress, only four women of twenty-nine official speakers were considered participants. Of these women only Sonia Raiziss of *Chelsea* magazine sat at the main table—as a panelist, not a speaker. Carolyn Kizer, founding editor with David Wagoner of *Poetry Northwest*, appeared on page 109 of the proceedings as "audience." Kizer, a poet, translator, and editor, several years before her own Pulitzer Prize and newly returned from teaching in India, spoke convincingly from the floor about the problematic use of English, the language of the British raj, in making contemporary Indian and Pakistani literature. Kizer was prescient in asking the assemblage to consider the ways language shapes identity.

In 1964 J. C. Oates's story, "First Views of the Enemy" brought cultural paranoia to our readers' attention. In 1965 she wrote in the magazine about gender issues. More recently, in 1998, Carolyn Kizer and Maxine Kumin, both chancellors of the Academy of American Poetry and contributors to *Prairie Schooner*, publicly resigned their positions to protest the inequity of gender and racial representation on that august body. Kumin's comments on the subject were important to our audience, therefore, they were published in our pages. For decades *Prairie Schooner* has published not only traditional genres but also documents, source materials, collaborations, informal writing and, in equal numbers, the works of women and men, the literatures of many cultures, and the languages of literature in America, which include Spanish, African American, French, Hebrew, Armenian, Latin, and others, as well as the mix of dialects and slang familiar to dwellers all over the world.

Ruth Behar, writer, MacArthur Fellow, and Cuban American anthropologist, wrote in these pages, "A poet cruel to history is cruel to poetry." In this anthology, readers will find poems and stories about the Tet in Vietnam, the Holocaust in Europe, the several bloody divisions in the Balkans, cultural appropriations, the anguish of the AIDS and the breast cancer epidemics, gender enactments, revisions and reversals, warfare, welfare, and the special relationships between partners, husbands and wives, parents and children, and teachers and students—all expressed in terms of cruelty and resistance, love and humor, the formal and traditional aspects of literary art as well as the informal voice speaking in private at once to itself and to a public audience. In two genres, poetry and fiction, this anthology also considers class, race, nationalism, the changing notions of displacement and home, language boundaries and their slurring, advice and imperatives, the cultural expansion brought by technology and media—television, magazines, cartoons, born in 1938 as an especially American form of art—and the vast changes medical technology has made in our bodies and our lives through chemical and hormonal therapy and surgery.

About suffering, poet Scott Cairns in "Musée," points out, wryly, that for artists, "every human torment [is] the fortunate occasion for their most passionate renderings." About aesthetics, critic and poet Jonathan Holden ironically joins antipoetic diction to formal rigor in "Such Beauty" to say,

I think that we humans
find pain interesting, that's all,
and warfare by far the most
interesting activity
that we have ever devised.

And, in spite of human divisions of race and language, often the occasions for warfare, poet Marilyn Hacker notices,

every other friend of ours is
ambiguous two generations back
mixed races swell the lexicon,
peach-cream through copper to obsidian:
Preta, negrinho, mulata, moreno.

By stretching her English text to include Spanish/Portuguese, Hacker challenges the boundaries of language as well as others that divide us.

Critic and poet Alicia Ostriker tells us that revising and correcting history, especially women's history, is one marker of twentieth-century art. Her long poem, "Surviving" begins, "It is true that in this century / To survive is to be ashamed." Part two says:

It is true that when I encounter another
Story of a woman artist, a woman thinker
Who died in childbirth, I want to topple over
Sobbing, tearing my clothing.

Carole Simmons Oles's remarkable restoration of nineteenth-century American astronomer Maria Mitchell's life, work, and imagined voice in her book *Night Watches: Inventions on the Life of Maria Mitchell* is represented here by two poems.

In addition to the abstractions we assume art resists, for example, suffering—others more specific appear—for example, hope, in Richard Jackson's long poem. The Bible, as expected, is present here in Mark Jarman's revision of the fall and, as a trope and a site for expansion, in Eric Pankey's work. Linda Pastan marries our body's craving for salt with the story of Lot's wife.

The single word that seems to chant the ground for our century's voice is, as David Lehman suggests, "can't." "Can't sing, can't go home again, Or alter the paths of the wandering planets, / Can't say no, can't wait for the wait to be over. . . ." To resist *can't* and *cant* has been, for seventy-five years, the job of *Prairie Schooner*.

How did we select the poetry and fiction for this anthology? We asked readers to consider all the work published in the magazine since 1980. Their recommendations were sent to the editorial staff. Our pleasure in reading this fiction and poetry was tempered by memories of superb pieces we couldn't include. Whatever the temptation, we resisted enlarging the pool except in the case of "Maggie of the Green Bottles" by Toni Cade Bambara, originally published in 1967, and the two short stories by Joyce Carol Oates published in 1964 and 1965. Individual poems and stories sparked changes in readers' responses, fast changes in taste that happen and must happen as new generations look at a body of accumulated work. We rediscovered work long forgotten and rejected pieces we remembered we'd loved. Revision of taste is one of the pleasures as well as one of the perils of life as a literary editor. Elizabeth Hardwick in the *New York Time Book Review* wrote a catalog of "the gifts necessary to an editor; that is evading, delaying, sliding, balancing friendship, courtesy and prudence against what are seen to be the immediate needs and possibilities of a periodical." We needed all of these gifts to decide to abandon most of the material from our special international issues.

For the past ten years we have published special issues of contemporary writing from Alaska, Australia, Czech and Slovak in translation, Canadian women writers, writing from China, Germany, Japan, Latina/Latino literature, and Jewish American Writing, reprinted by the University of Nebraska Press as *The* Prairie Schooner: *Anthology of Contemporary Jewish American Writing*. These issues most dramatically show our commitment to contemporary international writing. Each of these issues won critical recognition and popular success and sold out immediately. They have been used as texts in college classrooms where current anthologies simply were not available. *Prairie Schooner's* presence on the international literary scene is vibrant and we are committed to maintaining that presence in the new millennium. Ivan Klíma's story *The Washing Machine* from our Czech and Slovak issue—the last collection of work published before Czechoslovakia was divided—appeared on each and every reader's list, and represents this body of international work.

In January 1927 the first issue of *Prairie Schooner* was published in Lincoln at the land-grant University of Nebraska. The ninety-two pages, perfect bound, were wrapped in a cover paper called Goldenrod Sorg. English professor Lowry Wimberly was the chairman of a board of undergraduate editors that eventually came to include Edward Stanley, Edward R. Murrow, Loren Eiseley, and Mari Sandoz. According to the masthead the magazine cost was 40¢ a copy, $1.50 a year to the public. *"If there is sufficient interest in the publication, the publishers will continue the issuance. Immediate subscriptions will largely indicate the interest in the venture and will determine the fate of the magazine. This is a non-commercial venture. Income is dependent upon subscriptions, advertising, and donations."*

There was sufficient interest. Wimberly remained editor and shaper of the magazine for twenty-eight years with the help of his longtime editorial assistant, Frederick L. Christensen, who stayed on through the tenure of two additional editors and only retired from reading fiction manuscripts in the 1960s. The magazine became a home for young and established writers. After Wimberly's retirement in 1956, Pulitzer Prize winning poet Karl Shapiro took up the job as the second editor of the quarterly and renamed it *The Schooner*. He brought his esteemed reputation as a writer and critic and the experience of having edited Harriet

Monroe's *Poetry* magazine. To our early list of distinguished contributors Shapiro added Maxine Kumin, Randall Jarrell, Robert Penn Warren, Tillie Olsen, Anne Sexton, and the canonical names in anthologies of contemporary poetry in the '50s. The magazine flourished but the new name fell away.

After Shapiro's resignation over institutional censorship, scholar and poet Bernice Slote, who had been poetry editor under Wimberly and associate editor under Shapiro, became editor in 1963. In the magazine's fortieth year, Slote addressed the definition of the little magazine. She wrote, "Little magazines are founded on a genuinely heroic dare — to see if it could be done, to publish a kind of writing that needs doing, to give more good writers some space, to add to the energy and talent devoted to achievement in the arts, to reform something and take a stand, or simply to explore the idea of what a magazine can be. Of these, I think the best reason for founding and continuing a Little Magazine is to find and help the writer." She explained the name of the journal as a trope evoking the frontier, "not regionalism but a spirit of . . . adventure and action and endurance that could have some significance." During her tenure as editor, she published the work of Joyce Carol Oates, previously unpublished work of Willa Cather and the growing numbers of her critics; she inaugurated a series of issues of source material and criticism of American writers and "a Latin-American sampling with one of the few reports ever to come out of Paraguay, [and] two 'Letters from Selma' in which a businessman and a nun reported their visit South." She hired me as poetry editor and acting editor in her absence. English professor Hugh Luke became editor in 1980. For the spring 1983 issue, Dika Eckersley was commissioned to design "the first basic change of format since Volume One, Number One," as Luke wrote in his preface. Eckersley chose a cover photograph by Brian Oles of Maxine Kumin's house in New Hampshire, part of the farm she called Up Country in her Pulitzer prize book of the same name. A framed sampler on the wall clearly says, "In Heaven there are many Projects; Up Country, but a few." The sixtieth anniversary issue, bound once again in Goldenrod Sorg, was edited by Luke and me with the assistance of editorial assistant and business manager, Karma Larsen. New work by poets Stephen Dunn, Albert Goldbarth, Alberta Turner, and Walter McDonald and fiction writers Ellen Gilchrist and Kelly Cherry, as well as a previously unpublished play by Weldon Kees, marked the occasion. Larsen and I again worked together in 1986 to publish an especially popular special issue called *Nebraska: The Individual Voice*, the only issue in our seventy-five years to have a second printing.

Nebraska Educational Television producer Michael Farrell's photograph, "Pop always talked with his hands," served as frontispiece. When Hugh Luke retired in 1987, I became the fifth editor.

My favorite part of the job was the mail. Manuscript submissions from writers had been my chief responsibility, but now I also read the neglected letters addressed to the editor. Some of them came from early staff members who now were famous. Fine letters—often with photos—came from Marion Edward Stanley, who was born in Aurora, Nebraska, and became division editor of the AP and AP Wirephoto. For eighteen years he was head of NBC's Division of Public Affairs and Education. The first network TV series for college credit, "Continental Classroom," was his project. He started "Meet the Press" and three thousand other programs, published two novels, wrote for *Poetry*, and interviewed Robert Frost and Carl Sandburg on TV, and William Butler Yeats, his favorite, whom he remembered as "young and vigorous and, in fact . . . on the edge of his second blooming." Tuck Stanley died on May 17, 1989, but not before we had many of his letters in our files. (His nickname Tuck came from his undergraduate role as the friar in *Romeo and Juliet*.) His widow Gloria and their friends began what Tuck's son David has endowed as the annual $1,000 Edward Stanley Prize for Poetry at *Prairie Schooner*, our first and only endowed prize for writers.

"What might interest you," Edward Stanley wrote, "is the fact that I was one of the founding fathers of your fine magazine. I worked my way through [the University of Nebraska] as a reporter on the Lincoln Star . . . and was a friend of Lowry Wimberly" in 1927. "I met Wimberly one morning as I beat my way around the campus. He was not a dour man, but that is how he looked. He said, 'Don't you think we ought to have a literary magazine?' I said, 'Of course. Good idea.' And Lowry said, 'Good. I'll put you on the committee.' Which he did. I can't remember that we ever did meet, but I suppose we did. I think there were five of us. Ed Morrow was probably another . . . Ed and I were both reporters on the [Lincoln] Star." This founding committee came to include Loren Eiseley, Mari Sandoz, Weldon Kees, and Volta Torry, who later became editor of *Popular Science* magazine. Don Weldon, who wrote for *Prairie Schooner* as Weldon D. Melick, (his friendship with Torry later led to writing assignments for *Popular Science* that he called "Personality Pieces," interviews with famous people that made *him* famous). Don Weldon headed to Hollywood from UNL and became the youngest contract writer in Hollywood—fifty movie credits and a charter membership in the Writers' Guild of America. He wrote for *Photoplay* and the other fan magazines, the proving ground for "embryonic novelists, screenwriter, and syndicated columnists." He wrote for ten years for *Reader's Digest,* a job he got as the result of an interview with Jack Benny that was "practically dictated by George Burns."

Stanley and Weldon were not the only two successes on the committee. Another, on the masthead from 1929–31, was novelist Jim Thompson—his twenty-nine novels have had a revival and three of them, *The Grifters, The Kill-Off* and *The Getaway* (which has been produced twice) were made into movies. Thompson also wrote the screenplay for Stanley Kubrick's powerful antiwar film "Paths of Glory." Robert Polito's biography of Thompson, *Savage Art,* won the 1995 National Book Critics Circle Award and earned an Edgar from Mystery Writers of America as the best critical biography of the year. And when Polito called the office to ask about Thompson, we recovered another lost piece of the *Prairie Schooner* history. Thompson too was one of "Wimberly's Boys," as the group of talented writers he identified and encouraged came to be called. Another was folklorist Ben Botkin.

Lowry Wimberly, often described as "the dour"—(Bernice Slote told me he suggested "The Decay of the World" as the title for her M.A. thesis, but she declined his suggestion)—had the gift of inspiration. The complete list of his *Prairie Schooner* committee is very long and included Mari Sandoz, of course, one of his "boys," and Robert Lasch who was later a Rhodes Scholar, who worked on the *Omaha World Herald,* then the *Chicago Sun,* and who was for many years editor of the *St. Louis Post Dispatch.*

In a file in the office is a letter on Hughes Systems Development Laboratories stationary dated July 23, 1959, from J. Harris Gable, "Head of the Technical Library in the Systems Development Labs." Attached is his unpublished article, "The *True* Story of *PS*'s Founding," more complicated than I can represent. Mr. Gable reports that the real founders numbered three, Wimberly, himself, and Roscoe Schaupp, who later became a librarian at Eastern Illinois University. The passion of this writer for correcting the record and including his name in the distinguished company of the magazine's founders is impressive. Aircraft might have been thought to be enough for posterity.

Also in the files is a fine and heroic letter from Mari Sandoz dated June 11, 1937. Her home address was noted as 1226 Jay Street, now known as J Street. Under the press of budget reductions at the university, the magazine seemed about to be cut. Aware that the readers of her letter would know her national success as a writer, Sandoz wrote, "I realize that we of Nebraska have not always shown our full appreciation of the fine and faithful work of Mr. Wimberly, or of the cultural importance of the *Schooner* to us. Yet it was a matter of great pride to me that the magazine seemed of real moment in the eyes of the New Yorker and the Bostonian. Everywhere I went in the east I heard what a fine thing the state and the University were doing in maintaining a literary magazine of such high standards." She concludes, "Are we to let the *Schooner* die now?" Copies of this letter were sent to the Chancellor, the Dean of the college of Arts and Sciences, and the Chair of the English Department. Apparently the answer was no.

Recently Howard Junker sent us a memoir of his life as founding editor of the west coast magazine *Zyzzyva*. He wrote, "I just thought that if I got 50 guys together to put up $200 that would be plenty of money to start a magazine. A friend of my brother's who lived in San Francisco was a magazine start-up guy—he helped start *Mother Jones*—and he would have told me it takes $2 million to start a magazine. But I didn't ask." Obviously Wimberly and his boys and their successors didn't ask either because on January 2002, the three hundredth issue of *Prairie Schooner* will go to press. We have a small budget and the staff takes its editorial inspiration from the venerable reputation of the magazine. In the May 1931 issue of *Writer's Digest*, Lowry Wimberly wrote, "We are especially anxious to publish the work of promising young writers." And that is what he, and we, have done.

The first story published in the magazine was "The Vine," signed by Marie Macumber, whom we remember as Mari Sandoz. We have published early works of Ursula Hegi, Stephen Dunn, Maxine Kumin, Tim O'Brien, Reynolds Price, Marge Piercy, Linda Pastan, Richard Russo, and Susan Fromberg Schaeffer, Amy Clampitt, and more recently Antonya Nelson, Sherman Alexie, Minnie Bruce Pratt, Marcia Southwick, Marilyn Hacker, Toi Derricotte, Cornelius Eady, and many others. But the best names are the ones we can't use to impress potential readers. They're new writers and for the next ten years we'll be reading their work in journals such as ours, then books, and finally adding them to the lists of our proudest contributors who are Nobel Prize Laureates such as Roald Hoffman, Pulitzer Prize winners such as Rita Dove, MacArthur Fellows such as Eleanor Wilner and the names we see every year on all the *Best of* prize volumes for fiction, poetry, non-fiction, the *Best Writing from the South, The Beacon Press Best,* Pushcart Prizes and every prize given for literature in the us year after year after year.

Finally, our success comes from our always changing editorial staff.

Karma Larsen set us on the path of special issues with her Nebraska issue. Pamela Weiner's discipline with records helped us toward fiscal accountability and increased our circulation. Kate Flaherty streamlined our production methods and brought life to our publicity. Dika Eckersley reconfigured the look of the magazine and she continues issue after issue to create and design distinguished covers. Ladette Randolph, who was managing editor and senior reader of fiction for three years, has been our colleague in decisions both practical and literary and Erin Flanagan brings her ambition to that position as we begin our second seventy-five years. With a paid staff of two and the strong support of the department of English and the University of Nebraska Press, *Prairie Schooner* "rolls along, avoiding the quagmires of fads and schisms, steadfastly defining the American idiom" (*Literary Magazine Review*).

Hilda Raz
Editor-in-Chief, *Prairie Schooner*

Best of *Prairie Schooner*

TONY ARDIZZONE
1988

Larabi's Ox

In a ditch alongside the highway between Casablanca and Rabat lies Larabi's ox. Even in death the blue-black beast appears huge. Its open eye stares unfocused at the sky, streaked tangerine from the sun setting over the Atlantic. The ox's left foreleg, snowy white from hoof to knee, lies curled nearly to the swell of its stomach. The dying light lends its sallow horn a yellow cast. By the time Larabi finds his beast, the eye will be entirely milked over and covered with flies buzzing with greedy madness. Already the flies have settled on the blood clotted around the nostrils, lips, the black tongue bulging from the mouth. Other flies cling to the coarse hairs on the muzzle and the thinner lashes surrounding the eye, waiting their chance to bite something choice. Three egrets, white plumes unruffled in the still air, pick at a gash in the animal's side where its sweet blood has congealed, where a jagged spike of rib has torn through the skin. Beneath the skin the organs have bloated from the day's heat.

The ox has been struck by the shuttle bus from the Casablanca airport, then been prodded into the ditch by the bus's angry driver and by a dreamy boy pushing a red wheelbarrow loaded with two aluminum cannisters of milk. It is mid-morning on the highway to Rabat. The driver stands on the hot stretch of road in front of his idling bus, a curse on his lips, his foot eager to kick the stupid snorting animal his bus has just struck. The driver is dark, built as thickly as the steamer trunks stowed in the bus's cargo drawers. Despite the bus's air conditioning he has sweated through his shirt. Dark loops of sweat droop from his armpits. A rounded triangle of sweat stains the center of his chest. His pants cling to his thighs. He smokes so continuously that his first and second fingers are stained gold from nicotine. He has never had a driving accident. He believes in *maktub*, that what is written is sure to pass. Afraid to veer off the road and risk a flat or, worse, a broken axle, he drives down the road's center, with as much horn as wheel. The road belongs to the strong, he believes. The ox failed to understand this.

1

The stupid beast. It gasps on the road before him, sitting on its folded legs. Why, when other animals run from the bus, did this one stroll into its path? The driver cares nothing for the animal's pain. His sole concern is the worry that if the bus is damaged he may lose his job. For a moment he turns from the ox and a wide-eyed country boy, who hurries from behind a red wheelbarrow, and studies the front of the bus.

At least the headlight is intact, he thinks. The bumper and front panel are dented, spotted with blood. He glances back at the ox, fearing if he is not careful it will rear up and charge him. His hands try to jerk the bumper straight. Once he slit a sheep's throat for the feast celebrating the birth of his first son, and when he turned for a moment the animal stood and charged him. The dented bumper does not budge. After the birth of his second son he held the sheep to the ground. He jerks at the stubborn bumper. He straddled the animal and held the neck fast while the dumb thing's life spilled between his legs into the earth. He stares at the stupid ox, then steps into the bus and returns with a rag with which he begins wiping away the blood and the many dark hairs smearing the bumper and front panel and headlight.

He'll lose his job. The thought is too terrible to consider. His job is a big step up from what he used to do, which was drive a city bus. No, he was not in the wrong. The right of way belongs to the strong. He's no fellah from the countryside. He has opinions on many issues, his time spent behind the wheel being ample. Also he has observed much from the high seat of his bus. Force is what makes life work. No matter the situation, the world belongs to the strong.

He remembers when he was young, after they buried his mother and burned her things so the disease would not spread, her brother came and took him to Casablanca. All he knew was life of the fellahin. The brother told him to stop acting like a donkey. To dry his tears, learn to open his eyes, use his brain. The brother taught him how to lead tourists into shops owned by their friends, who would later share with him a percentage of whatever was bought. When he was older the brother taught him to steer and to shift the grinding gears of a friend's truck, and with luck and connections got him a job as a city bus driver. In the cool morning when the sun broke the darkness of the horizon, spreading over Casablanca's tan walls like a racing fire, and there were seats and room for everyone, the young driver saw that his countrymen could behave as decently as Europeans sipping mint tea. But in the thick heat of the afternoon when three buses wouldn't be enough—well, you risked your life sometimes trying to get aboard, to ride with the others, standing. Of course the weak ones were left behind at the curb, pushed aside, occasionally knocked down in the rush. With no room for them, he'd have no choice but to shut the door. Once, a woman with his mother's face was nearly trampled by a crowd thronging onto his bus. He watched her fall, remembers still her dark eyes and the curve of her raised arm as the mob swirled around her.

He sees his image in the headlight as he folds the rag he used to clean the front of the bus. In the headlight he is fat and upside down. The bumper and front panel look as they always look, he thinks. They must. A dent here, one there. And if someone were to point them out, why, the dents were always there, weren't they? No one needs to know the bus struck anything.

Then he hears the boy with the wheelbarrow sighing. The boy is filthy, wide-eyed, so thin his hips hardly hold up his ragged pants. He wears a man's T-shirt torn at the neck. The driver takes out a cigarette, then spits with disgust. He was just like him before he was rescued by his mother's brother.

"Oh, oh, oh," the boy says, his dirty hands fluttering in front of his face. He leans over the fallen beast, which thrashes its legs on the ground. The driver would like to slap some sense into the boy, at least to shut him up. He steps toward the boy, raising his hand. The beast lets loose a great quantity of shit. The ox must have been saving it for just this moment, the driver thinks. He lowers his hand. The shit lies repulsively in a mound, shimmering wetly. The stench is very high.

The driver considers for a moment the farmer who owned the animal. He might demand to be paid. Well, screw him. The stupid ox came out of nowhere, charged the bus. If blame is to be laid at someone's step, blame the fence the ox broke through or the sleepy shepherd boy who should have been watching it. The driver lights the cigarette, inhales deeply. There was no opportunity to stop without risking harm to the passengers. Of course, if accused he can blame the passengers. He nods, looking back at the bus. The passengers are pushed against the windshield, gawking out like sheep at a fence. One, a fat American in a fedora and safari shirt, is taking photographs.

The driver waves for the man to stop. "This damn American thinks it's amusing," he shouts into the bus's doorway. He speaks in Arabic to the group of Moroccans standing by the window.

"This is our life," one of the Moroccans answers, vigorously nodding, "the reality we live each day, and he makes of it souvenirs."

The American smiles at the driver, then snaps his picture.

Screw him, the driver thinks as he walks back to the ox. Already he has decided his bus hasn't struck a thing. The dents were there when he drove the bus from its station. He grabs the animal's horns, lifts its head, trying to pull it from the road. The ox was already on the highway. The muscles in the dark neck twist against his grip. The black tongue lolls in the mouth. The country kid will have to help him.

The driver rolls what has happened around in his mind. He wants to put the events straight. He was driving along until he stopped the bus for a few moments to move an animal blocking the road. Obviously something hit it, then sped off. A car, a truck, a motorbike, perhaps another ox. Who can say how the beast was hurt? Who else but he knows what took place?

Not too bad a way to go, the American in the safari shirt reflects. He nods at his thought, then looks again at the beast through his camera. Quick, out of the blue, mouth full of tasty grass. Maybe dreaming about a cool drink of water, green pastures, a juicy heifer. You step out onto a road and then honk honk, BAM! Welcome to the twentieth century. Probably broke the poor thing's ribs, punctured a lung, a few of the vital organs.

The American lowers his camera and pouts. He looks somewhat like an egg and knows it, feels sometimes like a big Humpty Dumpty as he plods about. His face is very pink and since the chemotherapy fairly hairless, and he is quite fat, particularly now that he no longer cares what or how much he eats. Funny how they can call them vital organs, he thinks, as if there's anything inside you that isn't. Well, there's the appendix. But who knows for sure? Life offers no reliability. You think your cells are inside your skin where they belong, minding their own business, behaving and carrying out their various God-given functions, and then you find out that a whole bunch has been traveling about your body acting like promiscuous sluts. Multiplying and dividing in places where there should be no arithmetic. He pushes his abdomen with the flat of his meaty hand and feels nothing but the hand's pressure. No pain. Funny how when it all goes haywire you don't even feel pain. He'd bet the animal on the road feels pain.

"He hit an immense black ox," he announces loudly, turning away from the windshield toward the Westerners, then the Moroccans, on the bus.

No one responds. He wishes someone would respond. Because whenever he remembers how his body turned Benedict Arnold on him, he aches to be touched, or at least acknowledged. He fears his loneliness is so strong sometimes it can be smelled. His eyes scan the others with visible urgency. Oh, see me and smile. No one does.

Pressed around him are several Moroccans, staring indifferently out the window or gesturing and talking with one another in Arabic. Others relax in their seats. A pretty American traveling by herself smokes a cigarette and fidgets, chewing her fingernails, pulling at the ends of her red hair, which is shoulder length, unwashed, breathtakingly lovely. What a shame beauty like hers is wasted on boys in their twenties, he thinks. When he was a boy in his twenties, he had the sensitivity of a toad. He remembers what a bumbler he'd been in bed. Like a bottle rocket. No sooner did he get all the way up than he popped. He shakes his head, feeling pity for the girl and all young women in general. Then he feels himself beginning to harden.

Oh Body, he thinks, how at times you amaze me. He covers the front of his pants with one hand and blushes, not having felt desire as strong as this in longer than he can remember. The young woman peers out her window, puffing dribs of smoke out the side of her mouth.

What a shame she smokes. What a shame she doesn't wash her hair. Hair that beautiful should be shampooed, gently dried, brushed, then held back from her face with fine combs. In a louder voice aimed at her he repeats, "Our driver has killed an ox."

Instead of looking up, the young woman ignores him, eyes and fingers busy with her cigarette and the ends of her hair.

Then he notices the older woman, reading in her seat. The drabness of her turtleneck and man's hiking boots and trousers makes him wonder if she's from England. Few American women dress that way, he considers, at least the ones he's had the fortune to know.

Is she in her forties? Fifties? Her complexion is quite fair. Her nose, forehead, the backs of her hands and her wrists are lightly brushed with freckles. Irish? Scotch? He imagines sitting next to her. What would he say? Surely she'll put down her book before they arrive in Rabat.

Then he sees the other American—or is he Spanish?—the one in the brown tie, gold-rimmed sunglasses. Corduroy jacket neatly folded next to him on the seat. Looking about like a cornered rat. No, he's from the States. You can tell by the button-down collar. Though the air inside the bus is still quite cool, the man is visibly sweating. Too tense a guy to go up to, sit down with, say how-de-do.

He turns and looks out the window, as the Moroccans around him at first give him room, then press in against him like a wave. They lean freely on him, touch his back, push against his legs, his arms, in their attempts to see out the windshield. He doesn't mind the contact, no, not in the slightest. It has been many years since he's been touched. He thinks perhaps that's why he has come to Morocco.

For a moment he closes his eyes and concentrates on the men around him. He feels their shoulders and hands rock against him, smells the sweet mix of their sweat and hair lotion and tobacco and some unidentifiable spice, listens to the lovely tumbling cadence of their speech. He turns, steals a glance at the young woman. She chews the ends of her hair, her tender face now buried in a guidebook. What a waste, he thinks. If only he could help her to be not wasted. He tips back his hat and gazes again out the windshield.

The boy with the heavy wheelbarrow is glad he was not hit. Surely if he had been, his father would beat him. He is taking the two cannisters of goat milk several kilometers down the road to his uncle. Then his uncle will sell the milk or take it where it will be made into cheese. The boy does not know what arrangement his father and uncle have made. All he knows is that he must not tip the wheelbarrow.

He has tipped many wheelbarrows in his short life. He has the welts to show for it. If he is as useless as his father and uncle tell him he is, he is sure to tip many more. Pushing a wheelbarrow is simple enough, difficult perhaps only over rock or in deep mud. But pushing a wheelbarrow usually led him to dreaming. As his uncle and father have told him, daydreaming distracts him and leads to mistakes. Dreamy boys tip wheelbarrows. He must not allow the wheelbarrow to tip.

Earlier, as the boy moved down the road, he daydreamed he was a horseman, like the ones he saw last summer in the magnificent fantasia held during the festival of Sidi Moussa el-Doukkali, a saint buried outside of Salé, where his father's family lives. Traveling to the festival had been the most exciting event of the boy's life. Sidi Moussa had lived on wild onions and the salty air and could appear and disappear whenever and wherever he wished, leaping through any distance, no matter how great. He gave bread to the poor. Each year he made a hajj to Mecca. He was the village's favorite saint.

The boy was imagining that he was a saint, a great horseman who lived on couscous and lamb and sheep's head and who could fly through the air with his horse, and who rode in every fantasia in Morocco. In a fantasia the country's best horsemen, dressed in turbans and their finest robes, gathered at the far end of a field, forming a line, their steeds meticulously combed and decorated in red tassels and brilliant saddle blankets. At the field's other end waits the eager crowd. A hush falls. Then the horsemen charge, bright white caps flowing, raising and then twirling their long rifles above their heads. The horses break into a gallop loud as thunder. The men scream, *"Allaho-akbar! Allaho-akbar! Allaho-akbar!"* Allah is the most great! The earth trembles. The crowd falls back and screams.

At the very last instant, when the crowd is certain it will be cut down by the horsemen like wheat beneath a sickle, the riders rein in and fire their rifles simultaneously into the air, and then the great horses rear and the riders stand victorious in their stirrups, again twirling their rifles above their heads. Then they retreat.

The boy imagines the red wheelbarrow is an elegant tassled bay, and he is starting the charge, crying, "*Allaho-akbar! Allaho-akbar!*" He pushes the wheelbarrow down the road with what for him is reckless speed. Then he hears the terrible honking bus. He raises his eyes to the sound. From his angle the bus appears to be charging a black ox standing alongside a slight ditch. How exciting, the boy thinks. A fantasia. Surely at the last moment the bus will brake. The ox takes a step onto the roadway. The boy readies his mouth with the sound of rifles. "Pa-tchoo! tchoo! tchoo!" the boy says. The bus speeds nearer, and the beast—Larabi's ox, the boy realizes—continues on its way, seeming to chew its tongue, the boy notices, gazing first vacantly at him and then casually in the direction of the honking. For a moment the boy has the giddy desire that the bus might actually hit the ox. No. Yes, yes, it would be something to see. Then horribly as all of time collapses to a single moment the bus does exactly as he wishes, glancing into the ox's side, causing the great animal to skid drunkenly up the road until its useless legs bend and then crumple and it tumbles down onto its side, neck arched, its horned head raised to the sky as it lows as if saying, "Oh, I am in such trouble and pain!" There is much dust then and honking, as the bus slides through the dust to a stop above the fallen animal.

For several moments the beast twitches and snorts, sides heaving like a punctured bellows. The driver rushes down from the bus, flares his nostrils, spits. The boy hears the man's dark curse and lowers his eyes. At that moment the animal begins emptying its bowels. The feces is soft, dark as pitch, and smells of fear and metal. Or is the metal just the taste on his tongue? The boy tries to taste his tongue, but it has turned to sand. He tries to swallow but cannot. He fears that by desiring the accident he has caused it.

The stench of the feces is so strong his eyes are tearing. He takes a deep breath and smells fear. Through the smell of fear he looks up, back at the ox. Blood bubbles like a spring from the wound where the bone protrudes. The bone is torn, tipped with pink. The boy steps over the mound of feces and puts out his hand to touch the bone. Perhaps he can push it back in place.

The driver tries to pull the beast to its feet. The ox seems to snore, as if asleep. The driver gives it a kick. The boy cannot comprehend why a man would kick an animal he is trying to save, though the boy knows that men often kick for no good reason the things around them. His two cannisters of milk reflect the morning sun with a glare that is dizzy and blinding. In the same blinding light the dying ox's side flutters wetly.

"Wake up," the driver shouts. Again he kicks the ox, which lies now on its side. "Hey, donkey boy! Help me with this damn thing."

"As you like," the boy answers with a heavy heart. He knows if he had not imagined the tragedy nothing would have happened.

Together they try to encourage the ox into the ditch beside the road, with the driver grabbing the beast's horns, and the boy tugging the animal's right foreleg. The ox doesn't budge, shaking its head free of the driver's grasp and kicking the boy's hands, all the while lowing plaintively. Blood pools on the road beneath it. At the end of each of its labored breaths there is a gurgling, soft as a stream. Then the ox's hind legs scissor the air, and the driver and the boy stand back. The ox tries to right itself. It tucks in its forelegs, kicks its legs. Then, as if understanding the man's intent, it rolls and works itself to its knees. The driver holds its horns, trying to twist the head toward the ditch. The ox follows its head, crawling on its knees through its blood and feces toward the man, who steps backward as he pulls its horns. Then the beast collapses alongside the road.

The morning sun blazes brightly in the corner of the bus's windshield. The passengers stare down from behind the tinted glass. The boy watches the driver pick up from the road a blood-stained rag and then fold it into smaller and smaller squares and then place the smallest square into his back pocket. Why does he want to keep the blood? the boy wonders. Tears fill his eyes. Oh, fantasia! Instead of a festival and celebration there is tragedy.

He returns slowly to the wheelbarrow. Without thinking, his hands fall to the wooden handles, which he lifts with a soft grunt. The boy knows he doesn't push his load so much as try to keep up with it. The weight of the load presses down on the wheel, which turns beneath the weight, covering the ground between where the barrow is and where it wants to go. His father told him it is the same with life. You run between the handles, trying your best to guide the wheel's direction and to prevent the load from tipping. The bus roars now like a horrible monster. The boy is careful to push his load around the slash of shit. The bus's gears engage with a clank. Then the bus starts up the roadway, moving through the blood.

For a moment the three—boy, driver, ox—are in a line perpendicular to the road. The bus is in the center, between the boy and the beast, which has stopped lowing and is nearly numb, feeling only a growing heaviness of breath and the familiar, teasing sting of the flies. The driver gives the bus gas, thinking no one else knows what has happened. The chugging sound of the bus's engine soothes him. No matter what, he will not give up the comfort of this seat. The American in the safari shirt and fedora waves at the boy with the wheelbarrow as he passes below. The boy does not notice the wave. His eyes dumbly watch the road and the two cannisters in front of him, as he trudges in the opposite direction. But then he looks up and sees behind the window the lovely face of the woman with red hair. Her face is turned fully toward the window. Her beauty surprises him. The boy thinks her large, heavy-lidded eyes look sad. He stares at her openly, smitten by the ripe fullness of her lips, as the bus pulls even with him. The young woman looks beyond him and the rocky field west of the road toward a blue sliver of the ocean, which she has just noticed, and which pleases her, brings a smile to her lips. She knew the road from the airport to Rabat ran parallel to the coast, though she did not expect the ocean to be this close.

The boy's heart catches when he sees her smile. He imagines she smiles at him because he is so handsome, so strong, so brave as to drive an ox into a ditch. The idea is too delicious for him to endure. His wheelbarrow strikes a sudden stone and all at once tips, one cannister shifting from the left side to the right with a bang, causing the cannister's top to pop off and some of the milk inside to splash out. The milk splashes onto the side of the road, which drinks it greedily, and into the belly of the wheelbarrow. The images of the woman's smile, the dizzy tipping, and the splashing milk tumble in the boy's mind as the roaring bus speeds past.

From a distance the boy's uncle watches the bus move past his nephew and the wheelbarrow. The uncle stands sideways on the inside slope of a slight ridge between the road and the pounding sea. In a moment the boy will notice him, he thinks.

He has just peed, not without effort and pain, straining with all his might to push out the last lazy drops that seem always to wish to remain. He is pleased that this morning he's been successful. He is sure the heavy drops contain grit from the food he has eaten in the past day. That's why it's so difficult to cleanse the body of them. Like the sediment you see settled on the bottom of a jug of clear water, so it is with a man's tubes, he believes. If a person is not careful, the grit builds up like silt at the bottom of a slowly moving stream. The grit clings to itself, forming peculiarly shaped pebbles. He has seen several such pebbles, picked up from the ground by men just his age after they'd painfully urinated. He knew a few men whose tubes became so choked with grit they died. There are far better ways to die than to die of clogged tubes, he thinks.

He shakes a stubborn drop from the mouth of his penis, then pushes his penis back inside the pantaloons he wears beneath his djellaba, which is wool, tan with sienna brown stripes. His dark eyes are set deeply in his skull. He has wrapped his shaved head in a white turban. Twice a month for a full day he fasts, and on the second day to break his fast he drinks bottled mineral water from Sidi Harazem, near Fez, to flush the grit from his bowels. During the thirty days of Ramadan, the ninth month, when Muslims forego all food, drink, and sexual relations from sunrise to sunset, his body purifies itself further, becoming a flame of thirst and desire.

At first the flame flares brightly. The edge of desire is keen. The body cries out in need, like a pampered child. But then after several days the needs stop crying out. The flame of physical desire flickers, dies back to an ember, and the person becomes self-contained, like a plant, the uncle thinks, which takes in nothing, surviving on itself. Then appetite becomes more suggestion than demand. The body becomes servant to the soul. The mind is then content, and the soul is better able to submit to the will of Allah. Fasting is a pillar of Islam, which means submission or self-surrender, a voluntary act whereby a person places his or her destiny in the hands of God and submits to God's rule as revealed through the commands given to the Prophet.

In the pocket of his leather *choukkara* his fingers touch his beads. The voice beneath his breath falls into prayer. *"La ilaha illa Allah."* There is no god but God. He runs the beads through his fingers as the prayer spills from his lips. The prayers have not yet become part of his body, companion to each breath, heartbeat. His hand still needs to feel the beads. But sometimes once he has started to finger the beads he is able to pray through to their knot without a distracting thought.

He watches his nephew stop to balance the cannisters in his wheelbarrow. Dawdler, inventor of excuses, dreamer and creator of unbelievable tales, the boy will need much discipline before he grows older, the uncle thinks. The man frowns, more from habit than displeasure. He deeply loves his nephew and would forgive him any sin. The boy is like the body, he thinks, full of need and desire. He is to the boy as the mind is to the body.

He notices far behind the boy an egret circle and then settle near a mound alongside the road. He does not know the dark shape is Larabi's dying ox. From where he stands it resembles a pile of freshly dug earth. He thinks no more of it, envying his brother, even though envy is a useless feeling and his brother is miserably poor. His poor brother lives in a shack made of scrap wood and tin with his wife, seven children, and skinny goats.

The sea rages against the rocky coast. The man turns into his shadow, fingers his prayer beads, reflects. "*La ilaha illa Allah.*" The waves pound the rocky shore, shatter into droplets. "*La ilaha illa Allah.*" The water recedes, and the shore resists, though with repetition and time the sea will reduce even the hardest rock to sand. "*La ilaha illa Allah.*" With time and repetition the body learns complete submission. "*La ilaha illa Allah.*" The rock and the sea act in accord with Allah's will.

The uncle looks off into the distance, to the south outside Casablanca, where there stands a refinery's flaming smokestack. This morning the sky over the refinery is especially gray, unclean. The man can remember when there was no flaming dirt in the sky. In time, he considers, even the refinery will be reduced. The candle will flicker, die. The towering cylinder of bricks will tumble. All of man's works will be reduced during the last hour, when the sun will be shrouded and the stars will no longer give light, when the mountains will vanish and the seas will boil over, and all people will be coupled with their deeds. Then the scrolls will be unfolded, and all will come to know what they have prepared for themselves. And the earth will be rocked in her last convulsion. The man returns his gaze to the furious whitecaps biting their way into the shore.

He knows his nephew nears, recognizes him, is thinking of a fantastic tale to explain why he is so late. Though the uncle is pleased to see his nephew, he clears his face.

Breathless, shouting with a high voice as he makes his approach, the boy tells him in a single tumbling sentence the story of the ox, the fantasia, the honking bus. As he begins to describe how the beautiful woman with hair the color of sunrise looked down and smiled with admiration at his bravery, the uncle chides him for the wasted milk puddled in the belly of the wheelbarrow. The uncle believes the entire tale is fantasy and is tempted to lecture the boy on the dangers of such idleness, but then he thinks better of it and holds his nephew to his chest and in greeting kisses both his cheeks, and the boy tells him no more of his story.

The boy tells no more of Larabi, the simple fellah, who, untold, will set out on foot in search of his stray beast as the tangerine sun streaks the sky and dips into the pounding blue Atlantic. No one will watch Larabi walk into the dying light, shielding his eyes with one hand, his other hand grasping the staff he uses to drive his herds. He will walk into the sun, to the sea. The birds in the air will lead him to it. At first Larabi's mind will deny what he sees, will tell him the animal is only resting, or asleep, or at worst has slipped, injured its snow-white left foreleg. Then when his eyes protest that the beast in the ditch is dead he will think that it only resembles his lively animal. Surely this dead, bloated beast is another man's misfortune, Larabi will think.

Then he will fall to his knees in mourning and in recognition of God's will, and his fingers will scratch sad furrows into the darkened earth.

TONI CADE BAMBARA
1967

Maggie of the Green Bottles

Maggie had not intended to get sucked in on this thing, sleeping straight through the christening, steering clear of the punch bowl, and refusing to dress for company. But when she glanced over my godfather's shoulder and saw "Aspire, Enspire, Perspire" scrawled across the first page in that hard-core Protestant hand, and a grease stain from the fried chicken too, something snapped in her head. She snatched up the book and retired rapidly to her room, locked my mother out, and explained through the door that my mother was a fool to encourage a lot of misspelled nonsense from Mr. Tyler's kin, and an even bigger fool for having married the monster in the first place.

I imagine that Maggie sat at her great oak desk, rolled the lace cuffs gently back, and dipped her quill into the lavender ink pot with all the ceremony due the Emancipation Proclamation, which was, after all, exactly what she was drafting. Writing to me, she explained, was serious business, for she felt called upon to liberate me from all historical and genealogical connections except the most divine. In short, the family was a disgrace, degrading Maggie's and my capacity for wings as they say. I can only say that Maggie was truly inspired. And she probably ruined my life from the get go.

There is a photo of the two of us on the second page. There's Maggie in Minnie Mouse shoes and a long polka-dot affair with her stockings rolled up at the shins, looking like muffins. There's me with nothing much at all on, in her arms, and looking almost like a normal, mortal, everyday type baby—raw, wrinkled, ugly. Except that it must be clearly understood straightaway that I sprang into the world full wise and invulnerable and gorgeous like a goddess. Behind us is the player piano with the spooky keys. And behind that, the window outlining Maggie's crosshatched face and looking out over the yard, overgrown even then, where later I lay lost in the high grass never hoping to be found till Maggie picked me up into her hair and told me all about the earth's moons.

Once just a raggedy thing holding telegrams from well-wishers, the book was pleasant reading on those rainy days when I didn't risk rusting my skates, or maybe just wasn't up to trailing up and down the city streets with the kids, preferring to study Maggie's drawings and try to grab hold of the fearsome machinery which turned the planets and coursed the stars and told me in no uncertain terms that as an Aries babe I was obligated to carry on the work of other Aries greats from Alexander right on down to anyone you care to mention. I could go on to relate all the wise-alecky responses I gave to Maggie's document as an older child rummaging in the trunks among the cancelled checks and old sheet music, looking for some suspicioned love letters or some small proof that my mother had once had romance in her life and finding instead the raggedy little book I thought was just a raggedy little book. But it is much too easy to smile at one's ignorant youth just to flatter one's present wisdom, but I digress.

Because, on my birthday, Saturn was sitting on its ass and Mars was taken unawares, getting bumped by Jupiter's flunkies, I would not be into my own till well past twenty. But according to the cards, and my palm line bore it out, the hangman would spare me till well into my hundredth year. So all in all, the tea leaves having had their say and the coffee grind patterns being what they were, I was destined for greatness. She assured me. And I was as certain of my success as I was certain that my parents were not my parents, that I was descended, anointed and ready to gobble up the world, from urgent, noble Olympiads.

I am told by those who knew her, whose memories consist of something more substantial than a frantic gray lady who poured coffee into her saucer, that Margaret Cooper Williams wanted something she could not have. And it was the sorrow of her life that all her children and theirs and theirs were uncooperative, worse, squeamish. Too busy taking in laundry, buckling at the knees, putting their faith in Jesus, mute and sullen in their sorrow, too squeamish to band together and take the world by storm, make history, or even to appreciate the calling of Maggie the Ram, or the Aries that came after. Other things they told me too, things I put aside to learn later though I always knew, perhaps, but never quite wanted to, the way you hold your breath and steady yourself to the knowledge secretly, but never let yourself understand. They called her crazy.

It is to Maggie's guts that I bow forehead to the floor and kiss her hand, because she'd tackle the lot of them right there in the yard, blood kin or by marriage, and neighbors or no. And anybody who'd stand up to my father, gross neanderthal that he was, simply had to be some kind of weird combination of David, Aries, and lunatic. It began with the cooking usually, especially the pots of things Maggie concocted. Witchcraft, he called it. Home cooking, she'd counter. Then he'd come over to the stove, lift a lid with an incredible face, and comment about cesspools and fertilizers. But she'd remind him of his favorite dish, chittlins, addressing the bread box though. He'd turn up the radio and make some remark about good church music and her crazy voodoo records. Then she'd tell the curtains that some men who put magic down but with nothing to replace it and nothing much to recommend them in the first place but their magic wand, lived a runabout life practicing black magic on other men's wives. Then he'd say something about free-loading relatives and dancing to the piper's tune. And she'd whisper to the kettles that there wasn't no sense in begging from a beggar. Depending on how large an audience they drew, this could go on for hours until my father would cock his head to the side, listening, and then try to make his getaway.

"Ain't nobody calling you, Mr. Tyler, cause don't nobody want you."

And I'd feel kind of bad about my father like I do about the wolfman and the phantom of the opera. Monsters, you know, more than anybody else need your pity cause they need beauty and love so bad.

One day, right about the time Maggie would say something painful that made him bring up free-loaders and piper's tunes, he began to sputter so bad it made me want to cry. But Maggie put the big wooden spoon down and whistled for Mister T—at least that's what Maggie and my grandmother, before she died, insisted on calling him. The dog, hungry always, came bounding through the screen door, stopped on a dime by the sink, and slinked over to Maggie's legs the way beat-up dogs can do, their tails all confused as to just what to do, their eyes unblinkingly watchful. Maggie offered him something from the pot. And when Mister T had finished, he licked Maggie's hand. She began to cackle. And then, before I could even put my milk down, up went Maggie's palm and bam, Mister T went skidding across the linoleum and banged all the seltzer bottles down.

"Damn fool mutt," said Maggie to her wooden spoon, "too dumb to even know you're supposed to bite the hand that feeds you."

My father threw his hand back and yelled for my mother to drop whatever she was doing, which was standing in the doorway shaking her head, and pack up the old lady's things posthaste. Maggie went right on laughing and talking to the spoon. And Mister T slinked over to the table so baby Jason could pet him. And then it was name calling time. And again I must genuflect and kiss her ring, because my father was no slouch when it came to names. He could malign your mother and work your father's lineage over in one short breath, describing in absolute detail all the incredible alliances made between your ancestors and all sorts of weird creatures. But Maggie had him beat there too, old lady in lace talking to spoons or no.

My mother came in weary and worn and gave me a nod. I slid my peanut butter sandwich off the ice box, grabbed baby Jason by his harness, and dragged him into our room where I was supposed to read to him real loud. But I listened, I always listened to my mother's footfalls on the porch to the gravel path and down the hard mud road to the woodshed. Then I could give my attention to the kitchen, for "Goldilocks," keep in mind, never was enough to keep the brain alive.

Then, right in the middle of some fierce curse or other, my father did this unbelievable thing, he stomped right into Maggie's room—that sanctuary of heaven charts and incense pots and dream books and magic stuffs. Only Jason, hiding from an August storm, had ever been allowed in there and that was on his knees crawling. But in he stomped all big and bad like some terrible giant, this man whom Grandma Williams used to say was just the sort of size man put on this earth for the "'spress purpose of clubbing us all to death." And he came out with these green bottles, one in each hand, snorting and laughing at the same time. And I figured, peeping into the kitchen, that these bottles were enchanted, for they had a strange effect on Maggie, she shut right up. They had a strange effect on me too, gleaming there up in the air, nearly touching the ceiling, glinting off the shots of sunshine, grasped in the giant's fist. I was awed.

Whenever I saw them piled in the garbage out back I was tempted to touch them and make a wish, knowing all the while that the charm was all used up and that that was why they were in the garbage in the first place. But there was no doubt that they were special. And whenever baby Jason managed to drag one out from under the bed, there was much whispering and shuffling on my mother's part. And when Sweet Basil, the grocer's boy, delivered these green bottles to Maggie, it was all hush-hush and back door and in the corner dealings, slipping it in and out of innumerable paper bags, holding it up to the light, then off she'd run to her room and be gone for hours, days sometimes, and when she did appear, looking mysterious and in a trance, her face all full of shadows. And she'd sit at the sideboard with that famous cup from the World's Fair, pouring coffee into the saucer and blowing on it very carefully, nodding and humming and swirling the grinds. She called me over once to look at the grinds.

"What does this look like, Peaches?"

"Looks like a star with a piece out of it."

"Hmm," she mumbled and swirled again. "And now?"

Me peering into the cup and lost for words. "Looks like a face that lost its eyes."

"Hmm," again as she thrust the cup right under my nose and me wishing it was a box of falling glass I could look at where I knew what was what instead of looking into the bottom of a fat, yellow cup at what looked like nothing but coffee grinds.

"Looks like a mouth loosing its breath, Great Granny."

"Let's not get too outrageous, Peaches. This is serious business."

"Yes ma'm." Peering again and trying to be worthy of Alexander and the Ram and all my other forebears. "What it really seems to be," stalling for time and praying for inspiration, "is an upside down bird dead on its back with his heart chopped out and the hole bleeding."

She flicked my hand away when I tried to point the picture out which by now I was beginning to believe. "Go play somewhere, girl," she said. She was mad. "And quit calling me Granny."

"What happened here today?" my mother kept asking all evening, thumping out the fragrant dough and wringing the dishtowel, which was supposed to help the dough rise, wringing it to pieces. I couldn't remember anything particular, following her gaze to Maggie's door. "Was Sweet Basil here this afternoon?" Couldn't remember that either but tried to show I was her daughter by staring hard at the closed door too. "Was Great Granny up and around at all today?" My memory failed me there too. "You ain't got much memory to speak of at all, do you?" said my father. I hung onto my mother's apron and helped her wring the dishtowel to pieces.

They told me she was very sick so I had to drag baby Jason out to the high grass and play with him. It was a hot day and the smell of the kerosene, soaking the weeds that were stubborn about dying, made my eyes tear. I was face down in the grass just listening, waiting for the afternoon siren which last year I thought was Judgment Day because it blew so long to say that the war was over and that we didn't have to eat Spam anymore and that there was a circus coming and a parade and Uncle Bubba too, but with only one leg to show for it all. Maggie came into the yard with her basket of vegetables. She sat down at the edge of the gravel path and began stringing the peppers, red and green, red and green. And, like always, she was humming one of those weird songs of hers which always made her seem holier and blacker than she could've been. I tied baby Jason to a tree so he wouldn't crawl into her lap which always annoyed her. Maggie didn't like baby boys, or any kind of boys I'm thinking, but especially baby boys born in Leo and Pisces or anything but in Aries.

"Look here, Peaches," she called, working the twine through the peppers and dropping her voice real low. "I want you to do this thing for your Great Granny."

"What must I do?" I waited a long time till I almost thought she'd fallen asleep, her head rolling around on her chest and her hands fumbling with the slippery peppers, ripping them.

"I want you to go to my room and pull out the big pink box from under the bed." She looked around and woke up a bit. "This is a secret you and me thing now, Peaches." I nodded and waited some more. "Open the box and you'll see a green bottle. Wrap this apron around it and tuck it under your arm like so. Then grab up the mushrooms I left on the sideboard like that's what you came for in the first place. But get yourself back here right quick."

I repeated the instructions, flopped a necklace of peppers around me, and dashed into the hot and dusty house. When I got back she dumped the mushrooms into her lap, tucked the bottle under her skirt, and smiled at the poor little peppers her nervous hands had strung. They hung wet and ruined off the twine like broken-necked little animals.

I was down in the bottoms playing with the state farm kids when Uncle Bubba came sliding down the sand pile on his one good leg. Jason was already in the station wagon hanging onto my old doll. We stayed at Aunt Min's till my father came to get us in the pickup. Everybody was in the kitchen dividing up Maggie's things. The linen chest went to Aunt Thelma. And the souvenirs from Maggie's honeymoons went to the freckle-faced cousins from town. The clothes were packed for the church. And Reverend Elson was directing the pianist's carrying from the kitchen window. The scattered sopranos, who never ever seemed to get together on their high notes or on their visits like this, were making my mother drink tea and kept nodding at me, saying she was sitting in the mourner's seat, which was just like all the other chairs in the set; same as the amen corner was no better or any less dusty than the rest of the church and not even a corner. Then Reverend Elson turned to say that no matter how crazy she'd been, no matter how hateful she'd acted toward the church in general and him in particular, no matter how spiteful she'd behaved towards her neighbors and even her blood kin, and even though everyone was better off without her, seeing how she died as proof of her heathen character, and right there in the front yard too with a bottle under her skirts, the sopranos joined in scattered as ever, despite all that, the Reverend Elson continued, God rest her soul, if He saw fit that is.

The china darning egg went into Jason's overalls. And the desk went into my room. Bubba said he wanted the books for his children. And they all gave him such a look. My mother just sat in the kitchen chair called the mourner's seat and said nothing at all except that they were selling the house and moving to the city.

"Well, Peaches," my father said. "You were her special, what you want?"

"I'll take the bottles," I said.

"Let us pray," said the Reverend.

That night I sat at the desk and read the baby book for the first time. It sounded like Maggie for the world, holding me in her lap and spreading the charts on the kitchen table. I looked my new bottle collection over. There were purple bottles with glass stoppers and labels. There were squat blue bottles with squeeze tops but nothing in them. There were flat red bottles that could hold only one flower at a time. I had meant the green bottles. I was going to tell them and then I didn't. I was too small for so much enchantment anyway. I went to bed feeling much too small. And it seemed a shame that the hope of the Aries line should have to sleep with a light on still and blame it on Jason and cry with balled fists in the eyes just like an ordinary, mortal, everyday type baby.

LAN SAMANTHA CHANG
1995

The Eve of the Spirit Festival

After the Buddhist ceremony, when our mother's spirit had been chanted to a safe passage and her body cremated, Emily and I sat silently on our living room carpet. She held me in her arms; her long hair stuck to our wet faces. We sat as stiffly as temple gods except for the angry thump of my sister's heart against my cheek.

Finally she spoke. "It's Baba's fault," she said. "The American doctors would have fixed her."

I was six years old—I only knew that our father and mother had decided against an operation. And I had privately agreed, imagining the doctors tearing a hole in her body. As I thought of this, and other things, I felt a violent sob pass through me.

"Don't cry, Baby," Emily whispered. "You're okay." I felt my tears dry to salt, my throat lock shut.

Then our father walked into the room.

He and Emily had become quite close in the past few months. Emily was eleven, old enough to visit my mother when it had become clear that the hospital was the only option. But now she refused to acknowledge him.

"First daughter—" he began.

"Go away, Baba," Emily said. Her voice shook. She put her hand on the back of my head and turned me away from him also. The evening sun glowed garnet red through the dark tent of her hair.

"You said she would get better," I heard her say. "Now you're burning paper money for her ghost. What good will that do?"

"I am sorry," our father said.

"I don't care."

Her voice burned. I squirmed beneath her hand, but she wouldn't let me look. It was between her and Baba. I watched his black wingtip shoes retreat to the door. When he had gone, Emily let go of me. I sat up and looked at her; something had changed. Not in the lovely outlines

20

of her face—our mother's face—but in her eyes, shadow-black, lost in unforgiveness.

They say the dead return to us. But we never saw our mother again, though we kept a kind of emptiness waiting in case she might come back. I listened always, seeking her voice, the lost thread of a conversation I'd been too young to have with her. Emily rarely mentioned our mother, and soon my memories faded. I could not picture her. I saw only Emily's angry face, the late sun streaking red through her dark hair.

After the traditional forty-nine day mourning period, Baba didn't set foot in the Buddhist temple. It was as if he had listened to Emily: what good did it do? Instead he focused on earthly ambitions, his research at the lab.

At that time he aspired beyond the position of lab instructor to the rank of associate professor, and he often invited his American colleagues over for "drinks." After our mother died, Emily and I were recruited to help. As we went about our tasks, we would sometimes catch a glimpse of our father, standing in the corner, watching the American men and studying to become one.

But he couldn't get it right—our parties had an air of cultural confusion. We served potato chips on lacquered trays; Chinese landscapes bumped against watercolors of the Statue of Liberty, the Empire State Building.

Nor were Emily or I capable of helping him. I was still a child, and Emily didn't care. She had grown beyond us; she stalked around in blue jeans, seething with fury at everything to do with him.

"I hate this," she said, fiercely ripping another rag from a pair of old pajama bottoms. "Entertaining these jerks is a waste of time." Some chemists from Texas were visiting his department and he had invited them over for cocktails.

"I can finish it," I said. "You just need to do the parts I can't reach."

"It's not the dusting," she said. "It's the way he acts around them. 'Herro, herro! Hi Blad, hi Warry! Let me take your coat! Howsa Giants game?' " she mimicked. "If he were smart he wouldn't invite people over on football afternoons in the first place."

"What do you mean?" I said, worried that something was wrong. Brad Delmonte was my father's boss. I had noticed Baba reading the sports page that morning—something he rarely did.

"Oh, forget it," Emily said. I felt as if she and I were utterly separate. Then she smiled. "You've got oil on your glasses, Claudia."

Baba walked in carrying two bottles of wine. "They should arrive in half an hour," he said, looking at his watch. "They won't be early. Americans are never early."

Emily looked up. "I'm going to Jodie's house," she said.

Baba frowned and straightened his tie. "I want you to stay while they're here. We might need something from the kitchen."

"Claudia can get it for them."

"She's barely tall enough to reach the cabinets."

Emily stood up, clenched her dustcloth. "I don't care," she said. "I hate meeting those men."

"They're successful American scientists. You'd be better off with them instead of running around with your teenage friends, these sloppy kids, these rich white kids who dress like beggars."

"You're nuts, Dad," Emily said—she had begun addressing him the way an American child does. "You're nuts if you think these bosses of yours are ever going to do anything for you or any of us." And she threw her dustcloth, hard, into our "New York Giants" wastebasket.

"Speak to me with respect."

"You don't deserve it!"

"You are staying in this apartment! That is an order!"

"I wish you'd died instead of Mama!" Emily cried, and ran out of the room. She darted past our father, her long braid flying behind her. He stared at her, his expression oddly slack, the way it had been in the weeks after the funeral. He stepped toward her, reached hesitantly at her flying braid, but she turned and saw him, cried out as if he had struck her. His hands dropped to his sides.

Emily refused to leave our room. Otherwise that party was like so many others. The guests arrived late and left early. They talked about buying new cars and the Dallas Cowboys. I served pretzels and salted nuts. Baba walked around emptying ashtrays and refilling drinks. I noticed that the other men also wore vests and ties, but that the uniform looked somehow different on my slighter, darker father.

"Cute little daughter you have there," said Baba's boss. He was a large bearded smoker with a sandy voice. He didn't bend down to look at me or the ashtray that I raised toward his big square hand.

I went into our room and found Emily sitting on one of our unmade twin beds. It was dusk. Through the window the dull winter sun had almost disappeared. She didn't look up when I came in, but after a moment she spoke.

"I'm going to leave," she said. "As soon as I turn eighteen, I'm going to leave home and never come back!" She burst into tears. I reached for her shoulder but her thin, heaving body frightened me. She seemed too grown up to be comforted. I thought about the breasts swelling beneath her sweater. Her body had become a foreign place.

Perhaps Emily had warned me that she would someday leave in order to start me off on my own. I found myself avoiding her, as though her impending desertion would matter less if I deserted her first. I discovered a place to hide while she and my father fought, in the living room behind a painted screen. I would read a novel or look out the window. Sometimes they forgot about me—from the next room I would hear one of them break off an argument and say, "Where did Claudia go?" "I don't know," the other would reply. After a silence, they would start again.

One of these fights stands out in my memory. I must have been ten or eleven years old. It was the fourteenth day of the seventh lunar month: the eve of Guijie, the Chinese Spirit Festival, when the living are required to appease and provide for the ghosts of their ancestors. To the believing, the earth was thick with gathering spirits; it was safest to stay indoors and burn incense.

I seldom thought about the Chinese calendar, but every year on Guijie I wondered about my mother's ghost. Where was it? Would it still recognize me? How would I know when I saw it? I wanted to ask Baba, but I didn't dare. Baba had an odd attitude toward Guijie. On one hand, he had eschewed all Chinese customs since my mother's death. He was a scientist, he said; he scorned the traditional tales of unsatisfied spirits roaming the earth.

But I cannot remember a time when I was not made aware, in some way, of Guijie's fluctuating lunar date. That year the eve of the Spirit Festival fell on a Thursday, usually his night out with the men from his department. Emily and I waited for him to leave but he sat on the couch, calmly reading the *New York Times*.

Around seven o'clock, Emily began to fidget. She had a date that night and had counted on my father's absence. She spent half an hour washing and combing her hair, trying to make up her mind. Finally she asked me to give her a trim. I knew she'd decided to go out.

"Just a little," she said. "The ends are scraggly." We spread some newspapers on the living room floor. Emily stood in the middle of the papers with her hair combed down her back, thick and glossy, black as ink. It hadn't really been cut since she was born. Since my mother's death I had taken over the task of giving it the periodic touch-up.

I hovered behind her with the shears, searching for the scraggly ends, but there were none.

My father looked up from his newspaper. "What are you doing that for? You can't go out tonight," he said.

"I have a date!"

My father put down his newspaper. I threw the shears onto a chair and fled to my refuge behind the screen.

Through a slit over the hinge I caught a glimpse of Emily near the foyer, slender in her denim jacket, her black hair flooding down her back, her delicate features contorted with anger. My father's hair was disheveled, his hands clenched at his sides. The newspapers had scattered over the floor.

"Dressing up in boys' clothes, with paint on your face—"

"This is nothing! My going out on a few dates is nothing! You don't know what the hell you're talking about!"

"Don't shout," my father shook his finger. "Everyone in the building will hear you."

Emily raised her voice. "Who the hell cares? You're such a coward; you care more about what other people think than how I feel!"

"Acting like a loose woman in front of everybody, a street-walker!"

The floor shook under my sister's stamp. Though I'd covered my ears I could hear her crying. The door slammed, and her footfalls vanished down the stairs.

Things were quiet for a minute. Then I heard my father walk toward my corner. My heart thumped with fear—usually he let me alone. I had to look up when I heard him move the screen away. He knelt down next to me. His hair was streaked with gray, and his glasses needed cleaning.

"What are you doing?" he asked.

I shook my head, nothing.

After a minute I asked him, "Is Guijie why you didn't go play bridge tonight, Baba?"

"No, Claudia," he said. He always called me by my American name. This formality, I thought, was an indication of how distant he felt from me. "I stopped playing bridge last week."

"Why?" We both looked toward the window, where beyond our reflections the Hudson River flowed in the darkness.

"It's not important," he said.

"Okay."

But he didn't leave. "I'm getting old," he said after a moment. "Someone ten years younger was just promoted over me. I'm not going to try to keep up with them anymore."

It was the closest he had ever come to confiding in me. After a few more minutes he stood up and went into the kitchen. The newspapers rustled under his feet. For almost half an hour I heard him fumbling through the kitchen cabinets, looking for something he'd probably put there years ago. Eventually he came out, carrying a small brass urn and some matches. When Emily returned home after midnight, the apartment still smelled of the incense he had burned to protect her while she was gone.

My father loved Emily more. I knew this in my bones: it was why I stayed at home every night and wore no makeup, why I studied hard and got good grades, why I eventually went to college at Columbia, right up the street. Jealously I guarded my small allotment of praise, clutching it like a pocket of precious stones. Emily snuck out of the apartment late at night; she wore high-heeled sandals with patched blue jeans; she twisted her long hair into graceful, complex loops and braids that belied respectability. She smelled of lipstick and perfume. So certain she was of my father's love. His anger was a part of it. I knew nothing I could ever do would anger him that way.

When Emily turned eighteen and did leave home, a part of my father disappeared. I wondered sometimes: where did it go? Did she take it with her? What secret charm had she carried with her as she vanished down the tunnel to the jet that would take her to college in California, steadily and without looking back, while my father and I watched silently from the window at the gate? The apartment afterwards became quite still—it was only the two of us, mourning and dreaming through pale blue winter afternoons and silent evenings.

Emily called me, usually late at night after my father had gone to sleep. She sent me pictures of herself and people I didn't know, smiling on the sunny Berkeley campus. Sometimes after my father and I ate our simple meals or TV dinners I would go into our old room, where I had kept both of our twin beds, and take out Emily's pictures, trying to imagine what she must have been feeling, studying her expression and her swinging hair. But I always stared the longest at a postcard she'd sent me one winter break from northern New Mexico, a professional photo of a powerful, vast blue sky over faraway pink and sandy-beige mesas. The clarity and cleanness fascinated me. In a place like that, I thought, there would be nothing to search for, no reason to hide.

After college, she went to work at a bank in San Francisco. I saw her once when she flew to Manhattan on business. She skipped a meeting to have lunch with me. She wore an elegant gray suit and had pinned up her hair.

"How's Dad?" she said. I looked around, slightly alarmed. We were sitting in a bistro on the East Side, but I somehow thought he might overhear us.

"He's okay," I said. "We don't talk very much. Why don't you come home and see him?"

Emily stared at her water glass. "I don't think so."

"He misses you."

"I know. I don't want to hear about it."

"You hardly ever call him."

"There's nothing to talk about. Don't tell him you saw me, promise?"

"Okay."

During my junior year at Columbia, my father suffered a stroke. He was fifty-nine years old, and he was still working as a lab instructor in the chemistry department. One evening in early fall I came home from a class and found him on the floor, near the kitchen telephone. He was wearing his usual vest and tie. I called the hospital and sat down next to him. His wire-rimmed glasses lay on the floor a foot away. One-half of his face was frozen, the other half lined with sudden age and pain.

"They said they'll be right here," I said. "It won't be very long." I couldn't tell how much he understood. I smoothed his vest and straightened his tie. I folded his glasses. I knew he wouldn't like it if the ambulance workers saw him in a state of dishevelment. "I'm sure they'll be here soon," I said.

We waited. Then I noticed he was trying to tell me something. A line of spittle ran from the left side of his mouth. I leaned closer. After a while I made out his words: "Tell Emily," he said.

The ambulance arrived as I picked up the telephone to call California. That evening, at the hospital, what was remaining of my father left the earth.

Emily insisted that we not hold a Buddhist cremation ceremony. "I never want to think about that stuff again," she said. "Plus, all of his friends are Americans. I don't know who would come, except for us." She had reached New York the morning after his death. Her eyes were vague and her fingernails bitten down.

On the third day we scattered his ashes in the river. Afterward we held a small memorial service for his friends from work. We didn't talk much as we straightened the living room and dusted the furniture. It took almost three hours. The place was a mess. We hadn't had a party in years.

It was a cloudy afternoon, and the Hudson looked dull and sluggish from the living room window. I noticed that although she had not wanted a Buddhist ceremony, Emily had dressed in black and white according to Chinese mourning custom. I had asked the department secretary to put up a sign on the bulletin board. Eleven people came; they drank five bottles of wine. Two of his Chinese students stood in the corner, eating cheese and crackers.

Brad Delmonte, paunchy and no longer smoking, attached himself to Emily. "I remember when you were just a little girl," I heard him say as I walked by with the extra crackers.

"I don't remember you," she said.

"You're still a cute little thing." She bumped his arm, and he spilled his drink.

Afterwards we sat on the couch and surveyed the cluttered coffee table. It was past seven but we didn't talk about dinner.

"I'm glad they came," I said.

"I hate them." Emily looked at her fingernails. Her voice shook. "I don't know whom I hate more: them, or him—for taking it."

"It doesn't matter any more," I said.

"I suppose."

We watched the room grow dark.

"Do you know what?" Emily said. "It's the eve of the fifteenth day of the seventh lunar month."

"How do you know?" During college I had grown completely unaware of the lunar calendar.

"One of those chemistry nerds from China told me this afternoon."

I wanted to laugh, but instead felt myself make a strange whimpering sound, squeezed out from my tight and hollow chest.

"Remember the time Dad and I had that big fight?" she said. "You know that now, in my grown-up life, I don't fight with anyone? I never had problems with anybody except him."

"No one cared about you as much as he did," I said.

"I don't want to hear about it." Her voice began to shake again. "He was a pain, and you know it. He got so strict after Mama died. It wasn't all my fault."

"I'm sorry," I said. But I was so angry with her that I felt my face turn red, my cheeks tingle in the dark. She'd considered our father a nerd as well, had squandered his love with such thoughtlessness that I could scarcely breathe to think about it. It seemed impossibly unfair that she had memories of my mother as well. Carefully I waited for my feelings to go away. Emily, I thought, was all I had.

But as I sat, a vision distilled before my eyes: the soft baked shades, the great blue sky of New Mexico. I realized that after graduation I could go wherever I wanted. Somewhere a secret, rusty door swung open and filled my mind with sweet freedom, fearful coolness.

" I want to do something," I said.

"Like what?"

"I don't know." Then I got an idea. "Emily, why don't I give you a haircut?"

We found newspapers and spread them on the floor. We turned on the lamps and moved the coffee table out of the way, brought the wine glasses to the sink. Emily went to the bathroom, and I searched for the shears a long time before I found them in the kitchen. I glimpsed the incense urn in a cabinet and quickly shut the door. When I returned to the living room it smelled of shampoo. Emily was standing in the middle of the papers with her wet hair down her back, staring at herself in the reflection from the window. The lamplight cast circles under her eyes.

"I had a dream last night," she said. "I was walking down the street. I felt a tug. He was trying to reach me, trying to pull my hair."

"I'll just give you a trim," I said.

"No," she said. "Why don't you cut it."

"What do you mean?" I snapped a two-inch lock off the side. Emily looked down at the hair on the newspapers. "I'm serious," she said. "Cut my hair. I want to see two feet of hair on the floor."

"Emily, you don't know what you're saying," I said. But a strange, weightless feeling had come over me. I placed the scissors at the nape of her neck. "How about it?" I asked, and my voice sounded low and odd.

"*I don't care.*" An echo of the past. I cut. The shears went *snack*. A long black lock of hair hit the newspapers by my feet.

The Chinese say that our hair and our bodies are given to us from our ancestors, gifts that should not be tampered with. My mother herself had never done this. But after the first few moments I enjoyed myself, pressing the thick black locks through the shears, heavy against my thumb. Emily's hair slipped to the floor around us, rich and beautiful, lying in long graceful arcs over my shoes. She stood perfectly still, staring out the window. The Hudson River flowed behind our reflections, bearing my father's ashes through the night.

When I was finished, the back of her neck gleamed clean and white under a precise shining cap. "You missed your calling," Emily said. "You want me to do yours?"

My hair, browner and scragglier, had never been past my shoulders.

I had always kept it short, figuring the ancestors wouldn't be offended by my tampering with a lesser gift. "No," I said. "But you should take a shower. Some of those small bits will probably itch."

"It's already ten o'clock," she said. "We should go to sleep soon anyway." Satisfied, she glanced at the mirror in the foyer. "I look like a completely different person," she said. She left to take her shower. I wrapped up her hair in the newspapers and went into the kitchen. I stood next to the sink for a long time before throwing the bundle away.

The past sees through all attempts at disguise. That night I was awakened by a wrenching scream. I gasped and stiffened, grabbing a handful of blanket.

"*Claudia*," Emily cried from the other bed. "Claudia, wake up!"

"What is it?"

"I saw Baba." She hadn't called our father Baba in years. "Over there, by the door. Did you see him?"

"No," I said. "I didn't see anything." My bones felt frozen in place. After a moment I opened my eyes. The full moon shone through the window, bathing our room in silver and shadow. I heard my sister sob and then fall silent. I looked carefully at the door, but I noticed nothing.

Then I understood that his ghost would never visit me. I was, one might say, the lucky daughter. But I lay awake until morning, waiting; part of me is waiting still.

RON HANSEN
1986

Nebraska

The town is Americus, Covenant, Denmark, Grange, Hooray, Jerusalem, Sweetwater—one of the lesser-known moons of the Platte, conceived in sickness and misery by European pioneers who took the path of least resistance and put down roots in an emptiness like the one they kept secret in their youth. In Swedish and Danish and German and Polish, in anxiety and fury and God's providence, they chopped at the Great Plains with spades, creating green sodhouses that crumbled and collapsed in the rain and disappeared in the first persuasive snow and were so low the grown-ups stooped to go inside; and yet were places of ownership and a hard kind of happiness, the places their occupants gravely stood before on those plenary occasions when photographs were taken.

And then the Union Pacific stopped by, just a camp of white campaign tents and a boy playing his harpoon at night, and then a supply store, a depot, a pine water tank, stockyards, and the mean prosperity of the twentieth century. The trains strolling into town to shed a box car in the depot side yard, or crying past at sixty miles per hour, possibly interrupting a girl in her high wire act, her arms looping up when she tips to one side, the railtop as slippery as a silver spoon. And then the yellow and red locomotive rises up from the heat shimmer over a mile away, the August noonday warping the sight of it, but cinders tapping away from the spikes and the iron rails already vibrating up inside the girl's shoes. She steps down to the roadbed and then into high weeds as the Union Pacific pulls Wyoming coal and Georgia-Pacific lumber and snowplow blades and aslant Japanese pickup trucks through the green, open countryside and on to Omaha. And when it passes by, a worker she knows is opposite her, like a pedestrian at a stoplight, the sun not letting up, the plainsong of grasshoppers going on and on between them until the worker says, "Hot."

Twice the Union Pacific tracks cross over the sidewinding Democrat, the water slow as an ox cart, green as silage, croplands to the east,

30

yards and houses to the west, a green ceiling of leaves in some places, whirlpools showing up in it like spinning plates that lose speed and disappear. In winter and a week or more of just above zero, high school couples walk the gray ice, kicking up snow as quiet words are passed between them, opinions are mildly compromised, sorrows are apportioned. And Emil Jedlicka unslings his blue-stocked .22 and slogs through high brown weeds and snow, hunting ring-necked pheasant, sidelong rabbits, and—always suddenly—quail, as his little brother Orin sprints across the Democrat in order to slide like an otter.

July in town is a gray highway and a Ford hay truck spraying by, the hay sailing like a yellow ribbon caught in the mouth of a prancing dog, and Billy Awalt up there on the camel's hump, eighteen years old and sweaty and dirty, peppered and dappled with hay dust, a lump of chew like an extra thumb under his lower lip, his blue eyes happening on a Dairy Queen and a pretty girl licking a pale trickle of ice cream from the cone. And Billy slaps his heart and cries, "O! I am pierced!"

And late October is orange on the ground and blue overhead and grain silos stacked up like white poker chips, and a high silver water tower belittled one night by the sloppy tattoo of one year's class at George W. Norris High. And below the silos and water tower are stripped treetops, their gray limbs still lifted up in alleluia, their yellow leaves crowding along yard fences and sheeping along the sidewalks and alleys under the shepherding wind.

Or January and a heavy snow partitioning the landscape, whiting out the highways and woods and cattle lots until there are only open spaces and steamed-up windowpanes, and a Nordstrom boy limping pitifully in the hard plaster of his clothes, in a snow parka meant to be green and a snow cap meant to be purple, the snow as deep as his hips when the boy tips over and cannot get up until a little Schumacher girl sitting by the stoop window, a spoon in her mouth, a bowl of Cheerios in her lap, says in plain voice, "There's a boy," and her mother looks out to the sidewalk.

Houses are big and white and two stories high, each a cousin to the next, with pigeon roosts in the attic gables, green storm windows on the upper floor, and a green screened porch, some as pillowed and couched as parlors or made into sleeping rooms for the boy whose next step will be the Navy and days spent on a ship with his hometown's own population, on gray water that rises up and is allayed like a geography of cornfields, sugar beets, soybeans, wheat, that stays there and says, in its own way, "Stay." Houses are turned away from the land and toward whatever is not always, sitting across from each other like dressed-up children at a party in daylight, their parents looking on with hopes and fond expectations. Overgrown elm and sycamore trees poach the sunlight from the lawns and keep petticoats of snow around them into April. In the deep lots out back are wire clotheslines with flapping white sheets pinned to them, property lines are hedged with sour green and purple grapes, or with rabbit wire and gardens of peonies, roses, gladiola, irises, marigolds, pansies. Fruit trees are so closely planted that they cannot sway without knitting. The apples and cherries drop and sweetly decompose until they're only slight brown bumps in the yards, but the pears stay up in the wind, drooping under the pecks of birds, withering down like peppers until their passion and sorrow is justly noticed and they one day disappear.

Aligned against an alley of blue shale rock is a garage whose doors slash weeds and scrape up pebbles as an old man pokily swings them open, teetering with his last weak push. And then Mr. Victor Johnson rummages inside, being cautious about his gray sweater and high-topped shoes, looking over paint cans, junked electric motors, grass rakes and garden rakes and a pitchfork and sickles, gray doors and ladders piled overhead in the rafters, and an old wind-up Victrola and heavy platter records from the twenties, on one of them a soprano singing, "I'm a Lonesome Melody." Under a green tarpaulin is a wooden movie projector he painted silver and big cans of tan celluloid, much of it orange and green with age, but one strip of it preserved: of an Army pilot in jodhpurs hopping from one biplane and onto another's upper wing. Country people who'd paid to see the movie had been spellbound by the slight dip of the wings at the pilot's jump, the slap of his leather jacket, and how his hair strayed wild and was promptly sleeked back by the wind, but looking at the strip now, pulling a ribbon of it up to a windowpane and letting it unspool to the ground, Mr. Johnson can make out only twenty frames of the leap and then snapshot after snapshot of an Army pilot clinging to the biplane's wing. And yet Mr. Johnson stays with it, as though that scene of one man staying alive was what he'd paid his nickel for.

Main Street is just a block away. Pickup trucks stop in it so their drivers can angle out over their brown left arms and speak about crops or praise the weather or make up sentences whose only real point is their lack of complication. And then a cattle truck comes up and they mosey along with a touch of their cap bills or a slap of the door metal. High school girls in skintight jeans stay in one place on weekends and jacked-up cars cruise past, rowdy farmboys overlapping inside, pulling over now and then in order to give the girls cigarettes and sips of pop and grief about their lipstick. And when the cars peel out the girls say how a particular boy measured up or they swap gossip about Donna Moriarity and the scope she permitted Randy when he came back from bootcamp.

Everyone is famous in this town. And everyone is necessary. Townspeople go to the Vaughn grocery store for the daily news, and to the Home restaurant for history class, especially at evensong when the old people eat gravied pot roast and lemon meringue pies and calmly sip coffee from cups they tip to their mouths with both hands. The Kiwanis Club meets here on Tuesday nights, and hopes are made public, petty sins are tidily dispatched, the proceeds from the gumball machines are talleyed up and poured into the upkeep of a playground. Johnson's Hardware store has picnic items and kitchen appliances in its one window, in the manner of those prosperous men who would prefer to be known for their hobbies. And there is one crisp, white, Protestant church with a steeple, of the sort pictured on calendars; and the Immaculate Conception Catholic church, grayly holding the town at bay like a Gothic wolfhound. And there is an insurance agency, a county coroner and justice of the peace, a secondhand shop, a handsome chiropractor named Koch who coaches the Pony League baseball team, a post office approached on unpainted wood steps outside of a cheap mobile home, the Nighthawk tavern where there's Falstaff tap beer, a green pool table, a poster recording the Cornhuskers' scores, a crazy man patiently tolerated, a gray-haired woman with an unmoored eye, a boy in spectacles thick as paperweights, a carpenter missing one index finger, a plump waitress whose day job is in a basement beauty shop, an old woman who creeps up to the side door at eight in order to purchase one shotglass of whiskey.

And yet passing by, and paying attention, an outsider is only aware of what isn't, that there's no bookshop, no picture show, no pharmacy or dry cleaners, no cocktail parties, extreme opinions, jewelry or piano stores, motels, hotels, hospital, political headquarters, travel agencies, art galleries, European fashions, philosophical theories about Being and the soul.

High importance is only attached to practicalities, and so there is the Batchelor Funeral Home, where a proud old gentleman is on display in a dark brown suit, his yellow fingernails finally clean, his smeared eyeglasses in his coat pocket, a grandchild on tiptoes by the casket, peering at the lips that will not move, the sparrow chest that will not rise. And there's Tommy Seymour's for Sinclair gasoline and mechanical repairs, a green balloon dinosaur bobbing from a string over the cash register, old tires piled beneath the cottonwood. For Sale in the side yard a Case tractor, a John Deere reaper, a hay mower, a red manure spreader, and a rusty grain conveyor, green weeds overcoming them, standing up inside them, trying slyly and little-by-little to inherit machinery for the earth.

And beyond that are woods, a slope of pasture, six empty cattle pens, a driveway made of limestone pebbles, and the house where Alice Sorensen pages through a child's World Book encyclopedia, stopping at the descriptions of California, Capetown, Ceylon, Colorado, Copenhagen, Corpus Christi, Costa Rica, Cyprus.

Widow Dworak has been watering the lawn in an open raincoat and apron, but at nine she walks the green hose around to the spiggot and screws down the nozzle so that the spray is a misty crystal bowl softly baptizing the ivy. She says, "How about some camomile tea?" And she says, "Yum. Oh boy. That hits the spot." And bends to shut the water off.

The Union Pacific night train rolls through town just after ten o'clock when a sixty-year-old man named Adolf Schooley is a boy again in bed, and when the huge weight of forty or fifty cars jostles his upstairs room like a motor he'd put a quarter in. And over the sighing industry of the train, he can hear the train saying Nebraska, Nebraska, Nebraska, Nebraska. And he cannot sleep.

Mrs. Antoinette Heft is at the Home restaurant, placing frozen meat patties on waxed paper, pausing at times to clamp her fingers under her arms and press the sting from them. She stops when the Union Pacific passes, then picks a cigarette out of a pack of Kools and smokes it on the back porch, smelling air as crisp as Oxydol, looking up at stars the Pawnee Indians looked at, hearing the low harmonica of big rigs on the highway, in the town she knows like the palm of her hand, in the country she knows by heart.

IVAN KLÍMA
1992

The Washing Machine

Translated from the Czech by Ewald Osers

She picked over her pile of dirty washing in order to fill the remaining space in the washing machine. It was a large machine, it could take six kilograms of washing, and this suited her because that way she only had to wash once a month. At one time, when the children were still living at home, she had of course washed more often, but always with displeasure. She hated all household chores because of their hopeless ineffectualness. The dust she'd wiped off would settle again within a few hours, the food she'd bought and cooked was irretrievably eaten up, the washed linen would get dirty again, just as the washed-up crockery, and the things she tidied away in their proper places would after a while return to where they didn't belong. They were an untidy lot, her daughters and her husband.

The daughters, of course, had left home, and as for Philip, where was he really? When had she last seen him? But his socks were still in the pile of washing. She picked them up one by one and tossed them into the open drum. One of them was a dark, rather dirty red. Surely Philip had never worn such a sock. She took it between her fingers: it was a good thick texture, probably genuine wool, heaven knew where it came from. Unless he'd got it from one of those girls of his, from some harlot he had, as always, concealed from her. He'd get some socks from her, or a scarf, and in return he'd give her—what did he give those women? Maybe jewelry, or money, or at least expensive clothes. She didn't bother about it, she'd never been interested in material objects or in money. She didn't know how much he was earning, let alone how much he was making on the side from his patients. She didn't want to know, and sometimes he actually resented that; it seemed to him that she didn't really appreciate his skill or his success.

She closed the washing machine, set the dial, and pressed the buttons. The water rushed into the drum and through the window she watched it flushing the white washing powder down. The gentle and continuous movement of the water calmed her. Now she would be able to return to the living room and enjoy a little free time. But she knew that she wouldn't be able to. Throughout her adult life, probably, she'd suppressed the wish to deal with her own time in her own way; instead she was discharging her duties.

Her life consisted of a series of duties. Toward her children, toward her parents, toward her friends, and of course toward Philip and his friends. Of duties at the institute and toward her colleagues at the institute, to her superiors and to her subordinates. Sometimes she was so tired, so worn out, that in the evening, when she was alone in her bath with the water noisily rushing into the basin, she would moan aloud, sob and lament, aware of the fact that the running water would drown her voice, so that her lamentations could not possibly disturb anyone. Later, with the passage of time, her duties diminished. Her daughters got married, friendships faded, and Philip spent less time at home. Lately that had been no time at all. She hadn't seen him for weeks on end, or at least that was how it seemed to her. But she still couldn't rid herself of the feeling that she had no right to spend time on her own pleasures.

How could she rest when there were so many things needing to be arranged, so many tasks discharged? How could she sit down at the piano and play, or creep into bed, when at the same time there were so many people having to work? How could she get pleasure from her work or delight in some invented happening in a book when so many living beings were suffering?

There was a click in the washing machine, a metallic groan, then the drum suddenly stopped and the motor revved up. She pressed a button and switched off the machine. For a while she gazed helplessly at the machine that had died on her, then she tried to start it up again. The motor moaned as it vainly tried to spin the drum. She thought she could smell the stench of burnt rubber. For safety she pulled out the cable from the socket. The sudden silence fell on her like a net. She floundered in it and tried to dispel her anxiety. This would have to happen to her today. Who'd come to repair a washing machine on a Saturday? If at least Philip would turn up, if at least there was a hope of him turning up. She could also ring up one or the other of her egregious sons-in-law, but they were sure to find some excuse for not coming.

She went to the telephone and for a while turned over the pages of her address book. She didn't have many friends, she only had a lot of acquaintances, but most of these would certainly not know their way about motors or any machinery. They were medical men, research scientists, and geologists. But then she noticed a name that meant absolutely nothing to her. Dušek. She'd obviously written it in herself, she recognized her own handwriting. And in brackets she had added: repairer. Repairer of what? Refrigerators, motor cars, or possibly washing machines?

She dialed the number. "But lady," a stranger's voice protested after listening to her, "don't you know that it's Saturday!"

"I need it to be repaired urgently, I beg you!"

"Couldn't it wait till Monday?"

"I've got to . . . we're about to leave; I beg you. I'll make it worth your while."

"Well, we'll see," the voice said. "But even if I come round now—I can't promise. If it's some part that's gone phutt . . ."

"Thank you so much. You're very kind!" She would have said some more nice things to him but he'd hung up.

She tried to recall the man's face. Maybe she'd never even seen him, maybe someone had given her his name and telephone number. But he was clearly a decent sort of person. Decent people were getting fewer all the time. Once she'd believed that Philip was a decent person, but later she'd discovered that he was selfish, self-indulgent, and a disgraceful liar. She'd never found out with how many women he'd deceived her. And he hoarded things, heaps of useless rubbish: old pictures, medals, coins, and even older containers and jars with Latin inscriptions. Oh yes, he had time for all that, it was only for her and the children that he never had any time. What use was his life really? Sometimes it occurred to her that it was better not to live at all than to live the way he did.

Her daughters had taken after him. She'd tried so hard to bring them up with love and for love, to teach them to care about the people around them, about people and not about things, for them to appreciate what was alive and not what was doomed to ruin, what would merely bury and choke them. She had not succeeded.

How long would it take the man to get to her place? And would he come at all? She crossed the room. The jars in the display cabinet were again covered with dust. Betonica, Serpentina, Valerianum, Pyrethrum-Speichelkraut—the money he must have squandered on these things and what was the use of them, whom did he benefit by them? The medals were lying about on their velvet cushions—the hours he would spend over them, the way he would caress them. When had he last caressed her? When had he last addressed her tenderly? Once, a long time ago, he'd call her his "little guinea pig" or "little mouse."

She brushed away her tears. From the window she could see down into the street, into that gray stony street, where not a single tree grew, where, apart from a few flowerpots on the balconies opposite, there was not a hint of greenery. Only shade, pavement, soot, and rusty pipes. And she was so fond of the open country. She would have liked to live in some little house near a wood, near a river, or at least near a stream. She'd have kept animals—rabbits, chickens, maybe even sheep. And she'd have had an orchard full of fruit trees.

That had been the only pleasure she'd allowed herself while her daughters were small: taking them into the country frequently. They'd drive beyond the city, Philip would be on duty or else he'd think up some other excuse, but he'd let them have the car, petrol was still cheap then, so they could set out for wherever their fancy took them. Along the motorway or, for a change, along the narrow little suburban streets toward the south. For a number of years they'd also rented a cottage not far from the Slapy reservoir. The wooden building stood on a rock that was so precipitous that if you looked out from the window you felt directly suspended above the surface of the water. Kobra had sometimes amused herself by throwing stones out of the window and waiting for the quiet yet somehow terrifying splash from down below. Sometimes she would herself throw out the remains of food and other refuse from the window. Their fall into the water had mostly been soundless, but rings would spread over the surface and after awhile disappear, and only the undisturbed and smooth sheet of water would remain. The way the surface closed up again, that dropping of things right into the depth somehow attracted her, and sometimes she had to step back from the window out of a vertiginous fear that she herself might give the waters the opportunity of closing up over her.

She couldn't recall when she had last stepped into that wooden cottage on top of the rock—it must have been ten years at least.

The telephone rang, it was Kobra, her elder daughter. "I'm not disturbing you in the middle of some work, am I, Mum?"

"I'm always in the middle of some work," she replied. "But now, to top it all, my washing machine's broken."

"Would you like to bring your washing over to me?"

"What an idea—it's all wet. Besides I can't even open the machine while there's water in it."

"I didn't realize you had your washing in it already. Anyone coming to look at it?"

"Yes. He should be here any moment."

"That's great," Kobra feigned interest.

She didn't say anything. Why had her daughter phoned? She didn't normally phone at this time—it was usually either in the morning or in the evening. Or if she wanted something.

"How's Dad? He hasn't shown up here for some time."

"I don't know. He hasn't shown up here either."

"Is he out of town?"

"Probably."

"And he didn't say when he'd be back?"

"He hasn't been telling me that for a long time."

"Sorry, Mum. It's just that they told me at the hospital . . ."

"What did they tell you at the hospital?"

"They expected him at the beginning of the week, but there's no sign of him."

"What am I supposed to do? They phoned me too, a few days ago. Wondered if he was ill. I told them that if he was ill I didn't know anything about it. But not to worry, he'd manage somehow."

"I'm sorry, Mum. I know you're having a rough time. But he'll be back, you know what he's like. And when he gets back, could he ring me?"

The sound of a bell came from the passage and she hurriedly said goodbye.

Through the spy-hole she saw a strange reddish face. An elongated goat-like head nodding on a long neck that seemed to be cut halfway across by a red scar. Small blue eyes were looking toward her from under colorless lashes.

"Here I am, lady!" He had a high, slightly stifled voice. In one hand he carried a bulging bag, the other was clutching a whitish rag. "Does this by any chance belong to you?" He held the thing out to her.

It was a sock. She took it between her fingers: a thick genuine woolen sock. Except that its color was different—grayish white.

"Where did you find it?"

"I made a mistake and climbed up to the next floor," he explained. "Right up to the attic. And there it was lying by the door."

"Thank you." She noticed that his gaze was fixed on something behind her back. It frightened her. What could the man be seeing there?

"You got some super things here, lady!" He pointed at the display case. "Real antiques, aren't they?"

"My husband. He collects anything you can think of." She felt alarmed by what she'd just said. "He chiefly collects medical items. These beakers and little mortars come from old pharmacies."

The man nodded his goat's head. The hair on it was short and sparse.

Philip's hair was dark and still thick. It smelled of a mixture of smoke and disinfectant, it smelled of hospital, and the smell always excited her.

"I wouldn't mind collecting things too," the man said in his high-pitched stifled voice. "Beautiful things in one's life are like spice in a goulash. But I haven't got the time."

She led him to the bathroom and went off to make some coffee for him. She was still holding the sock. How had it got upstairs? Where did the two socks come from and why was each a different color? Whose feet had they been on? Finally she threw it away with a feeling of revulsion and spent a long time rinsing her hands in the sink.

When she took his coffee to him the washing machine had been pulled away from the wall and its rear panel removed. The man was kneeling on the tiles, shining a pocket torch into its works.

"Can you do it?" she asked anxiously.

He turned his puce face to her, and as he was bending down, the scar on his neck seemed to be suffused with blood. "The control board's jammed. And where on earth would I get a new one?"

"Can't you get hold of one?"

"Lady, come down to earth!"

"I need—I need it working this day!"

The man shrugged. He straightened up, took the mug from her hand, and took a sip of coffee. "Good coffee," he smacked noisily. "Strong. The way I like it. Coffee should be like passion."

She fished out two hundred-crown notes from her wallet and placed them on top of the washing machine. "Please!" she said.

"I'd have to have a look round at home. No promise, mind." He took another sip of coffee. "Can't really tell what stuff there's knocking about at my place."

"I'll drive you there."

"That would be kind, lady!" He looked at her as though he was putting his hand on her shoulder and pressing it. She nearly cried out.

He lived at the edge of the town in a still unfinished two-story box with a garden. "I'll wait for you in the car," she suggested.

"No, come right in. I'll have something to show you."

They climbed a few stairs, went through a hall, and stepped into a room that struck her as unexpectedly spacious. The wall facing her was adorned by a wallpaper of a lake with a sunlit birchwood rising from its banks up the mountainside.

In the room there were only two easy chairs, a little table, a television set, and a control panel with switches on it.

"Won't you sit down?" He flicked one switch and below the ceiling a concealed light came on and from behind her back came the sweetish notes of a melody. "What d'you think of it?"

"You have a nice place here. Really nice."

"Ten years' work." He leaned over to her until she felt his breath. "Saturdays, Sundays, and every evening. My old woman helped me, can't say she didn't. But suddenly she went off her rocker, met some little pipsqueak, he was only ten years older than our oldest boy. So I'm now alone with all this stuff. I come home in the evening, sit down where you're sitting, turn on the music, and look at the lake. Looks real, doesn't it?" He moved a slide switch and the concealed lights were dimmed and at the same time turned red. The white walls were spattered with drops of blood that flickeringly flowed down to the floor. "Not bad, is it?"

"Very nice." And on her shoulder she felt a strange hand that was pushing her deeper into the chair.

"I'll leave you for awhile," he announced, "while I go and see what I can find."

"The light," she managed to jerk out as he'd reached the door. "You forgot to switch off the light effects."

"That's all right," he waved his hand.

She looked at the wall down which drops of blood flowed ceaselessly. Then she shut her eyes. The music was sweetly and thickly cloying to her face and trickling down to her neck. She fished out a handkerchief from her handbag and wiped her forehead, then she cleaned her hands with it for a long time.

Somewhere a door slammed in the house.

Why had the man made her come in? And why had she come?

Why was she so lonely? Why had her husband stopped loving her?

Why didn't her daughters visit her more often than just once a month?

Why was there so little love between people and so much coldness, hatred, and viciousness?

Here she was sitting in a strange house, having to listen to a stranger's misfortunes while she had more than enough of her own. Why did she have to sit here instead of sitting at home, waiting for Philip to enter and embrace her?

Why hadn't Philip embraced her for such a long time?

Why had nothing in her life ever come out the way she'd hoped? Who was punishing her all the time, and for what, when she was trying so hard to live a good and useful life, to fulfill all her obligations? And had the true punishment, the real and final punishment, arrived yet? She curled up in her chair and tears streamed down her cheeks.

The man appeared again. "Nothing," he announced. "But I'll have a look upstairs. If I could trouble you, lady, I'd take the liberty of showing you something."

She got up, wiped her sticky finger on her handkerchief, and followed him.

He led her upstairs to the first floor, and then farther up. "Careful," he turned back to her; "upstairs the handrail's missing." He opened a small metal door and through the space between his body and the doorpost she saw the roof beams.

What did it mean? Why had he dragged her up here? She was aware of a fit of trembling enfolding her. No, she wouldn't go in there, she wouldn't give in that easily, surely she didn't deserve anything like that—lying on some strange attic floor, covered with a sack and with blowflies buzzing around her.

On the little landing in front of the door the handrail was really missing. Glancing down she saw the stairwell. It was a lot deeper than she would have expected in a two-story house, and she stepped back from the abyss and pressed herself against the wall.

"If you please, lady," the man said and nearly bowed in front of the half-open door.

Dear God, heavenly father, protect me! She passed through the metal door. The attic was light, tidy, and hot. In the corner by the door was a neat pile of sacks and a cupboard with a lot of drawers stood leaning against the chimney-breast.

"Come in, I'll show you something, lady!" And he led her round the stack of sacks. A tattered rope hung from one of the massive beams. "Here," he demonstrated, "I tried to loop this up, but it didn't work out." His hands flew up and enclosed his skull, as if they were trying to lift it off, to sever it from his trunk and lay it down at her feet. "But I'm glad. Now I realize that there's plenty of time for that. Life's short, death is long—don't you agree?"

"You're right," she hurriedly nodded. Who was that person really?

"And now I'll show you something, lady!" In the farthest corner of the attic, on a low wall, hung some object covered with sacking. He stepped up to it and unveiled it.

She nearly cried out.

Before her she saw a huge Venetian mirror. The richly decorated frame glittered as if set with diamonds.

"What do you think of it?"

She saw her own face, her sallow, almost bloodless, and suddenly aged face. He was standing behind her, his hands behind his back, with his goat's head contracted in a smirk.

What if this isn't a living person, a real person, but a phantom, a dead shadow? Suddenly it occurred to her: what if this is Philip, with his face having just now assumed this revolting appearance, the real appearance of his goat's soul?

Maybe this was a punishment inflicted on him, a punishment for his pride, for his vanity, for his conceited self-assurance with which he would knock down all those who were weaker than himself, all those in whose hearts still flickered some human feeling.

And what would be her punishment?

Dear God, heavenly father, have mercy upon me!

The man behind her took a step toward her. What was he holding in his hand? Some instrument? Would she have time to glimpse it before he struck?

She closed her eyes. The floor beneath her rose and fell again.

"Some piece, isn't it?" He wanted her opinion.

"Magnificent!" she breathed.

"Cost quite a bit, too," he said. "But she sold it. She was quite old and almost totally blind. What use was a mirror to her?"

She was aware of his voice receding. She half-opened her eyes. He was no longer standing behind her. He was rummaging about in the cupboard. "Here's something," he announced. "Maybe it'll fit. We could drive back again, lady!"

Back home she made some more strong coffee for him. Then she stood in the hall and through the open door watched him working. He was whistling to himself.

Then he straightened up, plugged in the lead, pressed some buttons, and she could hear the motor starting up almost noiselessly and spinning the drum. He stopped the motor, replaced the rear panel, pushed the machine back against the wall, and washed his hands.

"How much do I owe you?" she asked.

"Just a moment, lady!" He again switched the machine on and turned the dial. She heard the familiar gurgle of the pump and the machine began to empty.

The two of them looked at the pinkish water running out of the rubber hose.

"Strange water you've got here, lady," the man said.

"That's from a sock," she breathed. "A badly dyed sock."

"That's it, then." He was still watching the pinkish liquid swirling about in the bathtub. "Suppose you let me have another two hundred. Spares are expensive nowadays!"

She handed him the green notes.

"Thank you, lady!" For a moment his gaze lingered on some object behind her, probably some antique, then he picked up his bag. "If you need me again, you've got my number."

"I have. And thank you. Thank you so much. You're a nice person."

She saw him to the door. Then she returned to the bathroom. She sat down on the edge of the bath and listened to the smooth spinning of the drum. Once more the pump gurgled and began to spew out the water. It was almost clear now, almost completely transparent, like tears, like a lot of tears, like a stream of tears this water was, she realized, and began to sob.

JOYCE CAROL OATES
1965

The Assailant

There are those strange, ugly times when your body seems transparent, your skin drawn too tight, something, so that the heightened beat of the heart and the minute hissing of blood through veins seems a concern not just of yourself but of everyone watching you. I knew this once but have forgotten it; sitting in the hospital waiting room I am reminded. Outside the hospital, past its bright green lawn and immaculate swept sidewalks, people are walking without this knowledge. It is spring, May. Why should they bother with this knowledge? If they glance at the hospital, it is a glance that does not sharpen but scatters their thoughts; for why should they be reminded of the transparency of their bodies under their handsome clothes?

And this is a weekday too; I am conscious, among the other people who wait, of being truant from something. Years ago I would have felt guilty at being out of school. Now, what am I absent from? At this time of day—ten-thirty in the morning—everyone belongs somewhere. We are those who have been selected out of ordinary routines because something has gone wrong. We are conscious of a mistake somewhere. Those we have come to visit are being propped up with pillows, tubes are being adjusted in them, blood pumped into their indifferent arteries: who knows what magic is being performed? The nurses are young and healthy and professionally impersonal. They know secrets of the kind we out here cannot be trusted with. Our bodies would refuse such knowledge. It is kept behind walls from us. When we leave the hospital and hurry out into sweeter air, they will tend our secrets for us and keep us from thinking. And, later, when our loved ones are dead, or recovered and free like us, we too can walk past the hospital without seeing it.

My friend sits beside me knocking ashes into the stained ashtray. It has a floor stand and is made of metal with markings to suggest wood; its early flashy brilliance is marred by rust spots. Bargain basement. A wad of pink gum with tiny teethmarks in it lies in the ashtray; fortunately, it is the kind of gimmicky ashtray you can manipulate into opening, so that the gum falls through and disappears.

My friend glances at me after he does this, but I have looked away. Impossible to keep up the strain of love if we share such things. . . . When I look back at him the gum is gone, he has recrossed his long legs, he smiles tentatively at me.

Time for the visit. My friend remains seated. He avoids the nurse's gaze, and the unlegal, unofficial nature of our relationship is advertised. He and I are nothing to each other, nothing that could be filed away. At the extremes of life and death we would part company. I follow the nurse along the corridor. The foyer must be a recent addition, for the floors and walls there were handsome. As soon as you leave the foyer the dingy, rather damp hospital itself begins . . . it has no dignity, disease and death. There is here the paid-for anonymity of county buildings with their clerks and counters, the anonymity of certain police stations and public libraries at the very centers of huge American cities. Dying must be easier in those gray impersonal surroundings, for their dimly white walls and chipped bed posts and noiseless wheeled carts have nothing in them to suggest a world to be envied. Or do I say this to myself to keep from feeling terror? The nurse walks ahead, in rubber-soled white shoes. All the money he pays, and what is so good about this . . . ? I try to be grim and practical; my father could admire no qualities in me except these.

And here, suddenly, he is. Propped up by pillows as I had imagined, and yet not the man I had imagined. He is still stunned and baffled. He is old. We think of our fathers not as they are but as they appeared to us one day—when we were ten, maybe, and everything was vivid and uncomplicated. We have no heart to think of them as they are, as if that were a betrayal.

"He likes the sunlight. He was sitting up for breakfast," the nurse says. She is pretty, with brown hair. In spite of her white uniform and the sure, practiced look of those hands accustomed to death, I think of her not as a function of the hospital but as a woman—someone my friend, waiting back there with the old rumpled *Saturday Evening Posts*, might find pleasing to look at.

I sit by the window, in a wicker-backed chair painted pale green. The hospital room is smaller than I remembered. So much money for this? But it is expensive, this death and dying, there is suddenly no room for the economical eye that charted us for so many years. The old man in bed watches me attentively, as if I might make a sudden movement. His eyes are still intelligent, though his face and body are wasted. Or are they intelligent? That is the sort of thing one carries back from the hospital, a little half-whispered remark to be made to friends who want to hear it. I sit and talk to him, leaning forward. I am aware again of my body as if it were transparent, and of the urgent set of my spine. What is that on his table? Something made of rubber, red-brown rubber? Everything frightens me. I talk on and on, about relatives, about the lawn at home, about the squirrels that dig holes in the lawn, about the man down the street with the annoying dog. . . . If some of these topics are familiar, good. My father wants to be told only what he already knows. This devastating stroke that has paralyzed his body and ruined his speech has done no more than point up what he has always been — but I am not allowed to think that. Something hurts my throat. I am not allowed to think such things of the dying.

I talk on. I am bright as the sunshine coming through the curtainless window, bright as the cheap handles of the drawers in the metal night stand. It occurs to me that I have blundered in the wrong room and am talking to someone else's father. Good, good. Someone then is in my own father's room, chatting away as if no one ever lived or died or suffered, but as if the horizons of human life were cleanly circumscribed by neighbors, relatives, dogs, the latest news from . . . friends thought forgotten, or friends of friends never really remembered.

"Aunt Thelma's neighbor, that one, you know, that won the car in the raffle, well, they went down to Florida with it and guess what. . . . They had an accident down there." I am dutiful and pleased with myself, to report such a thing. If only I had more misfortune to lay quietly on his bed! But his stroke was brought on by someone beating him — an unidentified assailant. "Unidentified assailant." They are not sure if he remembers this or not, so I should not make any reference to violence. Automobile accidents happen only to those who deserve them: he always felt that, obscurely. So I can talk about automobile accidents. But anything else might be bad for him: flowerpots falling accidentally out of windows onto innocent heads, children accidentally drowned in ditches, "man accidentally electrocuted while working with television set. . . ."

That unidentified assailant! I wonder, while I talk cheerfully to my father's wrinkled, mute face, what that assailant is doing now.

My father breathes quietly. Does he resent my body, transparent as it is? Marked for an assailant as it is? He cannot help but narrow his eyes at my talking mouth, wondering how it happened that he somehow brought that mouth into existence. He must begrudge the life he gave me; perhaps he is even bored with me. I am bored with the self he inspires in me. And as I fall into guilty silence, with that faint strained smile on my lips, I think of the more desirable self others inspire in me and of how that has always determined my love for them. As soon as I hurry back into the foyer and my friend glances up at me, another self will appear; this talkative self, this daughterly-maternal self, will be left behind with the antiseptic odor of the hospital. Another self! Of all absurd things, I catch myself trying to see my reflection in the hard shiny surface of the metal stand.

And yet I do love this man sitting motionless in bed. I love him, but we are paralyzed with each other. He is dying and I am living, and customarily, like people speaking different languages, we are fearful and bored in each other's presence. I can translate nothing of his into my own language. Painfully, he tries to speak—he cannot speak. Nonsensical sounds come from him. I listen with my spine urged forward in that foolish way, a way I just learned. Never have I sat like that before coming in this room. I listen; I frown; I stare at the floor. Nothing. I love him but cannot tell him so, for as soon as I said the word "love" that word would have no meaning. What little trinkets and souvenirs can we give to people on their way to die? At the end they must toss everything contemptuously aside, the way we clean out attics and drawers of things that belong to other people.

Afterward, my friend and I drive out toward the country, away from the hospital. It is nearing noon, evidently. People are out for lunch. At a school crossing my friend has to wait impatiently while a woman with a white band around her waist and chest holds up a sign that says STOP. Children run across the intersection; we watch them without interest. Negro and white children. They are energetic and vicious in the spring air; careless of color, they mingle and their blows are delivered brightly without discrimination. The woman lets her arm fall, wearily. My friend—whose face in profile is hard and has the illusion of being chipped, so deep is the cleft between the lips and chin—drives on.

We stop before reaching the country, at a park I've been in a few times: a grade school picnic once, I think. A fairly large park for the city. People are playing tennis on the courts as we stroll across the ragged grass. My friend is smoking a cigarette as if this were an offering to me—some normal distraction, something for him to do instead of talk. Like all men who are conscious of their bodies, the breakdown of someone else's body is an obscure embarrassment. He has never met my father and never will, my father would have hated him and he my father, yet he senses an alliance. Out of deference to that unknown man's suffering he frowns and pushes his sunglasses up, unnecessarily on his nose. We watch the tennis players. An Oriental boy dressed in white shorts, his chest bare and tanned. Marvelous graceful strokes; a flash of triumphant teeth. His opponent wears dark slacks and looks uneasy, though he plays well.

"I used to play tennis all the time," my friend says. "I won second place in a tournament once—just a city tournament."

But this saddens me, because though he is a young man his tone refers to something far in the past.

We walk on. In another court two girls are playing. Two women. They are poor players, but happy; we hear one call out to the other. My friend's teeth must be bared in an angry smile, for he hates the display of anything graceless. Once when I pulled my skirt up a little and side-stepped a newspaper fluttering down the street at me, he stared and said how graceful I was—like some kind of bird, like a swan? Only in flashes does he reveal himself.

As if we are following a map we pass the tennis courts and some disorderly picnic tables, and go into the woods. Here the paths are wide and rutted with bicycle tire tracks. The woods is thin; we can see traffic moving through it, out on the other street. Because we are very new to each other, everything is dreamy and tentative. He puts his arms around me and kisses me. I feel something against my back—the rough bark of a tree—and we say nothing, for we do not know each other well enough yet to be friends. We have nothing to say. In silence, like this, we are acting out a frayed drama that will be repeated this evening, right here, and the knowledge of our impersonality excites me. I love him, I think, though with my eyes closed I cannot remember what he looks like, exactly. He is here, he is touching me, there is more reality in his embrace than in the mysterious, abstract relationships between fathers and children, fathers and daughters. . . .

Then I understand: here is the assailant. "Unidentified assailant!" He is in my arms, and out of a mechanical urgency I caress his back, for isn't this what is always done? My father's assailant, with his rigid, critical profile and his mouth that is too soft and demanding, both at once, and his unidentifiable body pressed against me. He is the only honest person I have met. He is imitating nothing. Before the honesty of his passion everything lacks substance: the wearying sympathy, the hospital corridors that only seem to lead in one direction, the rooms with television sets droning inside, the nurses, the father enthroned in his last shrine, mysterious and vague with his appliances on the table or in the drawer, hidden, or in some nurse's care, ready to be switched on and switched off. If my friend is a liar sometimes—I know he is, he must be, for he so insists upon his truth—he is not a liar now. Only at this time men do not lie and are immortal.

I want to say, "What did you do to him? Why? Why did you jump out of that doorway and beat him? What did you use—a hammer? An iron bar? Why did you pick him, that particular old man?"

He draws back from me. His face is enough for me to love. My anxiety is not for him or for any nuances between us, but only to get everything over as quickly as possible—we will drive over to his apartment. We will drive over there at once. How tired I am of this transparency, and how I want to take on the innocence of passion and hide myself!

"What about *him*?" he says, for as he shakes aside the violence of passion some forlorn human memory touches him; he will become a liar again. He lifts one hand and the fingers part in a gesture of quaint, offered freedom. His eyebrows rise. "I mean, you're not going to—get upset, are you?" he says. "You're not going to get upset?"

J. C. OATES
1964

First Views of the Enemy

Just around the turn the road was alive. First to assault the eye was a profusion of heads, black-haired, bobbing, and a number of straw hats that looked oddly professional—like straw hats in a documentary film; and shirts and overalls and dresses, red, yellow, beflowered, dotted, striped, some bleached by the sun, some stiff and brilliant, just bought and worn proudly out of the store. The bus in which they were traveling—a dead dark blue, colored yet without any color—was parked half on the clay road and half in the prickly high grass by the ditch. Its old-fashioned hood was open, yanked cruelly up and doubled on itself, and staring into its greasy, dust-flecked tangle of parts was the driver, the only fair, brown-haired one of the bunch. Annette remembered, later, that as her station wagon moved in astonishment toward them the driver looked up and straight at her: a big indifferent face, curious without interest, smeared with grease as if deliberately, to disguise himself. No kin of yours, lady, no kin! he warned contemptuously.

Breaking from a group of children, running with arms out for a mock embrace, a boy of about seven darted right toward Annette's car. The boy's thick black hair, curled with sweat, plastered onto his forehead, framed a delicate, cruelly tanned face, a face obviously dead white beneath its tan: great dark eyes, expanded out of proportion, neat little brows like angels' brows—that unbelievable and indecent beauty of children exploited for art—a pouting mouth, still purple at the corners from the raspberries picked and hidden for the long bus ride, these lips now turning as Annette stared into a hilarious grin and crying out at her and the stricken child who cringed beside her, legs already drawn up fatly at the knees ——

In agony the brakes cried, held: the scene, dizzy with color, rocked with the car, down a little, back up, giddily, helplessly, while dust exploded up on all sides. "Mommy!" Timmy screamed, fascinated by the violence, yet his wail was oddly still and drawn out, and his eyes never once turned to his mother. The little Mexican boy had disappeared in front of the car.

Still the red dust arose, the faces at the bus jerked around together, white eyes, white teeth, faces were propelled toward the windows of the bus, empty a second before. "God, God," Annette murmured; she had not yet released the steering wheel, and on it her fingers began to tighten as if they might tear the wheel off, hold it up to defend her and her child, perhaps even to attack.

A woman in a colorless dress pushed out of the crowd, barefooted in the red clay, pointed her finger at Annette and shouted something—gleefully. She shook her fist, grinning, others grinned behind her; the bus driver turned back to his bus. Annette saw now the little boy on the other side of the road, popping up safe in the ditch, and jumping frantically—though the sharp weeds must have hurt his feet—and laughing, yelling, shouting as if he were insane. The air rang with shouts, with laughter. A good joke. What was the joke? Annette's brain reeled with shock, sucked for air as if drowning. Beside her Timmy wailed softly, but his eyes were fastened on the boy in the ditch. "He's safe, he's safe," Annette whispered. But others ran toward her now—big boys, tall but skinny, without shirts. How their ribs seemed to run with them, sliding up and down inside the dark tanned flesh with the effort of their legs! Even a few girls approached, hard dark faces, already aged, black hair matted and torn about their thin shoulders. They waved and cried, "Missus! Missus!" Someone even shouted, "Cadillac!" though her station wagon, already a year old, was far from being a Cadillac. As if to regain attention the little boy in the ditch picked up something, a handful of pebbles, and threw it at the car, right beneath Timmy's pale gaping face. A babble of Spanish followed, more laughter, the barefoot woman who must have been the boy's mother strode mightily across the road, grabbed the boy, shook him in an extravagant mockery of punishment: sucked her lips at him, made spitting motions, rubbed his head hard with the palm of her hand—this hurt, Annette saw with satisfaction, for the child winced in spite of his bravado. At the bus the American man's back swelled damply and without concern beneath his shirt; he did not even glance around.

Annette leaned to the window, managed a smile. "Please let me through," she called. Her voice surprised her; it sounded like a voice without body or identity, channelled in over a radio.

The boys made odd gestures with their hands, not clenching them into fists, but instead striking with the edges of their hands, knife-like, into the air. Their teeth grinned and now, with them so close (the bravest were at her fender), Annette could see how discolored their teeth were, though they had seemed white before. They must have been eating dirt! she thought vaguely. "Please let me through," she said. Beside her Timmy sat in terror. She wanted to reach over and put her hand over his eyes, hide this sight from him—this mob of dirty people, so hungry their tongues seemed to writhe in their mouths, their exhaustion turned to frenzy. "Missus! Missus! Sí, sí, Cadillac!" the boys yelled, pounding on the front of the car. The women, men, even very old people—with frail white hair—watched, surprised and pleased at being entertained.

"Please. Please." Suddenly Annette pressed on the horn: what confidence that sound inspired! The boys hesitated, moved back. She toyed with the accelerator, wanting to slam down on it, to escape. But suppose one of them were in the way. . . . The horror of that falling thud, the vision of blood sucked into red clay, stilled her nervousness, made her inch the big car forward slowly, slowly. And in the back those unmistakable bags of groceries, what would be showing at the tops? Maybe tomatoes, pears, strawberries—perhaps picked by these people a few days ago—maybe bread, maybe meat—Annette's face burned with something more than shame. But when she spoke her voice showed nothing. "Let me through, please. Let me through." She sounded cool and still.

Then she was past. The station wagon picked up speed. Behind her were yells, cries no longer gleeful, now insulting, vicious: in the mirror fists, shouting faces, the little boy running madly into the cloud of dust behind the car. He jerked something back behind his head, his skinny elbow swung, and with his entire body he sent a mud-rock after the car which hit the back window square, hard, and exploded. With her fingers still frozen to the steering wheel Annette sped home.

Beside her the child, fascinated, watched the familiar road as if seeing it for the first time. That tender smile was something strange; Annette did not like it. Annette herself, twitching with fear, always a nervous woman, electric as the harassed or the insanely ill are, saw with shock that her face in the mirror was warm and possessed. That was she, then, and not this wild, heart-thumping woman, afraid of those poor children in the road. . . . Her eyes leaped home; her mind anticipated its haven. Already, straightening out of a turn, she could see it: the long, low, orange-brick home, trees behind the house not yet big enough for shade, young trees, a young house, a young family. Cleared out of the acres of wheat and wood and grass fields on either side, a surprise to someone driving by, looking for all the world as if it and its fine light-green grass, so thin as to look unreal, and its Hercules fence had been picked up somewhere far away and dropped down here. Two miles away, on the highway which paralleled this road, there were homes something like this, but on this road there were only, a half-mile ahead, a few farmhouses, typical, some shacks deserted and not deserted, and even a gas station and store; otherwise nothing. Annette felt for the first time the insane danger of this location, and heard with magical accuracy her first question when her husband had suggested it: "But so far out. . . . Why do you want it so far out?" City children, both of them, the hot rich smell of sunlight and these soundless distances had never been forbidding, isolating. Instead each random glance at the land strengthened in them a sense of their own cleverness. Children of fortune, to withdraw from their comfortable pasts, to raise a child in such safety! —— It was fifteen miles to the nearest town, where Annette did her shopping and Timmy went to school, and forty miles to the city where her husband worked.

Annette turned into the driveway, drove slowly into the garage. Still in a trance, angry at herself, she got out of the car but stood with her hand still lingering on the steering wheel. A thin, fashionably thin young woman, for years more woman than girl, in a white dress she stood with a remote, vague smile, hand lightly on the wheel, mind enticed by something she could not name. Perplexed, incredulous: in spite of the enormity of what threatened (the migrant workers were hardly a mile away) she felt slowed and meaningless. Her inertia touched even Timmy, who usually jumped out of the car and slammed the door. If only he would do this, and she could cry, "Timmy! *Please!*" calm might be restored. But no, he climbed down on his side like a little old man; he pushed the door back indifferently so that it gave a feeble click and did not even close all the way. For a while mother and son stood on opposite sides of the car; Annette could tell that Timmy did not move and was not even looking at her. Then his footsteps began. He ran out of the garage.

Annette was angry. Only six, he understood her, he knew what was to come next: he was to help her with the packages, with the doors, open the cupboards in the kitchen, he would be in charge of putting things into the refrigerator. As if stricken by a sudden bad memory Annette stood in the garage, waiting for her mind to clear. What was there in Timmy's running out? For an instant she felt betrayed—as if he cherished the memory of that strange little boy, and ran out to keep it from her. She remembered the early days of her motherhood, how contemptuous she had been of herself, of what she had accomplished—a baby she refused to look at, a husband neurotic with worry, a waiting life of motherhood so oppressive that she felt nausea contemplating it: Is this what I have become? What is this baby to me? Where am I? Where am *I*? Impassioned, a month out of college and fearful, in spite of her attractiveness, that she would never be married, Annette had taken the dangerous gamble of tearing aside her former life, rejecting the familiar possessions and patterns that had defined her, and had plunged, with that intense confident sharp-voiced young man, into a new life she was never quite sure had not betrayed the old, stricken the old: her parents, her lovely mother, now people to write to, send greeting cards to, hint vaguely at visiting. . . .

Sighing, she began to move. She took the packages out of the car, went outside (the heat was now brilliant), put them down and, with deft angry motions in case Timmy was secretly watching, pulled down the garage door and locked it. "There!" But when she turned, her confidence was distracted. She stared at the house. Shrubbery hiding the concrete slab—basements were not necessary this far south—rosebushes bobbing roses, vulnerable, insanely gaudy, the great picture window that made her think, always, someone was slyly watching her, even the faint professional sweep of grass out to the road—all these in their elaborate planned splendor shouted mockery at her, mockery at themselves, as if they were safe from destruction! Annette fought off the inertia again; it passed close by her, a whiff of something like death, the same darkness that had bothered her in the hospital, delivered of her child. She left the packages against the garage (though the ice cream in its special package might be melting) and, awkward in her high heels, hurried out the drive. She shielded her eyes: nothing in sight down the road. It was a red clay road, a country road that would never be paved, and she and her husband had at first taken perverse pride in it. But it turned so, she had never noticed that before, and great bankings of foliage hid it, disguised its twistings, so that she could see not more than a quarter mile away. Never before had the land seemed so *flat*.

She hurried. At the gate the sun caught up with her, without ceremony. She struggled to swing the gate around (a few rusty, loosened prongs had caught in the grass); she felt perspiration breaking out on her body, itching and prickling her, under her arms, on her back. The white dress must have hung damp and wrinkled around her legs. Panting with the exertion, she managed to get the gate loose and drag it around; it tilted down at a jocose angle, scraping the gravel; then she saw that there was no lock, she would need a padlock, there was one in the garage somewhere, and in the same instant, marvelling at her stamina, she turned back.

Hurrying up the drive, she thought again of the little Mexican boy. She saw his luxurious face, that strange unhealthy grin inside his embracing arms—it sped toward her. Cheeks drawn in as if by age, eyes protruding with—it must have been hunger—dirty hands like claws reaching out, grabbing, demanding what? What would they demand of her? If they were to come and shout for her out in the road, if she were to offer them—something—milk, maybe, the chocolate cookies Timmy loved so, maybe even money? would they go away, then, would they thank her and run back to their people? Would they continue their trip north, headed for Oregon and Washington? What would happen? Violence worried the look of the house, dizzied Annette: there were the yellow roses she tended so fondly, rich and sprawling against the orange brick. In the sunlight their petals, locked intricately inside one another, were vivid, glaringly detailed, as if their secret life were swelling up in rage at her for having so endangered their beauty.

There the packages lay against the garage, and seeing them Annette forgot about the padlock. She stooped and picked them up. When she turned again she saw Timmy standing just inside the screen door. "Timmy, open the—" she said, vexed, but he had already disappeared. Inside the kitchen she slammed the bags down, fought back the impulse to cry, stamped one heel on the linoleum so hard that her foot buzzed with pain. "Timmy," she said, her eyes shut tight, "come out in this kitchen."

He appeared, carrying a comic book. That was for the look of it, of course; he had not been reading. His face was wary. Fair like his mother, blond-toned, smart for his age, he had still about his quiet plump face something that belonged to field animals, wood animals, shrewd, secret creatures that have little to say for themselves. He read the newspaper like his father, cultivated the same thoughtful expression; encouraged, he talked critically about his schoolteacher with a precocity that delighted his father, frightened Annette (to her, even now, teachers were somehow *different* from other people); he had known the days of the week, months of the year, continents of the world, planets of the solar system, major star groupings of the universe, at an astonishing age—as a child he approached professional perfection. But Annette, staring at him, was not sure, now, that she could trust him. What if, when the shouting began outside, when "Missus! Missus!" demanded her, Timmy ran out to them, joined them, stared back at her in the midst of their white eyes and dirty arms? They stared at each other as if this question had been voiced.

"You almost killed him," Timmy said.

His voice was soft. Its innocence showed that he knew how daring he was; his eyes as well, neatly fringed by pale lashes, trembled slightly in their gaze. "What?" said Annette. "What?"

The electric clock, built into the big white range, whirred in the silence. Timmy swallowed, rustled his comic book, pretended to wipe his nose—a throwback to a habit long outgrown, hoping to mislead her—and looked importantly at the clock. "*He* hit the car. Two times," he said.

This was spoken differently. The ugly spell was over. "Yes, he certainly did," Annette said. She was suddenly busy. "He certainly did." After a moment Timmy put down the comic book to help her. They worked easily, in silence. Eyes avoided one another. But Annette felt feverishly excited; something had been decided, strengthened. Timmy, stooping to put vegetables in the bottom of the refrigerator, felt her staring at him and peered up, his little eyebrows raised in a classic look of wonder. "You going to call Daddy?" he said.

Annette had been thinking of this but when Timmy suggested it, it was exposed for what it was—a child's idea. "That won't be necessary," she said. She folded bags noisily and righteously.

When they finished mother and son wandered without enthusiasm into the dining room, into the living room, as if they did not really want to leave the kitchen. Annette's eyes flinched at what she saw: crystal, polished wood, white walls, aqua lampshades, white curtains, sand-toned rug, detailed, newly cleaned, spreading regally across the room—surely no one ever walked on that rug! That was what *they* would say if they saw it. And the glassware off in the corner, spear-like, transparent green, a great window behind it, linking it with the green grass outside, denying a barrier, inviting in sunlight, wind, anyone's eyes approaching——
Annette went to the window and pulled the draw drapes shut; that was better; she breathed gently, coaxed by the beauty of those drapes into a smile: they were white, perfectly hung, sculptured superbly in generous swelling curves. And fireproof, if it came to that. . . . Annette turned. Timmy stood before the big red swivel chair as if he were going to sit in it—he did not—and looked at her with such a queer, pinched expression, in spite of his round face, that Annette felt a sudden rush of shame. She was too easily satisfied, too easily deluded. In all directions her possessions stretched out about her, defining her, identifying her, and they were vulnerable and waiting, the dirt road led right to them; and she could be lured into smiling! That must be why Timmy looked at her so strangely. "I have something to do," she murmured, and went back to the dining room. The window there was open; she pulled it down and locked it. She went to the wall control and turned on the air conditioning. "Run, honey, and close the windows," she said. "In your room."

She went into the bedroom, closed the windows there and locked them. Outside there was nothing—smooth lawn, lawn furniture (fire-engine red) grouped casually together, as if the chairs made of tubing and spirals were having a conversation. Annette went into the bathroom, locked that window, avoided her gaze in the mirror, went, at last, into the "sewing room," which faced the road, and stood for a while staring out the window. She had never liked the color of that clay, really—it stretched up from Louisiana to Kentucky, sometimes an astonishing blood-red, pulsating with heat. Now it ran watery in the sunlight at the bend. Nothing there. Annette waited craftily. But still nothing. She felt that, as soon as she turned away, the first black spots would appear—coarse black hair—and the first splashes of color; but she could not wait. There was too much yet to do.

She found Timmy in the living room again, still not sitting in the chair. "I'll be right back, darling," she said. "Stay here. It's too hot outside for you. Put on the television—Mommy will be right back."

She got the clipping shears out of the closet and went outside, still teetering in her high heels. There was no time to waste, no time. The yellow rosebush was farthest away, but most important. She clipped roses off, a generous amount of stem. Though hurried—every few seconds she had to stare down the road—she took time to clip off some leaves as well. Then she went to the red bushes, which now exclaimed at her ignorance: she could see they were more beautiful, really, than the yellow roses. Red more beautiful than yellow; yellow looked common, not stunning enough against the house. It took her perhaps ten minutes, and even then she had to tear her eyes away from the lesser flowers, over there in the circular bed; she did not have time for them—unaccountably she was angry at them, as if they had betrayed her already, grateful to the migrant workers who were coming to tear them to pieces! Their small stupid faces nodded in the hot wind.

Timmy awaited her in the kitchen. He looked surprised at all the roses. "The big vase," she commanded. In a flurry of activity, so pleased by what she was doing that she did not notice the dozens of bleeding scratches on her hands, she laid the roses on the cupboard, clipped at leaves, arranged them, took down a slender copper vase and filled it with water, forced some roses in, abandoned it when Timmy came in with the milk-glass vase (wedding present from a remote aunt of hers). The smell of roses filled the kitchen, sweetly drugged Annette's anxiety. Beauty, beauty—it was necessary to have beauty, to possess it, to keep it around oneself! How well she understood that now.

Finished abruptly, she left the refuse on the cupboard and brought the vases into the living room. She stood back from them, peered critically . . . saw a stain on the wood of the table already; she must have spilled some water. And the roses were not arranged well, too heavy, too many flowers, an insane jumble of flowered faces, some facing each other nose to nose, some staring down toward the water in the vase in an indecent way, some at the ceiling, some at Annette herself. But there was no time to worry over them, already new chores called to her, demanded her services. What should she do next?——The answer hit her like a blow, how could she be so stupid? The doors were not even locked! Staggered by this, she ran to the front door, with trembling fingers locked it. How could she have overlooked this? Was something in her, some secret corner, conspiring with the Mexicans down the road? She ran stumbling to the back door—that had even been left open, it could have been seen from the road! A few flies buzzed idly, she had no time for them. When she appeared, panting, in the doorway she saw Timmy by the big white vase trying to straighten the flowers. . . . "Timmy," she said sharply. "You'll scratch yourself. Go away, go into the other room, watch television."

He turned at once but did not look at her. She watched him and felt, then, that it was a mistake to speak that way to him—in fact, a deliberate error, like forgetting about the doors; might not her child be separated from her if they came, trapped in the other room? "No, no, Timmy," she said, reaching out for him—he looked around, frightened—"no, come here. Come here." He came slowly. His eyes showed trust; his mouth, pursed and tightened, showed wariness, fear of that trust. Annette saw all this—had she not felt the same way about him, wishing him dead as soon as he was born?—and flicked it aside, bent to embrace him. "Darling, I'll take care of you. Here. Sit here. I'll bring you something to eat."

He allowed her to help him sit at the dining-room table. He was strangely quiet, his head bowed. There was a surface mystery about that quietness! Annette thought, in the kitchen, I'll get through that, I'll prove myself to him. At first cunningly, then anxiously, she looked through the refrigerator, touching things, rearranging things, even upsetting things—a jar of pickles—and then came back carrying some strawberry tarts, made just the day before, and the basket of new strawberries, and some apples. "Here, darling," she said. But Timmy hesitated; while Annette's own mouth watered painfully he could only blink in surprise. Impatiently she said, "Here, eat it, eat them. You love them. *Here.*" "No napkins," Timmy said fearfully. "Never mind napkins, or a table cloth, or plates," Annette said angrily—how slow her child seemed to her, like one of those empty-faced children she often saw along the road, country children, staring at her red car. "Here. Eat it. Eat it." When she turned to go back to the kitchen she saw him lifting one of the tarts slowly to his mouth.

She came back almost immediately—bringing the package of ice cream, two spoons, a basket of raspberries, a plate of sliced chicken, wrapped loosely in wax paper—— She was overcome by hunger. She pulled a chair beside Timmy, who had not yet eaten—he stared gravely at her—and began to eat one of the tarts. It convulsed her mouth, so delicious was it, so sweet yet at the same time sour, tantalizing; she felt something like love for it, jealousy for it, and was already reaching for another when she caught sight of Timmy's stare. "Won't Daddy be home? Won't we have dinner?" he pleaded.

MARLENE NOURBESE PHILIP
1993

Stop Frame

Is 1958. On a hot, dry island. Somewhere. In the Caribbean. Is 1958 and
I hearing the screams of Dr. Ratfinger's patients—the whole village of
Bethlehem hearing the screams of Dr. Ratfinger's patients and knowing
them as their own. Everybody screaming like this at least once before on
a visit to Dr. Ratfinger's office.

Ratfinger not really his name, but Ratzinger, and is me, Gitfa, and
Sara who christening him Ratfinger. We writing his new name on a piece
of paper and burning it under the big chenette tree in my yard as we
repeating on obeah spell we making up. After that he was always Dr.
Ratfinger to us—it suiting him better.

He always there—in the village—Dr. Ratfinger. (It seems like that
now.) He coming during the war. *The* War. That is how everybody calling
World War II—*the* War. My mother saying one morning they getting up
and brip brap just like that there he be—Dr. Ratzinger—high and dry in
his house—one of the biggest in the town of Bethlehem. And is from the
rooms he calling his surgery—at the front and side of his house—that
the screams of friends and neighbors coming.

War babies—me, Gitfa, and Sara—is how our mothers calling us. All
born at the same hospital in town, within a day of each other at the end
of *the* War, so we not really war babies, but we feeling really important
when people calling us "the war babies." I couldn't be remembering any
of the things I talking about, my mother saying, since I was born after
the war. "You too young to remember the screams of Dr. Ratzinger's
patients," she telling me, but I knowing otherwise.

And why should I be trusting her memories any more than I trusting
mine? My own crick-crack-monkey-break-he-back stories . . .

My own fictions . . .

I could—if I wanted—make Dr. Ratfinger tall and lean . . . give him the
pale skin, thin nose, and fair coloring of the Aryan. Blue eyes! I could.
If I wanted. Make Dr. Ratfinger six feet six inches tall, make him thin,

61

make him fair, make him blond. I could give him all those "things" *and* a Doberman, as well as a large and perfect specimen of an Aryan wife, all blond hair, fair-complexioned, and reddening in our sun. I could. Or, if I wanted, I could make him short—five feet one inch, perhaps—and fat, with one of his eyes—his pale blue eyes—slightly unfocused, lending him an eerie air of malice, disease, and mystery . . . and *if* I were to give him a monocle, that would make the whole episode even more strange to a young girl on a tiny Caribbean island—far away from events like "the final solution," panzer divisions, and the Desert Fox. Many, many years later she would read of those—she could, if she then wanted, fill in the gaps with whatever fictions (or memories) she chose.

The reality of the fiction is me—Miranda—hanging round Man Fat store, the only store in Bethlehem, listening to the singing and songing of his voice: "Ahtinahmilk, ahpoundahrice," as the neighbors filing in with their ration cards and filing out—"Ahtinahmilk, ahpoundahrice," and the line hot, the line sweaty and winding its way in and out of the store to the refrain.

Sometimes on a Saturday, I finishing my work quick quick, avoiding my mother and going to Man Fat store and buying Kazer Balls that redding-up your tongue and teeth and filling up your cheek so you looking like you having a toothache, and I playing with Mikey, Man Fat little son, who just learning to talk.

"Mikey," I saying to him, "what's that?" and I pointing to the tins of condensed milk that Man Fat handing over the counter.

"Milk-ah."

"What's that, Mikey?" and I pointing to the sugar.

Mikey smiling at me and saying, "Sugar-ah." And I laughing, and all the people in the store laughing, and Mikey laughing and liking how everybody looking at him as he adding 'ah' to everything he saying—"milk-ah, sugar-ah, bread-ah, salt-ah."

And when nighttime falling, I hearing the bombs dropping on London over the wireless, except my mother telling me, in the flat voice she using when she don't want me arguing with her, that bombs stop falling *before* I born. But I hearing them all the same. I hearing them *and* seeing Cousin Lottie too, who living with us since she having a stroke and not walking, lying high high up in her four-poster brass bed that I polishing plenty Saturdays. Everytime a bomb falling Cousin Lottie farting. Long and loud. "Take dat, Hitler, take dat," she saying as she letting go each blast. And sometimes when I creeping into her room and crawling into bed with her, she whispering and telling me that each one of us have to do something. "That is me own war effort," she laughing and telling me, "me-one own." Is so that whenever me, Gitfa, and Sara playing and one of us farting out loud, all of us saying together, "Take dat, Hitler, take dat!" and we laughing out big and loud and hard like we already big women.

"So, Miranda," my mother saying to me one day as we sitting down at the kitchen table for the evening meal, "is why you biting the man hand?" I watching the hot water pouring out from the spout of the old black kettle she holding, into the yellow and blue enamel bowl, and the steam rising and the kitchen filling up with the smell of coconut oil the cassava farine parch in.

"I telling you, Ma, I not liking the way he touching my tongue and telling me how it not going to hurt." My mother spooning some of the farine on to my plate and covering it with fish and gravy. "Hear him, Ma—'Dis vill not hurt—you vill not feel any pain—only ze pressure.' " I talking like Dr. Ratfinger now and I seeing the laughing running all over her face, but she holding it in.

"Eat," is all she saying to me.

"And I remember how he making people scream, Ma, so I biting him, Ma—hard hard."

And is Dr. Ratfinger turn: is he who screaming and yelling at me and I thinking he hitting me. But he not doing so. Instead, he refusing to fill my tooth, so I suffering weeks and weeks of the tooth hurting. And my mother packing the rotting hole with cloves that smelling sweet and sharp at the same time.

One morning she getting up, setting her face like when she and my father having a quarrel, putting on her good print dress and going to Dr. Ratfinger and "please-sir" apologizing for me, begging for him to fill my tooth and even promising I not biting him again; my mother not "please-sir-ing" anybody, especially somebody white like Dr. Ratfinger, and that morning when she combing it, she pulling and tugging my hair and showing how she angry with me, but it hurting her seeing me hurting so she "please-sir-ing," but he not having anything to do with me and that is just fine, because I hating Dr. Ratfinger and his hands—his white puffy hands with fingers like fat white worms. And I not caring at all I looking like I have a Kazar Ball in my mouth all the time.

"Dis vill not hurt—you vill only feel ze pressure—only ze pressure." First me. Then Gitfa. Then Sara—each of us saying this slow slow and we sticking pins in the figure we making of Dr. Ratfinger. The dough white and soft and I praying my mother not missing it from the bowl she covering with a red-checked towel and leaving to rise in the sun on the sill of the kitchen window. Sara making the body, Gitfa the legs and arms, and me the head, since I was the one biting him. I taking some straw from where the chickens nesting and putting it on the soft white ball of his head, and then with my finger I poking in two holes for his eyes where his face supposed to be. When I putting the two marbles in these holes Sara saying:

"How come you giving him one green and one blue eye?"

"Because," is all I saying as very slowly I pushing his eyes deeper and deeper in his face and the dough not stopping me. I not telling them that these marbles chipped and I not giving my good marbles to Ratfinger, even though "is for a greater good" as my mother always saying when she doing something she not liking.

"Is why you pushing them in so far?—you can't even see them."

"Leave me alone—I not telling you how to make his body."

I smashing a piece of coal into little black bits and putting two for his nose-holes, and with the other little bits making a straight line across for his mouth.

Gitfa putting a stick in one of his hands for the drill and we all laughing at that, but is when we seeing what Sara doing that me and Gitfa sucking in our breath and looking at each other and feeling a little frighten: Sara making a little totie and two little balls and sticking them below the black piece of coal she marking Ratfinger navel with. None of us saying anything—we just stooping down looking at the separate parts of Ratfinger—then still not talking we putting it together—head to body, and we pinching the dough together—hard; body to arm, arm to hand, pinch the dough, leg to foot—hard. Then we trying to sew clothes on him but the dough so soft we leaving him naked. Is then we start sticking pins in him and we putting him on a long piece of stick. Without saying anything we knowing we having to move to where nobody seeing us.

Way down the back of the garden we moving, to where the dasheen— "the best dasheen bush in Bethlehem" my mother saying—growing in a wet sticky patch of black mud, almost to where the forest starting. First we lighting the fire, then we tying our heads with pieces of cloth like we thinking the obeah women doing, and each one of us taking turns holding Ratfinger on the stick and chanting "Dis vill not hurt—only ze pressure you vill feel," while the others stamping the ground and making sounds like a drum—"boom de boom—dis vill not hurt—boom de boom—only ze pressure," as the flames licking him and crinkling his hair right away. "Dis vill not hurt" and the bits of coal glowing bright bright in his face along his smile; "only ze pressure" and we seeing him turning light brown, then dark brown and now the coal in his navel glowing like the ones on his face, "Dis vill not hurt, only ze pressure" and we dancing round the fire and trying to catch the power. Then we stopping and watching Ratfinger burn in the hell we hearing about in Sunday school, as the stick catching fire too and falling in the fire with him.

"I wonder how he liking ze pressure now," I saying, and gentle gentle I probing my rotten tooth with the tip of my tongue and still feeling the pressure and pain.

"Look how black he getting," Gitfa whispering as we watching Ratfinger cooking in the fire.

"Just like Nurse Pamela," Sara saying.

"Nurse Pamela Blantyre!" my mother using the voice that telling me and anybody who listening that she knowing plenty plenty histories about her. "Yes, Nurse Blantyre—but look at she nuh," and she curling her lips round the words in a way that saying she not lowering herself and telling you everything she knowing, but the tone saying what she knowing filling up hours and hours of talking. "She with her pouter pigeon chest."

Me, Gitfa, and Sara agreeing with my mother, because Nurse Blantyre not looking like she having two breasts like our mothers and other women in the village, but her whole front area round, smooth and corset right up to her neck and her bottom cocking out.

Nurse Blantyre black like Dr. Ratfinger white, a black so deep that when you looking at her you feeling you losing yourself in it and not wanting to come out, and people saying she loving with the dentist. But people in the village of Bethlehem also saying she is a zamiist and loving women, and me, Gitfa, and Sara talking and whispering about this and wondering what it is people meaning when they saying Nurse Blantyre loving men and women, and I just knowing is not something I asking my mother about.

One day me, Gitfa, and Sara peeping through the window of Ratfinger office and we seeing Nurse Blantyre speeching off Mrs. Standall who believing herself plenty cuts above everybody else in the village, especially somebody like Nurse Blantyre who having a black skin, because she, Mrs. Standall, tracing her ancestry "right back to a white sailor who settled on the island a long time ago." "Huh," is what my mother saying whenever she hearing this and adding that that was nothing to be proud of, since anybody with an ounce of sense knowing sailors having syphilis and gonorrhea *and* the morals of a dog. "And not just any old dog either, but a dog in heat." Then she biting down on her mouth which telling me I not to be asking her what syphilis or gonorrhea is. But I knowing what dogs doing in heat, so I know she not thinking much of sailors. Furthermore, my mother adding, she herself tracing her own ancestry right back to African royalty that "de damn white people tiefing and bringing to work for them on the island," and Mrs. Standall ought to be knowing, she adding, that the only thing a red skin meaning is that you have a crook, robber, or rapist in your family, and she could be putting that in her pipe and smoking it.

What me, Gitfa, and Sara seeing when we looking through the window is Nurse Blantyre pushing out her chest even more and telling Mrs. Standall that Dr. Ratfinger was very *very* busy and that she having one of four choices: she could stand and wait, or she could sit and wait; as she saying this Nurse Blantyre puffing herself up even more, then she going on, "You can leave *and* come back," and Nurse Blantyre stopping now, and me, Gitfa, and Sara holding our breath for what coming, "or, you can leave and *not* come back."

I nudging Gitfa in the side, Gitfa nudging Sara and we laughing fit to burst outside the window. Me, Gitfa, and Sara holding our breath and watching how Mrs. Standall's red skin getting even redder, and she flaring her nose-holes wide wide and turning on her heel, walking out, and slamming the door behind her. We not knowing who we laughing at more—because we not liking Nurse Blantyre or Mrs. Standall.

When a patient screaming, is Nurse Blantyre who holding his arms to the side of the chair while Dr. Ratfinger carrying out his worst. *I* know. He touching my tongue and if I not biting him, he doing the same thing to me. Me, Gitfa, and Sara hearing that big big men who working hard splitting rocks in the road, putting up a fight and is Nurse Blantyre who sitting on them or holding them in place easy easy. We frighten for so by Dr. Ratfinger and his nurse.

Nothing we doing getting rid of him though. We waiting and waiting for something to happen to him after our obeah ceremony, but he only getting fatter. And I waiting and waiting with my toothache. *The* War. And my stubbornness. Until the visiting dentist coming to the island. And that was a long long time. The word in the village of Bethlehem was that Dr. Ratfinger meeting with "important collar-and-tie big shots" and sending people to the mad house, and this frightening us even more than the pain sometimes. People saying he also putting electrical wires to your head and shocking you until you begging for mercy. He and Nurse Pamela, people saying "tight as po and bottom" and having "a ting going." Neither me, Gitfa, nor Sara knowing what "a ting going" meaning, but we just knowing it having to do with man and woman business. We hearing the talking and arguing all round us and we listening when we not supposed to be: "I telling you de man is a Nazi, and if he is a Nazi, dere is no way he doing it with her." My father voice coming into the bedroom where I lying quiet quiet.

"But Nurse Pam not black," my mother answering back. "You know what I mean—her skin might be black, but de family mix-up . . ."

"Me don't care how mix-up she is—as far as those Nazis go she is a member of an *inferior* race. Me read about it—they even killing Jews and they have white skins!"

"All I know is that when it comes to that thing between man and woman, man does say he have all kind of principles, but is like what Cousin Lottie say—a standing prick knows no mercy in a widow's house at night, or any woman house for that matter. And not only at nighttime either. And *I* am going to bed."

I telling all this to Gitfa and Sara and we laughing like big people and nodding our heads as if we understanding what our parents talking about. But what me, Gitfa, and Sara knowing is that we hating Ratfinger and nothing too evil for him to do. And when we behaving bad is threaten our parents threatening us with him and so we wanting to put an end to Ratfinger.

Is so we starting the mango wars. Ratfinger liking mangoes plenty plenty; he priding himself on his Julie mangoes which everybody knowing is the queen of mangoes. Late late one night, when is only duppy and sucouyant about, me, Gitfa, and Sara meeting outside Ratfinger house, slipping the latch on his gate and going into his back garden.

"Is a good thing he not having Long mango or Starch mango eh," I whispering to Gitfa and Sara, and we all laughing because the Julie mango trees not much bigger than us, so I shining my torch and easy easy we reaching in between the branches and pulling off every single mango, even the young green ones no bigger than marble and lime. Me, Gitfa, and Sara stripping every single mango tree in Ratfinger yard that night, and we leaving all the green mangoes in a pile outside his front door. For days after, up and down the village, inside and outside our houses, even in the school yard where the other children skipping and clapping hands to the singing about how Ratfinger "mad and bad" and "somebody tiefing he mango and leaving he trees naked," we hearing how Ratfinger don't have no more mangoes for the season, how he angry and wanting to know who "committing this predial larcency." Everybody laughing and saying nobody tiefing nothing since he still having he mangoes, and the market women happy because they only seeing him coming and quick quick they doubling their price. But nothing stopping Ratfinger and Nurse Pamela—we still hearing screams coming from his surgery.

That is how we deciding on another plan. When Sara first whispering it to me as we sitting up in the plum tree in her yard, my eyes opening wide wide and I putting my hand to my mouth and laughing out loud, and even more when I seeing Gitfa doing the same thing when Sara telling her. Is Sara who getting the cow-itch grass, and one day when he making somebody scream, I sneaking into Ratfinger car—after I greasing my hands with lard—and I rubbing the grass all over the car seat. We hiding behind the hedge then, and when we seeing him coming out and getting into his car we holding our breath, and then laughing and laughing when he getting out fast fast and running back into the office scratching his behind. We sitting behind the hedge and peeing ourselves we laughing so hard, as we watching Nurse Pamela trying to scratch it for him.

That night when everybody sleeping we getting up and meeting outside Ratfinger house again. Is Gitfa turn this time and she climbing through the window in his surgery and rubbing Nurse Pamela chair with the cow-itch grass. And we laughing as we thinking what happening the next day when Nurse Pamela coming into the office and sitting down in her stocious way and starting to scratch what my mother calling her "cockmollify behind."

"Is the same Mrs. Standall self," my mother saying the next day. "The one who she speech off only a few days ago, who passing by and taking her home and putting some medicine on her behind." We all sitting round the kitchen table eating supper; the laughing running round and round inside me as I listening to my mother, and when I hearing how Nurse Pamela rushing out the surgery scratching and screaming it breaking out and I hiding it behind my hand and my enamel cup. My mother fixing me with her eyes as if she suspecting me but she not asking anything. I giving my best marble—the big one that is part blue and part clear glass, the same one I winning off my cousin, Theo—to anybody if I could be seeing Nurse Pamela that day.

The next day me, Gitfa, and Sara celebrating and since is Saturday we running around town like we owning it, and in we own way we was owning it. When the woman who selling tickets not looking, we sneaking under the curtains and into the Strand, the only cinema in Bethlehem and watching *King Kong Meets Tarzan.*

"Is not Jane that that King Kong holding—where Tarzan?" Gitfa whispering to me and I whispering to Sara. And we feeling frighten as the ape waving and waving the little, tiny white woman over the big tall building with a spike.

King Kong looming big big in my memory: he stands eighteen inches tall behind the glass display case—"A jointed steel frame, rubber muscles, and a coat of rabbit fur. Stop frame animation moves the model slightly . . ."

It is 1988. On a damp, cold island—a long long way away from 1958. On a hot, dry island. Somewhere. " . . . expose a frame of film, move the model again . . ."

Stop frame: me, Gitfa, and Sara sneaking under the curtain, over the Empire State Building, into the dark dark theater, finding seats, grabbing each other, and screaming for so as King Kong and Tarzan coming up big big on the screen.

Stop frame: " . . . use miniatures . . . glass shots . . . real and model aircraft" as King Kong waving Jane—"No, is Fay Wray that!"

Stop frame: Dr. Ratzinger. Ratfinger—was he a Nazi? It was a long time—a very long time—after he had left us and the screams had died down, that I learnt what the word meant, although it didn't matter that I didn't know—the way my mother saying the word "Nazi," holding in it everything that evil, and I believing Ratfinger was a Nazi who fleeing Germany, and carrying out experiments on the people of Bethlehem. But bad teeth not caring about politics and despite all the mango wars and the cow-itching, Ratfinger still having patients.

Stop frame: move the model slightly—did Sara know about Nazis? She was Jewish. If she did, she and I never talked about them, running round the town of Bethlehem as if we owning it.

Stop frame! Me, Gitfa, and Sara sneaking under the curtain, into the darkened cinema, finding seats and grabbing each other for comfort in the scary parts of the Tarzan movie.

Stop frame! Tarzan—what did I know about Africa? Nothing except "me Tarzan, you Jane."

Stop frame: Tarzan, Nazis, Africa.

Stop frame! you von't feel ze pain, just ze pressure—the weight of memories—a tooth impacted, pushing, pressing against gum against bone—the hard white bone of history, and I remembering the tooth black and rotting—the white memory eating and eating away at the creeping black which making the hard white soft, crumbly, and Ma packing it again and again with the dark brown powder she making from cloves, and it stopping the aching—the memory—

Stop frame: my mother lying; stop frame: my mother lying on the floor; stop frame: (move the model slightly) my mother lying on the floor screaming; stop frame: my mother lying on the floor screaming that she drinking poison; stop frame: my mother lying on the floor screaming that she drinking poison and she killing herself.

Stop frame.

Move the model slightly:

"So, Ma, is why you doing it?"

"Doing what, chile?" She watching me pour the water—steam rising, but no smell of coconut oil. Only the slightly acrid smell of tea.

"You know, Ma—pretending you killing yourself?"

The bowl of tea nestling in her cupped hands; the fingers, gnarled by arthritis and work into a network of roots, tremble ever so slightly and the rheumy eyes lift to look at me—once—before returning to the tea. As if wanting to veil the past, the present—the world itself! from her gaze, age pulling a blue cast over the brown eyes—blue, like my best marble! and I remembering how she packing my rotting tooth with cloves. "Huh—that Ratzinger!" is all she saying for a while. "He was really something, that man—just refuse to take out your tooth."

"That was because I bit him, Ma—remember?"

"Just refuse to take out your tooth! . . . Uh uh." The surprise and anger still there in her voice.

"Why, Ma? Why did you do it?"

The smile she smiling just like the tone of voice that telling me "thus far and no further" and is like the veil over her eyes getting darker—more blue. "You know what I always saying, chile, a memory just like a rotten tooth—if it hurting too bad, you must be taking it out."

"And what if you can't take it out, Ma?" I challenging her right back with my tone.

"Then you pack it with a little cloves, chile." Is like her eyes looking through the blue curtain to another place: "And some forgetting," she adding quietly.

"And wait for the dentist?" Anger and remembered pain roughening the edges of my voice. My tongue tip gently touches the spot where once the tooth ached, exploring old areas of pain, seeking some life where a long time ago ache had splintered into throb and lance and stab—each nerve with its own hurting life—and come together again in a roar as loud, as red as the dye of the Kazer Ball coating my mouth. The cold white porcelain gave nothing back to my questioning tongue. All feeling had gone with the rotting tooth.

"Yes, you wait, chile. You wait for the visiting dentist."

SUSAN POWER
1993

Watermelon Seeds

Sometimes I want to take this baby out of me before it's alive and breathing and wanting too much. Catch it before it grows from being a seed. I never wanted Donald to put this baby in me. It's hard enough just the two of us.

"This goddamn kid is doomed," Donald says around a long swig of beer he takes in like air and breathes out like a malt dragon. "This kid is going to be so screwed up I can hear it already. Damn, can't you shut it up?!"

If I ever snatched that brown glass bottle from Donald's mouth, stripped his lips and told him—*I don't want it either! I don't want it fighting me in there!*—I know WHAT would HIT THE FAN. I'd break the sound barrier flying off the end of Donald's broken fist.

I curl up sometimes with one hand on my stomach, whispering things like, "I'll make you grilled cheese sandwiches," because I have these dreams where I can hear the baby crying. It is curled around my intestines and holding on with hands smaller than a silver dollar. The baby shakes its wizened Donald face and tells me it won't come out. No way.

"Bagged at sixteen, that's really sad," my mother told me just last week, with chicken-greasy fingers poked in her mouth. She should know, she had me when she was that age. She would never say that kind of thing in front of Donald but we were in her kitchen sharing cold leftover chicken and sorting through coupons with five city blocks beween Mama's mouth and Donald's ears.

She used to come over to our place nearly every morning for breakfast, reading us our "Omarr's Horoscope" from the *Chicago Sun-Times*, but now I go over to her apartment after setting out Donald's bacon strips and burned grits because Donald says it starts his day off wrong to see me sitting across the kitchen table like an expectant cow. As if he goes off to work and has a rough day. He doesn't. We live off his disability and the

72

beadwork he taught me to do which we sell at powwows ranging from Michigan to Minnesota. Of course, Donald advertises the beadwork as his own because he's a Chippewa Indian from Lac du Flambeau, Wisconsin, while I'm Mexican from Dad's side and Polish from Mama's.

"Nobody wants to buy any Taco-Polack stuff," Donald says. "They want genuine Indian shit, so keep to my designs."

In a hat box way in back of my side of the closet I keep a collection of secret work. I use tiny cut seed beads that sparkle to sew the pictures, stringing just three beads at a time like Donald taught me. I wear a thimble on each finger to help shove the needle through the leather; it can tear up your fingers to do this kind of work.

I hide my beaded pictures because they aren't Indian designs like Donald wants, but a reflection of what I see in our neighborhood, what some people call the *Chicago Hills*; the white trash ghetto Ozarks in the Uptown Area. There are Indians and Puerto Ricans, but mostly hillbillies living around here, just a few evil-smelling blocks from Lake Michigan and all the big white boats docked at Belmont Harbor. One of my beaded pictures is a scene of Donald burning one of those boats, a really big one. He hasn't ever burned a boat but he talks about how good it would feel to sink one out of sight. He says, "Strike one for the good guys," and tips his beer bottle toward the east where all those boats are tied down and covered up. I don't know what he means. I don't even know why he's one of the good guys.

When I try to draw him out, try to understand him better the way those psychologists on "Oprah Winfrey" say you should before you give up on a person, I stub my toes. Donald won't talk much about his growing-up years.

"You want to hear a litany of self-pity, go over to your mother's," he told me when I asked about his past. Sometimes when he's way into the bottle, on a real bender, he mumbles a detail or two. So I know he and his brothers did a lot of spear-fishing to keep food on the table, and might have even speared game of the two-legged variety; a stepfather whose name he cries out in his sleep. *Carter.* I'm still trying to piece that story together.

I asked him once why he left Wisconsin for Chicago and he told me, "You can get lost in the city, so they hate you less."

I wrote it down in my red diary locked with a gold key, but no matter which way I look at it, I don't understand. At least Donald gave me a picture of himself taken when he was my age. He is so handsome in that picture, with thick black hair greased and combed high off his forehead, the short sleeves of his T-shirt rolled back to show off his muscles. He is a full-blood Indian version of Elvis in that picture, and the Donald I will always love. My eyes have learned to carve him out of the man I live with.

Donald is thirty years old but looks older because his wrinkles are deep as cracks in a pounded wall. I know from his nightmares that his stepfather is responsible for a lot of the hammering he has taken. His hard drinker's belly rides over the beaded belt buckle I made him for Valentine's Day. His stomach squirms and rumbles like his insides are angry.

Donald is impulsive, something Mama is still trying to account for because it contradicts the description of his Taurus sign as taciturn, measured, slow to action. I think Mama's been looking for an alignment of planets at the time of his birth. He switches back and forth on me, like the night I told him about the baby. At first he bellowed. He kept saying, "It will NEVER work, it will NEVER work." But then the next morning I woke up in the bed alone, my feet covered with what felt like a mound of cookie crumbs. I pulled down the covers on Donald's side of the bed and stared. Donald had uprooted clusters of plum-covered hydrangea bushes and placed them beside me. The flowers were full and fat as pompoms, springing from perfect green leaves shaped like spades in a deck of cards. The roots, still clinging soil, tangled at the bottom like wild blonde hair.

I heard Donald in the kitchen humming "Spanish Eyes" while he made breakfast. I guess he had forgiven me and the baby. At least for a time.

Technically we're not starving. Donald gets a disability check from the Army for when a new recruit shot him in the thigh at target practice and messed up the big bone in there. That and the little bit I make from beadwork keep us in flour and vegetable oil for fry bread, and dark beans and lean hamburger for my endless chili. But today I want a triangle of pork chop as thick as my thumb to surprise Donald. I know he'll smell it from the landing four flights down. It will urge him upstairs, getting stronger and stronger, hitting him like a meat cloud outside our door.

The grease will still be lining his mouth and oiling the tips of his fingers when he comes to bed, smelling the smoke in my hair. We will kiss the flavor off each other until Donald falls asleep with his forehead laid flat against my neck, and an easy expression unwrinkling him. At least, that's how it should be.

When I imagine the pork chops and me in an apron with my hair twisted up, eyes turned soft brown under daubs of pearl-pink eyeshadow,

I find myself staking out Water Tower Place on the Magnificent Mile. I have on my ugliest jeans and fastest sneakers. I am watching the ghosts shop.

A pair of women who must be mother and daughter are looking in the I. Magnin shop window, a block away from Water Tower Place. The mother is saying, "Don't get too many mini-skirts. Next season you just *know* they'll lower the hemlines and you'll have to go out and start from scratch. That's no way to build an efficient wardrobe."

The daughter rolls her eyes. It looks like she doesn't have on any makeup so I know she wears the expensive kind of cosmetics, the perfumed kind as subtle as disappearing ink.

All up and down this section of Michigan Avenue that looks like it spills right into the lake at its end, I see people straight out of nighttime soaps like "Dynasty" or "Falcon Crest." They are too perfect for me to take seriously. Their hair and nails are so neat, so polished, they are like aliens who have taken the place of the real thing. Michigan Avenue is *Invasion of the Body Snatchers* all over. It's spooky.

I'm ready for action. I am near invisible, but all-powerful. I can feel my heart beating in my throat, my chest, at my wrists, even whamming down by my ankles. I have the fastest feet in the world. I wait patiently and carefully; it's important to find the right purse belonging to the right lady. Just when I think I'll never find her, she walks right in front of me. She is perfect: young, beautiful, tall. She smells wonderful and attracts the stares of men who turn their heads to watch her pass.

For a few heart-slamming moments I take control of her life. I step on her shadow and touch her shoulder. She thinks I'm some guy making a pass. I let her take one good startled look at my face before I grasp the leather handle of her purse and pull for my life. The bag is suede, as soft as the beautiful lady's moisturized skin. I am half a block away before she gets her voice back and there is no catching me now.

I take the purse to a pretty little gazebo in Lincoln Park and sit with my legs crossed, pretending the purse is mine. I casually go through its contents and discover a whole life in that purse. An hour earlier I didn't know its owner and she didn't know me, but now I'm reading her as plainly as a gypsy reads palms.

I like the photographs best. There's a stack of them in the wallet, pictures of her parents and boyfriend. She even has old school pictures of herself going back to when she had braces and oily skin. I think of my own school pictures Mama arranged on her wall, going around in a circle like a clock. The picture from tenth grade ends up next to the one from kindergarten like I'll jump from being fifteen to age five. That's probably the way Mama thinks I'm living my life.

I keep the money but I decide to mail the purse and its contents back to the owner, to the address on her driver's license. I don't even keep the credit cards or the little gold locket on a broken chain I find in a zippered pocket. It adds a whole new dimension to my power to return what I have taken. This is the way Donald must feel when he cries me an apology.

I'm three months pregnant when Mama surprises me. She really lets me have it. Usually she keeps her opinions to herself, partly out of habit from the days when my father was still alive, and partly because she says kids will always do the opposite of what you tell them.

I go over to her place really early for breakfast. She looks up from the astrology column when I walk in. Her look pins me in the doorway. I cross my arms in front of my chest but that doesn't help because my arms are striped with blue welts. They look like fancy twirling batons.

Mama grabs me and drags me into the bathroom. Her palm pushes against the back of my head, supporting it at the base the way a mother cups the head of a baby so it doesn't wobble loosely on its neck.

"Look. Take a good look at yourself," she yells. She pushes my head so close to the cabinet mirror my breath makes curls of steam. "How do you like it? Your eye all out to here? You're just so attractive, Lois. You take my breath away."

After she says that she leaves me, taking away her hand. My whole body goes limp like a rubberband shot against the wall, and I fall to the ground. For a long time the only important thing is staying on the cool tile floor, counting the six sides of each tile and studying how they fit together, feeling the grit against my cheek. I don't ever have to get up off the floor again.

Mama comes back after a while and sits on the edge of the tub. I'm looking at her open-toed slippers. Purple frost nail polish is chipping off her toenails. She sighs and I close my eyes so I can stay curled up at her feet.

"I don't mean to make it worse," she says. "It pisses me off. I guess I feel responsible because it's what you saw with me and that S.O.B. father of yours. But I wouldn't take it off him now, okay? You hear me? No way I'd stand for that shit now."

Mama leaves and I have the feeling she will never say anything about this again.

I want to tell her it's fate that brought Donald and me together, so I guess it's fate that will work out the ending. Not her. She doesn't even know the whole story:

I didn't go back to school after some hillbillies got me in the girl's bathroom and did a job on me. The heavy one, JoJo, with sharp overlapping teeth and a hacksaw haircut sat on my back and held me down while Ginny and Melora used toenail clippers to cut my hair. After that they poured bleach on my head and turned my brown hair a brittle yellow-white the color of grapefruit pulp.

"You ever seen a white Mexican before?" JoJo pulled me up by the collar and turned me around so I faced Ginny and Melora's teeth and gums, shoved out of their mouths like laughing fools. HAW HAW HAW. The bleach burned the skin on my neck and scalp, and I had to wipe my forehead to keep it from drizzling into my eyes.

"She looks so bad she could be arrested for being in public," said Ginny, and when they doubled over with giggles, I took off. I never even went back to open up my locker and get some tapes I had in there, good dance tapes it took forever to make off WLS Radio.

Mama cut my hair better and evened the yellow until it grew out, but for a while there my skinny face looked just like the death mask she has hanging on her living room wall. It is a mask of my father's face, made after his heart attack and before his cremation. Mama says she needs all the proof she can get that he is dead, dead, dead, so she keeps his ashes in an old plastic Cool Whip bowl under her bed, and his death mask on the wall over the TV set. One of her boyfriends punched a hole in the mask between the lips, and stuck a cigarette in there. I don't like it because it makes him look like he is alive, pushing right through the wall and coming after us.

Donald started out as one of my mother's boyfriends, but I took him over. He wasn't working, and I wasn't leaving for school like Mama thought. The minute she left for her waitressing job I set him up with a beer and we watched cartoons together. Pretty soon Donald was making time with me in my bed.

"It's more comfortable in there," he said, nodding toward Mama's room, but it was bad enough I stole him away. I wouldn't use her bed. Donald was shy and wouldn't ever undress all the way, although he liked me stripped like a little stick.

Mama didn't forgive me and Donald for falling in love behind her back until we moved out and got our own place. Then she was full of advice and always coming over with fancy recipes she'd never tried herself, or material for matching bedspreads and curtains. She even took out a Sears charge card and helped us buy some furniture.

"I want you to do it right," she explained when I asked her why she was helping. "You're starting too early, just like me. But maybe with people behind you from the get-go you'll make it."

Mama wasn't as understanding when I told her I was pregnant. I really hadn't meant to ruin her day, but I had to tell her about the baby, like it was a Coming Attraction she wouldn't want to miss. Maybe I picked a bad time. Mama was all excited about a blind date she was going on later that evening. A real date with dinner and a movie and dressing up. She asked me over to watch her model clothes, and help her pick out a dress that might change her whole future.

She was taking her hair out of tight curls pinned to her head, scattering bobby pins and looking vulnerable with half her hair stuck like glue to her scalp and half of it hanging down in corkscrew ringlets. She looked for a second like she would understand, so I opened my mouth. I repeated something I'd read in a science textbook: "The species will propagate."

It stopped Mama dead in her tracks. "What are you talking about?" She suddenly noticed the bobby pins and stooped to collect them.

"I'm having a baby."

Mama took air down the wrong pipe and choked. I started forward to slap her on the back but she pulled away. She threw the bobby pins right at me, in a shower, the way people chuck rice at a wedding. Mama and I fell into a black hole of time that felt like "The Twilight Zone." We didn't move or speak. Finally Mama snapped her head to the side. She was looking at my school pictures circling on her wall.

"Well, I either accept it or I don't," she said, mostly to herself. "There's no going back now." She flicked the bangs out of my eyes so she could stare at me.

"Aren't you the typical Pisces?" she sighed. "Flaky, dreamy, never living in the real world. But here's the kicker, Lois, baby. Now the real world's got itself *right in you.*"

In July Donald decides to go back to Lac du Flambeau for a visit. I want him to take me with him and introduce me to his family, but he won't.

"Nah," he says, "my ma would just get on me for robbing the cradle."

"Will you tell them about the baby?"

Donald is packing his old Army duffle bag. He rolls his clothes very tightly so it looks like his bag is full of snakes and sausages. He shakes his head, no.

"We're not married. What am I going to say? *Hey, I'm shacked up with this goofy Mexican and about to have a kid?* Don't be squirrelly."

That's when I get my idea. If Donald hadn't accused me of being squirrelly it wouldn't have occurred to me. The day he leaves it rains, so I can't carry out my plan, but the day after that is perfect. The sun is high and bright, the clouds have all been swept to Canada. Gray-backed seagulls from the lake glide over buildings like wisps of smoke.

I wear one of Mama's old bikinis under a T-shirt and shorts, and pack myself a towel. At Murray's Market I buy a *Teen Magazine*. I roll it in the towel because its pages are slick and shiny, and I don't want to smudge them with my sweaty hands. I'm almost four months pregnant but still not showing. That much is obvious when I get to Oak Street Beach and peel off the shirt and shorts. I am sharing the sand with hundreds of people my age who don't even suspect that I'm an intruder. I'm not what I seem. Flopped on my stomach to read *Teen Magazine* without the sun glaring in my eyes, I forget the second heartbeat pounding in my belly.

A bunch of kids who go to Francis Parker Academy—an elite school— invite me to play volleyball with them. Volleyball was my game before I left high school. I enjoy the way the ball smacks against the inside of my arms, held taut to direct it over the net. I like bumping into the guy with hair as gold as a Ken doll's. My team wins three times straight and the guy with gold hair asks me for my number. I give him an old number, from the apartment Mama and I lived in years ago. I wouldn't mind seeing him again. I wouldn't mind touching that gold hair of his. But all I need is Donald finding out. Donald would pitch a fit on my head.

When Donald gets back from Lac du Flambeau he doesn't notice my suntan. He has brought back enough fish to fill our freezer and my mother's. I like opening the freezer door to look at all the blind-eyed fish stacked closely together. They remind me of the Bible story where Jesus feeds the masses with a few loaves of bread and a few fish. I have this crazy feeling our own supply will go on forever.

His first night back Donald holds me gently after we've gone to bed. His touch is so warm and light I begin to feel that no skin can separate us tonight. All the tiny little particles scientists say scoot around to form our bodies have reorganized themselves. My quarks stir themselves up with Donald's, so in the span of only a few minutes we have become one person.

"You're all I've got," Donald murmurs. He is starting his warm-up dance in our bed. The covers roll off his hard, creased body. Rhythm is taking him over, making his hands shake.

"Lois," he says, and it is the best thing I have heard all night. "Lois," Donald whispers in the dark like he has just said he loves me.

Donald ignores me when I finally start to show. He spends more time with his friends. Donald's two best friends, Edsel FastWolf and Glen Fredericks, are Sioux. They are two self-proclaimed goodtime boys who beat it out of Rapid City, South Dakota when they were just kids. The way Glen tells it, they left just in time.

"Whites in Rapid City feel about Ind'ins the way the KKK in Mississippi feels about blacks. You hear what I'm saying?"

"You know it . . ."

"You said it . . ."

Donald and Edsel back him up like they're a singing group.

Glen and Edsel come over on weekends, never during the week, because despite their big talk they are hard workers. Edsel is Inspector Number 76 at a cheese factory, and Glen is a lineman for the phone company.

All three of them use the same old lines when they drink. Today, as I'm washing the dishes, I catch myself mouthing their words along with them, under my breath: "Those Bulls are getting supernatural. They're going to take home seventy wins this season, you watch. Yeah, you mean if Dennis Rodman or Billy Laimbeer don't kill one of them first. Hey, I ever tell you about that little Navajo girl with the wood leg?"

Some people can learn plays by heart or recite poetry. I can regurgitate these bonding sessions like a tape recorder.

From behind I can't tell Edsel and Glen apart. They both have shoulder-length brown hair drizzling down their backs into half-hearted split-end ponytails. Their hair is not thick and black like Donald's. I have never seen them without their beaded White Sox caps pulled down low over their eyes. They like to reminisce about Vietnam, or maybe they just have to.

"Hey, we were primed for Vietnam," Glen is saying, "because we had lifetime training. It's guerilla warfare in some of those little redneck towns." Glen squints into his bottle as he talks. He has a big dimple in his left cheek that makes it look like he's smiling all the time. Edsel is the quiet one. His fine, large hands rest comfortably on his thighs, and he nods his head at whatever Glen is saying. Every now and then he strokes the hairs on his upper lip with an index finger. That scraggly mustache has been a work-in-progress for as long as I've known him.

When Donald is with Glen and Edsel he forgets he never made it past boot camp. All of a sudden he was there beside them when they shipped out, he took a bullet for Edsel, he carried Glen on his back to a chopper under fire. He is one fierce Rambo warrior with a steel plate that resonates when he toasts a beer bottle against his thigh.

As usual, they forget I'm there. So I go in the bedroom to work on my secret beadwork. I'm trying to finish one of my favorite pieces that I've been beading for two months. It pictures Glen, Edsel, and Donald together in Vietnam, just like Donald's fantasy. They are in a dry, yellow field; the brittle grass is gold like cornsilk. They're wounded and waiting for help. Donald is between Glen and Edsel with an arm around their shoulders. They are all looking up at the sky.

I used to think I had control over the scenes I create but now I'm not so sure. I hate the way they are so alone in the picture, but I can't seem to change anything. If I stare at it for too long as a whole piece, I start to cry because I know what my needle won't let me stitch. Hope.

"You're my brother."

"You are my brother."

Voices from the living room curl under the bedroom door and I open it a crack to peek at the men. The friends have hit the weeping stage and are close to passing out. They punch each other's arms, their heavy turquoise rings leaving bruised circles.

"I love you, man."

"No, I love you."

"I love both of you."

Their overlapping words are a round song. No one hears them but me.

I'm six months pregnant and can hold the baby in my cupped hands. Sometimes its feet press against my palms, pushing off them like they're a springboard at the YMCA pool. Me and the baby go over to Mama's for breakfast, the same as always.

Mama is on the floor of her bedroom, still in her babydoll nightgown and large hair rollers. It suddenly occurs to me that I don't know the true color of Mama's hair. She and Lady Clairol are tight; Mama changes hair color the way other people change clothes. I don't know why she bothers to roll her hair over fat pink sponges since she teases it into one of those tired old beehive hairdos every day of her life.

Mama nails me with her speckled green eyes. "Look what I got here." She points to papers strewn on the floor, stranding her on a small island of carpet. "Did you know I kept all your report cards?"

I shrug. Me and the baby sit down on her unmade bed and I flip through TV Guide. I hope Phil Donahue has a really hot show today, like the ex-wives of celebrities dishing the dirt. I like the way they carry on and talk about how $5,000 a month alimony is chicken feed.

"You were a good student. Look at this. Come *here*." Mama pulls me down on the floor, into her atmosphere of White Shoulders perfume. She keeps thrusting report cards in my face, one after the other, going all the way back to kindergarten.

"So?"

"*So?* You got a B+ in your Civics Speech class and all you can say is, *So?* What I'm saying is, you've still got avenues. You should finish high school, maybe go to night school and I could watch the baby. Or—"

I'm trying to cut in but she slices the air with her hand like she's dicing onions.

"—Or you could just study at home for the G.E.D. One way or the other. It would be criminal not to get your diploma. Just criminal."

"You never got yours," I tell her. And she looks pretty much alive to me, sitting there in her emerald-colored babydoll nightgown that really brings out the green of her eyes.

"There," she says, satisfied. "You've just made my whole case. Why would you want to do like I did? I'd swap with you in a second to get another chance."

"What about Donald?" I ask her. I'm used to Donald being the last word.

"What *about* him? He's got fourteen years on you but he's the child. For the life of me, I don't see what the big attraction is. What do you like about him?"

Mama thinks she's got me. She thinks I'm quiet because I can't come up with a single example. But the truth is, I don't know where to start. The truth is also that some of the things I'd like to tell her would sound silly: when Donald isn't drunk his eyes are soft, like brown soil. He has great big hands that look as if they hurt him because the skin is stretched so tight over knotted knuckles, his fingers are pumped too full of blood. He had these special tattoos made on his knuckles. He said he got the idea from an old Robert Mitchum movie, *Night of the Hunter*. One hand has LOVE written across the knuckles, and the other spells out HATE. He can do the whole monologue Robert Mitchum did in the movie about the struggle between Love and Hate, and when Donald finishes he always cries, drunk or sober.

I have three pockmarks on my forehead from when I had the chicken pox as a baby. Donald uses his pinkie finger to trace them into a triangle. He calls it, *the Bermuda Triangle*.

"I got lost in here," he whispers in my ear. "I met you and just got lost. Went overboard. This is where you keep your tricky love spells, huh?"

Donald is the cleanest person I know. He says it goes back to the military. Donald is maybe the only man on this earth who can go on a three-day drunk where he can't even tell you his name, and still shower, shave, and splash on some Old Spice before staggering back to the scene of the crime.

"Donald never forgets an anniversary. He gets me flowers every time," is what I finally tell Mama.

"Oh? And he probably gets you flowers after beating the crap out of you too?" Mama looks like she wants to slap me. I even flinch, but instead she pulls me into the meanest, hardest hug I've ever had. We're kneeling on the report cards. I'm watching my tears fall all over the fourth grade card with its crawling As and Bs; my tears are smudging them until they look like a foreign alphabet, or maybe some of those Chinese characters.

"If I can't make you see that you have choices," Mama sobs, "I'm going to go crazy!"

Mama releases me suddenly and me and the baby lurch sideways onto the carpet. Mama scuttles to the bed on her knees, shoving her hand under the bed like she's grabbing for the tail end of a cat. She pulls out the Cool Whip bowl with Dad's ashes inside. Mama sits cross-legged in front of me. She has pretty, slim legs. I guess she's not an old lady yet.

Mama doesn't remove the lid, but taps it sharply with a blood-red fingernail. "This dead S.O.B. sold me a line and I bought it. I bought his whole world view for cry sakes. They didn't have these talk shows and magazine articles back then about what you could expect from a man. You hear that? What *you* can *expect*. You've got to want something for yourself," she tells me. "You deserve to get something."

"I'll have the baby," I tell my mother. And me and the baby go home.

It's a week before Christmas and the baby is due any day now. It can pop out at any second. Donald was drinking eggnog while we watched the Dr. Seuss special, "How the Grinch Stole Christmas," but now he is drinking something stronger and is starting to look like the Grinch himself.

"Kids' stories always cop out at the end," he is telling me. "What does that teach a kid? I come from a big family, and one after the other we all learned that this happy ending garbage is just a lot of bullshit."

"I don't know, Donald. You're too profound for me," Mama says and winks at me. Donald ignores her and her remarks which is fine with me. I don't want a fight.

"You take those Whos down in Who-ville," Donald says, pulling me closer to him so he can be sure I'm paying attention. " . . . Look like goddamn furry roaches, don't they? If they were so happy without all their Christmas shit—gifts and toys and food and decorations—then the Grinch should've just kept it. That'd teach little kids something. That'd give them some real values. Some kids won't get anything, just like we didn't most years. But a story like that would prepare them."

Mama yawns and rises from the couch. She kisses me goodbye.

"I think I'll take off. This is getting too heavy for me," she tells Donald and leaves.

"What does your mother know?" Donald asks me. I shrug. I want to tell him that I don't know anything myself. The closer I get to having the baby, the less I remember. Yesterday I spent an hour trying to get through the times tables up to 12, and when I couldn't even get past the 3s, I just sat there crying. Maybe I know less and less because the baby knows more and more? What if this is a genius baby?

I know I'll have a nightmare about it tonight. Something horrible like I give birth to a talking baby. It talks just like Donald, swearing at me from the moment the doctor slaps it on the butt. Then it looks at me, hanging upside-down in the doctor's hands. At first I think it's the spitting image of Donald, right down to those LOVE and HATE tattoos stenciled on its tiny fists. But then I see its eyes. They aren't warm like brown soil. They are black and empty like little watermelon seeds.

Donald is thoroughly drunk now. His nose is as red as that reindeer's they sing about on the radio. He is getting so angry his forehead is sweating.

"So, where is it?!" he yells at me all of a sudden. I back up against the TV set. I haven't sat down once all evening because if I do, I'll be stranded. I can't trust Donald to help me up again.

"Where is what?"

"That DOOMED kid of ours!"

"Don't say that. It isn't doomed." Static makes my blouse stick to the television screen. Maybe that's what gives me this suicidal courage to face Donald. Maybe I'm not real, just another character looking out of the TV. Donald is on his feet now.

"What else do you call a kid nobody wants?"

"DON'T LET IT HEAR!" That's the first time I've ever yelled at Donald and my throat burns. I'm waiting for Donald to do something. I'm waiting for his hand to twist in my hair or peel the skin off my face, or at least for his voice to spray hot words like all those crazy rounds of bullets on

"Miami Vice." Donald just stands there, tense and awkward, until our breath is pressing us against the walls.

"You thought of any names yet?" he whispers, cracking the knuckles of his right hand.

"No," I breathe, and it's safe now to take a few steps closer to him.

"Figures," he mutters, and turns around in one twist of the heel. He knocks his knuckles against the wall on his way out of the apartment without looking at me. He slams the door but I don't hear him going down the stairs. When I peek out of the peephole in the door I can see that he is still standing there, right outside, so close to the door his magnified head curves and hovers before my eyes like a black planet.

Donald is subdued and won't give me any more trouble tonight, but I can't relax; now the baby is mad. It's heavier than it was a half hour ago because it is sulking. Donald is still motionless in the hallway when his child, unnamed and unborn, balls up its tiny hands into fists and begins pounding me from the inside.

REYNOLDS PRICE
1993

An Evening Meal

Sam Traynor had got the reprieve two days ago—the five-year cure of his stomach cancer—and he'd spent both days in quiet pleasure, not unstrung but high on a joy he'd hardly known since boyhood. Because his parents were long dead though, and he'd lived alone since chemotherapy made him reckless for weeks on end, he had no close friend to tell the news. A woman who worked at the next desk over and the doorman in his apartment building seemed at least to notice a change. The doorman remarked on the tie Sam spent thirty dollars for, in celebration; the woman said "Sam, are you wearing blush?" (it was healthy color). And that was all, for human response. Sam wouldn't phone his aunt or her sons; they'd offered so little when it would have counted.

So after work that pleasant Friday, he walked ten blocks to eat at a diner he'd last visited the week before surgery, not even sensing a near ambush. It was not his favorite restaurant, then or now; but he'd planned this evening in further celebration—or the risk of one. That last visit, he was also alone; but a new waiter was working the counter, a boy just off the plane from Amalfi and as good to see as any face that rushed toward Sam too fast to use, in his early days. The boy had accepted his invitation, turned up after the diner closed and—through a whole night—lent Sam his stunning body and smile, free as air.

And never again. When he left at dawn, he thanked Sam, saying "I liked you, sir." Sam stopped him there with a silent hand and fixed the moment in his mind where he knew it was safe as long as he lived. Five years later though, the boy wouldn't be there—surely not. His name was Giulio, called Giuli; and still his memory seemed worth the risk.

But there he was after all, at the grill end, when Sam took a stool up near the cash register. A few pounds thicker but lit with a heat that spread from inside him, the generous fearless eyes of a creature better than humankind anyhow. He was talking intently with an ancient woman in a genuine cloche hat, stained pink velvet. The one other worker in sight was a girl who served the counter and the booths by the street wall. Final daylight was strong at the windows, colored green by water-oak leaves.

Right off, Sam knew he'd give no sign. If Giuli glanced his way or walked by, Sam would look right at him but not speak first. That would test many things—how much the wait had changed Sam's looks, how deep his face had registered on Giuli that one dark night, what Sam's whole life might hold from here out, a whole new life. He was calmer than he'd expected to be and was halfway through a bowl of good soup before Giuli passed to ring the woman's check.

No look Sam's way; and once the woman passed back of Sam, blowing a dry old kiss at Giuli—and Giuli had actually turned to Sam and asked if the crackers were fresh enough—still no door swung open between them. Giuli grinned but in a general direction.

Sam knew it was strange, but he wasn't disappointed. The most he'd hoped for was some shared memory and the chance of Giuli's pleasure in the news. It was plain anyhow that Giuli's forgetfulness was real when their hands touched to exchange the crackers. The skin was warm as before and tougher. On the right ring finger, Italian-style, was a wedding band.

By the time his turkey sandwich was ready, Sam had agreed they'd touched near enough. They'd silently proved they were still alive and had asked for no more; but then Sam's mind set off on its own, watching a clear line of pictures that came from the night they'd shared nearly all they had. The same pictures had been a main help through the six hard months after surgery and x-ray—Sam's old skill as a home projectionist of well-kept memories. In lucky hours he could shut his eyes and play through a useful number of scenes—from minutes to days—in keener detail than when they were new, tasting individual pleasures and thanks strong as ever. There were twenty-some scenes from his adult years, eight of which were masterworks of time and light; and the scene that centered on the early Giuli contended for best. In the next half-hour, through his sandwich and tapioca pudding, Sam had again everything Giuli gave him and needed no more.

He believed that at least till he asked for his check and Giuli brought it, clearing the dishes in graceful ease—not a clink or scrape. But one more time their hands brushed; and Sam was startled by the wash of gratitude poured out in him—an unexpected need to say his own name, then allude to their meeting and tell Giuli what that memory had meant to a man condemned by a ring of doctors to die in a month. *It hauled me back*; Sam knew that much. At first a cold-scared hunkered patience of constant pain; then slowly an easier slog through time, dense at first as hip-deep seaweed.

Terrified and then edgy as the wait was, it came to feel better than what went before; and the new years turned out, of all things, celibate. In eighteen hundred ominous nights, however often Sam ran the scenes, he'd never once felt compelled to reach for another man near him. A bigger surprise by far than his cure; and he sometimes wondered if the x-ray had done it, burning out some nerve for longing. Or was it simply fear of more sickness? Whatever, Sam took the world through his eyes now. With no real blame and no regret, though he'd sometimes wonder *Am I dead and punished? Or maybe it's Heaven.* Alone on his stool, he actually laughed.

Giuli turned from cutting a blueberry pie and seemed to nod toward a table beyond them—a nod and a frown to hush the air, then a dark-eyed sadness.

Sam hushed and tried to see a reflection in the glass pie-cabinet; it curved too sharply. So when he'd sat another two minutes, dawdling through the last of his coffee, he laid a small stack of bills on the check, caught Giuli's eye and said "Keep the change," then turned on his stool.

Four yards ahead—close to the door, in a four-seat booth with the low light on him—a single man was huddled inward on himself as tight as if a blunt pole had pierced him, threaded his chest and bolted him shut. He might just weigh a hundred pounds; his rusty hair was parched and limp. His eyes hit Sam's a moment, then skittered.

It's Richard Boileau, already dead. Sam guessed it that fast; but since the man's eyes wandered to the window and watched the street, Sam stayed in place and tested his hunch. He'd last seen Richard in '78, the November morning after they'd proved through a long bleak night how well they'd learned each other's least weakness and how they could each flay the other with words. Then as daylight had streaked the roof, Sam suddenly found the one path out. He stood from the bed they'd shared for three years, picked up a few good things from the bureau—his father's gold watch, a comb of his mother's, his wallet and knife—and said "All right, the rest is yours."

The rest had literally been the rest—Sam's clothes, books, records, two years of a diary, a few nice pieces of furniture he'd more than half paid for. All well lost and Richard with it, the dazzling tramp, hungry as any moray eel, cored-out by a set of monster parents. Through the years Sam heard second-hand of his whereabouts, always in town at a new address; but the two had never collided till now, if this was Richard.

For whatever reason, of Sam's old loves—vanished or lost—it was only Richard he'd thought of as dying, purple-splotched with Kaposi's sarcoma or drowning in lung and nerve parasites. Each day he'd read the obituaries, crouched against the name on the page; and while he chalked off friend after friend, Richard stayed inexplicably free. Even in Sam's own worst days though, when radiation seared his gut in third-degree lesions, he somehow knew he'd outlast the havoc inside his skin while Richard Boileau would certainly die in this new plague. And not from an endless hunger for bodies—scrupulous Sam could have picked a killer any calm night—but from some cold rage in Richard's mind to leave a string of his riders appalled.

But is this helpless scarecrow Richard? In two more seconds Sam all but knew. The worn blue shirt that swallowed the long neck was one Sam had left—a red *S.T.* still edged the pocket, sewed by Sam's mother. Had a stranger bought it at the Salvation Army? Sam turned away to steady himself.

By now Giuli was back by the grill, laughing with a cook that had just turned up, a rangy boy with a knife-blade profile.

Sam thought of quietly walking their way and asking if they knew the man in the booth—was he a regular; what was his problem?

But the young cook met Sam's eyes, gave a wave with his spatula, then kissed Giuli's jaw—their eyes were identical; they had to be brothers. Guili called out *"Grazie,"* smiled at the whole room, took a short bow and scrubbed at his neck.

Sam stood up and faced the booth. The man was still pressed close to the window, though Sam could see there was nothing to notice, nothing Richard would have spent ten seconds on. The fact freed Sam; he stepped across, took the opposite bench two feet from the man's head and said "See anything good out there?"

The man turned gradually and, at close range, the skin of his upper face was transparent—that thin and taut on the beautiful skull.

Sam thought he could see a whole brain through it, a raddled mind, whatever it knew or had lost for good. But Sam stayed still till he'd drawn a direct look from the eyes—they'd kept their color, an arctic blue. Then he said "Is it Richard?"

No move or sign from the frozen face.

Sam tried a new way. "Bertrand? Remember?" In the early days he'd sometimes called Richard "Bertrand Le Beau," when nothing yet had dulled the shine.

At first the name seemed to penetrate. The eyes widened and the dry lips cracked.

But then a quiet voice said "You know him?" The waitress was there with a dry slice of toast and a cup of milk that gave off smoke. She set it by the man's right hand and spoke to him gently, "This'll warm you fast."

Sam took the risk and looked to the girl. "You know his name?"

The man might have been on the moon, engrossed.

The waitress smiled. "I know he's been bad off a long time. I know this is what he eats every night. But he's gaining strength now—aren't you, friend?" She touched the wrist that was nearly all bone.

The man faced her, his smile a ruin. He managed to lift the cup of milk though and drink a short swallow.

The waitress tapped Sam's shoulder lightly. "Sit with him some. He never sees people; make him drink his milk." As she left, she asked Sam if he was still hungry.

He shook his head No; but when she was gone, he saw she'd left an idle fork and spoon on the table, bound in a napkin. He took out the clean spoon, stirred the milk, drank a spoonful himself; then slowly over the next ten minutes, he fed Richard Boileau the whole cup.

RICHARD RUSSO
1985

The Dowry

"That was certainly quick," my wife frowned when I returned to the car.
"So much for your predictions."

I handed her the visas and the Mexican insurance, both of which she
deposited in the glove compartment.

"Can I ride up front with you guys?" Allison asked.

"No," said her mother. "We've got a long drive, and there's no reason to
be cramped. Besides, you don't even like your father and me, remember?"

"True," she admitted.

She stared out the window sadly, and I felt for her, remembering how
it had been when I saw my first border town. I had been a few years older
than Ali, a supposedly worldly college freshman, but what I had felt then
I now recognized in her expression—an odd combination of guilt and
fear. There were swarthy, idle men milling about everywhere, and they
all seemed interested in us and the rental trailer we were towing. They
pointed and made us the topic of their conversation. My wife cheerfully
gave the finger to one of the men who stared too openly, but he just smiled
back at her. Shanty homes were built at crazy angles all the way up the
hilly slopes that contained the town, and Ali, in order not to have to face
the open stares of the men who surrounded us, studied the shanties a
little fearfully, as if she saw one in her future.

"Ignore them," I suggested to Susan, who was less easily intimidated
by the staring men than our daughter. When I backed carefully into
traffic, a taxi careened by, blaring its horn. Susan gave the fleeing cab the
finger too.

"Stop that," I told her.

"I will not," she said.

"All right, but if a fight breaks out, I'm going for you."

"I'll be better when we get farther south. I hate the border."

"I don't see why," said Ali from the back seat. She was learning sarcasm.

"You'd better get used to being a sex object," I said.

"I know I'm a sex object," Ali said.

"I was referring to your mother. So far, you're just an object, until you define your gender." I smiled at her in the rear view, and she gave me her mother's favorite gesture. I looked over at Susan, but she just shrugged at my unspoken accusation. Breasts were a tough subject for poor Ali, who had begun to develop over a year ago, but the initial promise remained as yet unfulfilled. The disappointment rankled her, as did her mother's figure, which was still very good.

"Who wants to bounce through life like Mom anyhow?" she said.

"Your mother doesn't bounce," I said. "She jiggles."

"God," Susan said. "How far *is* it to San Carlos anyway?"

As we approached the outskirts of town, the traffic thinned and we all began to relax. At the customs check, I pulled over and Susan handed me the visas. I rolled three one dollar bills into tubes and palmed them, so that the tops were just visible. The denominations were anybody's guess.

"This guy looks like he wants to shoot you, Pop," Ali said. In fact, the federali who came over did not look overjoyed to see us. He noticed the money when I got out, but the sight failed to cheer him. I followed him around back to the trailer and opened it for him. He glanced inside.

"You got any guns?"

"Of course not."

"Visas."

I handed them to him along with the rolled bills. He pushed the money away.

"Anything wrong?" Susan said, when I had locked up and got back in the car.

"Not as far as I know. But that's the second time my modest bribe has been refused. Things have sure changed down here."

After a few minutes the man who had taken the visas returned and handed them through the window. When I asked if we were free to go, he gestured without bothering to turn around.

"Did that mean yes?" Susan wondered.

"I guess we'll find out." I put the car in gear.

"Nice country," Ali said.

"Pipe down," I told her. "You haven't seen it yet."

"I like it better at home. I want to go to high school. What's going to become of me?"

"Your girlfriends will catch up to you mentally and you'll catch up to them physically."

"Thanks, Dad."

It was starting to get dark by the time we got to Hermosillo. We decided to forego dinner and push on. Ali munched Oreos for awhile, then plumped a pillow against the door and closed her eyes. The Sonora desert flew by, dark and desolate. There was no moon yet, and the oncoming vehicles blinded us when they were still a mile away. The darkness was that perfect.

"You should take it easy on her," Susan said. "She's taking this whole sabbatical business pretty well."

"I know. Are you excited?"

"Sure," she admitted. "I just hated the border."

"It's the worst of it."

"Could we get a maid?"

"I don't see why not. With the devaluation we can probably afford it."

We drove on in silence for awhile, until Susan slid across the seat to snuggle. "Do you still think I'm a sex object?"

"Go ahead and answer her, Pop," Ali said from the back seat. "I'm asleep."

The condo was everything Charlie Stewart had said it would be. He had shown us photos, but I hadn't really believed them. It was right on the beach and the first thing we heard when we got out was the waves lapping up against the shore. The moon had just come over the ridge across the bay. Ali, who had finally fallen asleep for real, rubbed her eyes. As we stood there a couple clopped up the beach on horseback, moving silhouettes, passing in front of the large moon. "Holy shit," Ali said.

"How would you have expressed your admiration if you hadn't a near genius IQ?" I asked.

We were all very tired from the trip. I left the trailer packed and Susan didn't even bother to put sheets on the bed in the master bedroom. The two smaller bedrooms faced the ocean. Ali took one. The other would be my workroom. We opened the windows and the warm sea breeze rustled the curtains. Ali said she heard the riders return up the beach later in the night, but by then I had zonked.

Susan had already met the neighbors when I stirred. They were Mr. and Mrs. Henderson. "Alice wants to take us on a local tour," Susan said. "Do you mind? It's just the women."

I said that was fine.

"She says her husband Dan will be over to help you unpack."

He didn't show up though, and I spent what remained of the morning lugging. That didn't matter because the May morning was very beautiful and the sound of the waves kept me company. I even hoped that Dan wouldn't show up and spoil things. When I finished, I put on a pair of gym shorts and went for a swim. The water was warm and I swam a long way before coming back in and collapsing on the beach. It was a little cool at first when the breeze came, but the sun was warm and I could feel my skin tighten as it dried. Rather than burn, I went back inside and put on a shirt.

When the girls weren't back by noon, I left a note and strolled up the beach toward the large hotels. They were a lot farther than they looked, and by the time I got there I was hungry and ordered a crock of shrimp out on the terrace, along with a Bloody Mary. The shrimp came well iced with cocktail sauce and plenty of limes. When they were gone, I ordered another crock, this time along with some cold Mexican beer. I had the whole sabbatical year ahead of me and the sun was warm. It was wonderful to sit there and not worry about anything. Susan and Ali would find me if they wanted to, or not if they didn't want to. I couldn't decide which would please me more, to have them join me on the terrace, or spend the whole afternoon by myself, drinking cold Mexican beer and eating shrimp.

People came and went on the terrace. They were all Americans. The waiters were Mexicans, dressed up in red bolero jackets. Mine was trying desperately not to sweat in the hot sun. Had he been able to sit in the shade and drink beer as I was doing he'd have had no problem, but as things were, a dark circle of perspiration formed beneath his armpits. I wondered if he was likely to be fired for this offense, and the more I drank, the more likely it seemed. I decided to make sure that didn't happen, because he was a very good waiter. If they tried to fire him for sweating, I would defend him to the end, take my business to the hotel next door if need be. I began to almost hope they would try to fire him, so I could show the waiter that he had a real friend.

By mid-afternoon it was quite hot and only a few of the tables on the terrace were occupied. At one was another American who had been there when I arrived. The two of us were apparently in sync because my friend the waiter brought our drinks together three times in a row and we raised our glasses across the terrace in a toast. He looked like he might be a few years older than I, a little thick around the middle and a little thin on top. When the breeze blew, his baby fine hair stood on end like a flame until he smoothed it down again. This he must have done fifty times. I kept wondering why he did not change chairs so the wind would be going the way his hair was, but the idea apparently never occurred to him. After a while he came over, and I motioned for him to take a chair. "You're new," he said. Up close he had a very boyish face, which made me wonder if I had gauged his age correctly. He was quite drunk.

When I said we had just arrived in San Carlos, he offered to shake hands. "Dan Henderson," getting up about halfway out of his chair, balancing precariously.

"Ah, yes," I said and introduced myself. "You were supposed to help me unload my trailer this morning."

He flushed bright red, the way only fair-skinned people can. "Jesus God," he said. "Jesus God, I'm sorry."

He was so obviously penitent that I almost laughed at him. "Don't be," I smiled.

"Todd, I feel God-awful."

"Please don't. I was just kidding."

"I feel God-awful. Let me buy you a drink. Tell me what you're drinking."

The beer bottle was right in front of him, but when the waiter came, Dan Henderson ordered tequilas and more limes. "And stay close," he advised the Mexican. "Moocho closo."

We drank the tequila and Dan ordered two more. I wondered how many he would have to buy before he felt better about not helping me with the trailer. I was willing to find out because the tequila tasted good. I hadn't drunk it straight with limes since my college days.

My companion raised his glass and tried to clink mine, spilling about half of his tequila in the process and then pretending it wasn't important. "On behalf of San Carlos," he made a sweeping gesture, "welcome to you and your lovely family."

I thanked him and San Carlos. He said he was an investor and had done rather well in something or other, and invested every nickle in something else and that had done very well too and now he was taking a year off before going back to work. A vacation from worry, he said. He hated to worry and he wondered if I wanted to know why.

"Why?" I said.

"S'only money," he said. "What good is it?"

"It buys tequila," I pointed out for the sake of argument.

"Not happiness," he said seriously.

"No," I admitted, "just tequila."

Having reached agreement we drank up, and when the waiter brought us two more, I paid for them, and that finally settled the issue. Money did buy the tequila. In fact, remarkably little money had bought a lot of tequila and shrimp and Mexican beer. I'd started with a little over ten dollars worth of pesos and it wasn't gone yet.

I was though. Or pretty close to it, and so was Dan Henderson, who I could tell was still thinking that money couldn't buy happiness. I wondered why that particular cliché had taken such powerful possession of him. He forgot about me entirely and stared at his own pile of pesos so bitterly that I felt sorry for him. I also wished that he would cheer up, because I didn't want to share his depression and I was very afraid he was going to explain the cause of it. I was wrong though. He snapped out of it and grinned at me drunkenly, and I grinned back at him.

Before long we were friends. Around four in the afternoon I thought of Susan and Ali and told Dan Henderson that I had to head back up the beach. He looked very disappointed until I told him he could come too. I wasn't too surprised to discover it was hard to stand up. Tequila is still the sneakiest booze I know, but we made it, nevertheless. Dan Henderson stuffed the rest of his pesos that wouldn't buy happiness into his slacks. I left what remained of mine on the table. It couldn't have amounted to very much, but I was too drunk to figure percentages in pesos, so I just made a mental note to remember in the morning and make it up to the waiter on another occasion if it turned out I had gypped him.

"You aren't going to *leave* all that," Dan Henderson said, pointing at the pile of paper and coins.

"Yes," I said.

"Put it in your pocket," he said, his voice low and conspiratorial. "They don't expect it here."

"Then it will be a surprise."

I started away, toward the beach, but he did not follow. When I turned back, he was still standing there staring at the money, and I could see that he was thinking about picking it up and thrusting it at me. If he did, there would have to be an ugly scene about it, and I didn't want that. Instead, he took out some of his own pesos and dropped them on the table. "You're abs'lutely right," he said. "S'only money."

"It won't buy happiness," I said, half fearing that the reminder would make him depressed again, but it didn't. We weaved our way up the beach for a long time. Twice I turned around and looked back toward the hotel, afraid that we had missed the condo. There were a lot of them and I wasn't sure I'd remember what mine looked like. All I knew for sure was that I was drunk and that I lived next door to Dan Henderson, and that was who my companion claimed to be. If he was lying, or if he passed out, I was in trouble. We kept moving toward some mounds on the beach. One of them moved and I recognized Ali in her new one piece bathing suit. She studied me critically. Neither Susan nor Alice Henderson bothered to get up.

"God, you're beautiful," Dan Henderson said, his thin hair standing up in the breeze like a flame. His observation took me off guard because I thought for a moment that he was talking about my wife, who did look pretty nice, now that he mentioned it, all creamy skin and suntan butter. I was wrong though. He was talking about his own wife, who was, if one cared to be generous, about as plain a middle-aged woman as I'd ever seen. He apparently was sincere though, for he dropped to his knees and began to nibble her foot. Alice kicked him away. On the surface, the gesture was playful, but I could tell she had caught him pretty good. He tried to cover up the fact that the kick had hurt, but it must have.

"You did a crummy job of unpacking," Susan said. She knew I was drunk but wasn't sure how badly. She would listen to my reply and that would tell her. Speech was the first, if not the only, skill I lost when I was far gone.

"I'll bet my lazy husband let him do the whole thing by himself," Alice Henderson observed.

"Not true," I said. "I couldn't have mamaged without him." Dan gave me the most grateful look I'd ever received.

"Mamaged?" Ali said.

"Yes," I said. "Mamaged. Look it up."

She doubted herself for a moment. Ali was an avid Scrabble player and while she had a wonderful vocabulary for a twelve year old, I was always employing words she didn't know, some of which I made up to get rid of letters I didn't know what to do with. She knew I cheated but was never sure when and hated to risk calling me.

She had me this time though. "Challenge," she said confidently, and everyone laughed.

"Go inside and get me something to drink," Alice Henderson told her husband, and he hopped up to do as he was told. "I'm sure glad you all have moved in," Alice said, "before I lost my mind with boredom. It's about time we had new blood."

There was something about the way she said all that which made it sound like a criticism of her husband, and I realized right then that I wasn't going to like Alice Henderson. She had to know that her kick in the chops had hurt Dan, but it did not bother her.

I went inside and fell asleep on the bed. Susan had put fresh sheets on and they smelled wonderful. They were better than I deserved. I woke up much later when Susan came in. It was always pleasant to awaken to the sight of her undressing. She didn't want any part of my drunken admiration, however, for which I couldn't blame her. "Alice says her maid will do our place twice a week for three dollars."

"Never," I said.

"Really."

"Three dollars?"

"According to Alice. Is that all right with you?"

"Of course."

"I think it's going to be a great year," she said. "I'm so glad we decided on it."

I got up and out of my clothes so that I could get in bed for real. From our bedroom window I could see the Henderson place next door all lit up. I wondered whether inside, out of the breeze, my new friend's hair still stood on end like a flame.

The maid was named Maria. She was a pretty girl, the way pretty Mexican girls are pretty, and she was very happy for the opportunity to clean the condo twice a week. Her English was much better than my Spanish, so when we conversed, which was seldom, we spoke English. My only complaint with the girl was that she couldn't be made to understand that my work room was off limits. Either she didn't understand or she was afraid that by not cleaning one room she would be vulnerable to the possibility of not being paid the full amount. Apparently the Hendersons paid Maria by the month, because when we paid her first week in advance she was surprised and very happy. But it in no way altered her resolve not to clean and straighten my room, at which times I was forced out onto the patio until she finished.

"Apparently I missed out by not being young and Mexican," Susan observed. "You bite my head off at the slightest interruption."

"I would do the same to her if I could summon adequate Spanish, but I dislike being cruel to people unless I can manage it gracefully."

After a few days we all settled into a routine. I worked in the mornings while Susan and Ali explored, sometimes with Alice Henderson, sometimes by themselves. Alice wasn't a bad guide when it came to places, but she'd somehow managed to live in Mexico for over a year without learning more than a few words of Spanish and was a wealth of misinformation on a variety of subjects. The uneasiness we all felt at the border completely dissipated, the way it always does when you get into the interior. The girls took the car and went confidently on long excursions. Sometimes we ate lunch together. Other times I wouldn't see them all day. After lunch I usually took a swim and headed up the beach to one of the hotels where I would sit on the terrace and read what I had written in the morning and see if any of it made sense. Sometimes it did and that made me feel good. I even began to worry that I might finish ahead of schedule, but I resolved to slow my pace if that became a real danger. I didn't want to lose my justification for being in San Carlos. Ali complained at first about not having American television, but before long she rediscovered books, and in the evening we played Scrabble by the hour. She even got a little better about guessing when I was making up words.

About the only problem I had was avoiding Dan Henderson, who would have interrupted my work if I had let him. He knew that when I locked myself in my workroom he was to leave me alone, but once I ventured out into the open air, he figured I was fair game. He haunted the hotels every afternoon, and it didn't matter to him if he saw that I was hunched over a sheaf of notes. All I could do was be unpredictable, working on the terrace of one hotel one day, another the next, and trust that once he was settled he would be too lazy to come looking for me. He drank every afternoon the way he had that first one, weaving dutifully back up the beach around five or so, anxious to nibble on one of Alice's tough toes. He never got anywhere that I could see.

My favorite part of the day was early morning. Susan and Ali were late sleepers and that freed me to drive into Guaymas two or three times a week when the morning chill was still in the air. I usually went to the mercado for pastries and fruit to bring back for breakfast. The market was always bustling no matter how early I got there, the same men in tan shirts milling about outside. The Guaymas mercado occupied an entire block, and that particular block did not look that different from the others, for it was ringed with small shops and stalls, the entrances to the mercado itself always congested with idle men. The average tourist might have walked by twice a day for a month and never guessed what was inside.

Which was just as well, all things considered, because it was a different world. Even in the morning it was very hot. Halves of skinny Mexican cows lay gutted on the block waiting for somebody to butcher them. Flies, thousands of them, darted from one spot of blood to the next, crazy with good fortune. Everywhere the smell of shrimp and fish mingled with that of warm meat and cooking in the tiny, cramped, three stool family lunch counters where the poorest working men breakfasted on menudo and rice, sweating from the heat generated by the sputtering grill that was close enough to touch. I liked the mercado because it was busy and honest about the flies and the smells. American tourists who did manage to find the market mostly retreated to their hotels, happy that they didn't have to eat food that came from there. I don't know where they thought the hotels got their food from. I showed Susan the mercado one day and she was pretty good about it, but she continued to do all our weekly shopping at the more expensive American style market where English was spoken and the customers were reassured with cellophane.

Most of the time I bought little more than a fresh pineapple and enough Mexican pastries to last us a couple days. I was always overcharged and occasionally short-changed, but by such paltry amounts that I never objected. It was just a local tax on being an American, and all things considered that was fair enough. When a family of three can breakfast for two days on roughly a dollar and a half, they are miles ahead of the game.

Still, I very nearly did not go back to the mercado after my first visit. On my way out I was met by a deformed woman who had been seated up against the inner wall, surrounded by several children, one of whom rested quietly on the woman's shoulder. She got to her feet with some difficulty so she could hold out her hand. She said nothing, but pointed to her ragged children. One of the woman's eyes was badly damaged. There was next to no iris, and while her good eye fixed me squarely, the other looked away, indifferent. I could tell that the hand was outstretched as a matter of habit, without much real hope. I had not yet pocketed my change from the pastries, so I gave it to the woman, who turned away without saying anything. A dark-skinned man leaning against the wall shook his head at me. He looked disgusted, as if he'd seen me kick the woman. Outside, as if they had learned about me through some sort of telepathy, I was suddenly surrounded by children, all with hands extended, all chattering in Spanish. The bigger ones pushed the little ones aside to jockey for position. For a moment it was impossible to move in any direction and as the sea of bodies pushed against me I was afraid that I might fall into their midst. The idle men at the entrance to the mercado smiled at each other, and I hated them blackly. When I finally got back to my car, I just sat there until the crowd of children were gone. When I turned the key in the ignition, there was a scratching on the driver's side window. That was exactly what the boy was doing, scratching not rapping. He was just able to see inside by standing on his toes. I met his dark brown eyes and shook my head, and then he went away.

One morning on the way back from the mercado I saw a girl who resembled Maria walking along the side of the highway. I slowed, and that's who it was. It had never occurred to me to wonder how she got from Guaymas to San Carlos to do her work. None but the wealthier Mexicans could afford San Carlos, especially since the devaluation. Maria explained that she usually caught a ride with a relative who drove a truck. That got her as far as the San Carlos turnoff, then she walked the last mile and a half. She said she would have walked a good deal farther. As she talked, I marvelled again that she considered herself a very fortunate girl to have so many American houses to clean, because such work was not easy to come by, and there were many girls who came all the way out from Guaymas to do just one house, whereas she herself had five and made a good wage, though there were many people in her family who depended on her earnings. Some of the other girls worked cheaper than Maria, she admitted, glancing carefully over at me, but she was of the opinion that they were not worth the savings, although some Americans were seduced by the lower rate. She herself would not work for less than top dollar and only for nice American families like mine, who paid what they said they would pay. She was quite a little businesswoman, was our eighteen-year-old Maria, and very religious too, which was why she had not worked for the bad father who had lived there before us.

The reference to Charlie Stewart I did not understand until much later. A friend of mine for some years, he taught "The Bible as Literature" at one of the Arizona universities when he wasn't writing slightly pornographic romantic potboilers under a female pseudonym. They made him an awful lot of money, much of which he gave away. There was also a lot of which he kept. Enough to finance a condo vacation home. I was one of very few people who knew he wrote the potboilers, and even fewer knew about the condo. Giving it to us for my sabbatical year had been very generous, and he refused to hear of any rent.

"Did you know that our friend Father Stewart is leading a dual life?" Susan asked me one July afternoon. "Alice says he has a different girl with him every time he comes down here."

"Really?" I said. I don't know why that should have surprised anyone as cynical about religion as I, but it did.

"Yes, yes," Susan said, her eyebrows arched significantly.

Since there was a salt shaker handy I gave it to her. "Alice is malicious. You know that."

"Not in this case. She didn't even know he was a priest until I told her."

"I wouldn't be too sure," I said. Maria had known, and she must have found out from someone. Her disapproval finally made sense.

"Why do you insist on disliking Alice?" Susan wanted to know.

"Because I like Dan."

"Can't you like them both?"

"No. *I* can't."

"You always take sides."

That was true. I couldn't help myself.

"Dan's a drunk."

"That's beside the point. Alice isn't a nice person. If she were, I would like her. When have you ever known me to dislike a nice person?"

"You dislike my mother."

"Think of another example," I suggested. "One that proves your point, not mine."

Susan let that one go, which suggested she had something on her mind. "Alice told me something yesterday. I've been thinking about it ever since."

"If it's about Charlie, I don't want to hear it. I'm glad he's getting laid, if he's getting laid. If I had a real problem, I'd take it to him sooner than about anyone I know."

"It's not about Charlie," she said. She looked so worried and serious that I put down what I was doing and gave her my full attention. "Alice says that in Mexico City parents sometimes maim their children to make them more pitiful. So they can beg."

I had heard similar stories, but I did not know if they were true. I could tell that Susan thought they were, and the possibility hurt her deeply. I took her hand across the table and gave it a squeeze.

"It's all right, isn't it?" she said. "Our being down here and every-thing."

I said I thought it was.

"It seems wrong sometimes. We have too much."

Then an idea occurred to me. "Why did Alice tell you that story?"

"I don't know," Susan said, but she didn't meet my eyes.

"Tell me," I insisted.

She hesitated, then finally gave in. She had been going to give money to a beggar, and Alice had prevented her with the story.

"See?" I told her.

"You're right about Alice," she admitted. "But that doesn't mean the story isn't true."

I suggested we go outside for awhile. It was dusk and we always enjoyed sitting on the patio with a glass of wine, letting the outside world shrink toward us with the dark.

In July, Ali fell in love. The whole thing began when we chartered the boat. I hadn't been able to interest Susan in deep sea fishing, but Ali was all for it. She was all for anything that gave her a sense of purpose, and the alternative was tagging along with her mother and Alice Henderson. I think my darling Ali shared her father's ungenerous opinion of Alice, though we never discussed the matter. At any rate she got pretty excited about spending a whole day with me, which was probably an index of her boredom. The first few weeks she had enjoyed, before the novelty of sunning on the beach began to wear off. She was berry brown and she didn't know what to do next.

The boat I chartered was captained by a swarthy, toothless fellow who appreciated the case of beer I brought on board in an ice chest. He drank several before we were even out of the bay and I expected the boat to start traveling in circles, but the captain knew what he was doing with both boat and beer. His mate was a skinny, brown-skinned boy about Ali's age. He got all the bad jobs—baiting hooks, gutting the fish, sponging down the deck. He did all of it cheerfully, hopping around in a very worn pair of tennis shoes, sockless. He apparently spoke no English, and his Spanish came in such quick, explosive volleys that neither Ali nor I could understand much. Ali's Spanish was fast becoming better than my own. Maria had adopted her, and the two spoke slow careful Spanish whenever Maria was around. Ali was doing so well that she insisted we suspend strict rules so she could use Spanish words when we played Scrabble. I went along, provided she got a Spanish dictionary, because she had enough of her father in her to make up a word when it suited her, and I wasn't about to give her another whole language to do it in.

I could tell that Raul—that was the boy's name—was going to be the hit of the trip. He attended Ali from the beginning, even offering, if I understood correctly, to rub lotion along the small of her back where she couldn't reach, a duty my charmer nevertheless allowed me. The captain nodded at them knowingly, and flashed me a toothless grin. I gave him one back, full of teeth. It really was sweet to watch them, they were so awkward. I could tell that for the first time in her life, wearing a bikini really meant something to Ali. During the last month or so, her figure had improved dramatically, and she was full of her approaching womanhood and scared as hell. Raul shared her awkwardness, facing seaward from time to time, probably to conceal his boyish erection. I had a great time drinking beer and watching them throw sparks.

Around mid-afternoon I hooked a small sailfish, and while he was running, I slipped off the fighting chair and turned the fish over to Ali. I knew she was scared, but she was also dead game, and she planted her pink-tennied feet on the runner and fought the fish nobly until she was very tired, trying to follow my rather bad instructions, which she could understand, along with the much better advice of the boy and the toothless captain, which she couldn't. In the end the fish got off and I could see by her eyes that she was relieved, though she professed disappointment ("Oh, buggers!"). I think Raul was more disappointed than anybody, for he had watched her tense, working limbs with admiration and was really hoping for her.

A couple of days later when I came back from my afternoon work session at the hotel, I saw Ali talking to a boy on the beach. When she saw me coming she ran to meet me and the boy disappeared.

"Who was that?" I said.

"Raul, of course."

"Of course," I said. Silly me. I have no idea how the boy found out where we lived. He may have walked up and down the miles of San Carlos beach until he ran into her for all I know. "Invite him in," I suggested, but she said he was gone. I knew that, and I had not meant right that minute, but thirteen-year-olds with growing breasts don't pick up on everything, even when they're smart as hell.

From that day forward, Raul haunted the condo, and after a while he got to the point where he would wave a hello to me, but he never did come in. Apparently, he was related in some distant way to Maria, who learned of the boy's infatuation for Ali and was unable to talk him out of it. When I asked her one morning (I often gave her a lift to San Carlos on my way back from the mercado) why she had wanted to, she refused to explain, but I could tell I was supposed to know.

The other person dead set against my daughter's flirtation with the Mexican boy was Dan Henderson, who took the trouble to search me out one afternoon. I was at the fourth hotel he tried and I could tell he'd been at each of the first three for a while. He sat down heavily in the chair across from me and my notecards, his baby-fine hair standing on end in the gentle breeze, and studied me seriously. "You know how much I love your Ali," he began.

"I won't let her date a married man, Dan. That's final."

He reacted to my joke as if I'd jabbed him hard. "Jesus Christ, Todd," he said. "Jesus Christ. You shouldn't joke about her. She's a swell kid."

"I know that, Dan," I told him seriously.

"Then protect her, for God's own sake. Send that kid away."

"Why?"

But he was adamant, almost in tears, his hair aflame. "I don't care," he said. "Call me a bigot. Call me whatever you want, but protect her, for Jesus' sake."

"I will," I promised him. "I do."

But he made me promise again, several times, protesting how much he loved my kid. It was really rather touching, in a nasty, racist sort of way.

When I mentioned the scene to Susan that night, while Ali and Raul were out walking on the beach, she wasn't surprised. "You can guess why he's like that, can't you?"

"No," I said. "I've never understood that kind of thinking, frankly. Not in people who have had some advantages, anyway."

"You don't know why he goes out drinking every afternoon?"

"He likes to drink?"

Susan gave me her 'where have you been' look. "It's Alice. That's when her friend comes over."

I hated like hell to be slow, but there was no way around it. "What friend?"

"I should think Dan would have told you."

"I wish someone would."

"Well, Dan . . . can't."

"Can't what?"

"The big can't. At least he couldn't for a long time. He claims he can again now, but there have been no demonstrations. Anyway, Alice isn't one to sit around idly . . ."

I was stunned. I shouldn't have been, a big, worldly, steely-eyed realist like me. But I was anyway. "That cunt," I said. It was a word I had never used in my wife's presence before.

She became instantly angry. "Isn't that typical?"

"It stinks," I said, because it really did.

"Sure," Susan said. "What if it were the other way around? If it was Dan with some little chiquita on the side, would you think anything of it? But let a woman take the same initiative and it's suddenly a capital offense."

"Initiative?"

"Why not. For a few bucks a week Alice can have a young Mexican stud and a little happiness."

"She doesn't deserve a young Mexican stud," I said. "I'm not even sure she deserves a little happiness. Not at Dan's expense, anyway. It's probably her fault to begin with. I'd have my problems too if I had to climb on top of that woman."

That was a crummy thing to say, of course, and Susan seemed almost relieved that I'd said it. She hadn't felt that comfortable defending Alice, but I had handed her the argument by surrendering the high ground. So there was nothing left to do but go out on the patio and slam the door. Which I did.

Ali and Raul were a ways down the beach. I sat down and watched them. They were like a couple of young colts, clumsy and awkward. All legs. I felt sorry for them. After a while Raul trotted off down the beach and Ali joined me on the patio.

"How's love?" I said.

"Oh, Dad."

"Don't oh dad me."

"What were you and mom fighting about? We could hear you all the way down the beach."

"Nothing to do with you."

"Okay," she said cheerfully. One of the things I loved about her was the way she never doubted the truth of what I told her. I made a mental note to try and be worthy of that trust. "It's not easy," she says. "He never has any money and he won't let me pay. And I think he's ashamed of me with his friends."

"You seem to be communicating pretty well."

"He's proud."

"Aren't we all."

We sat in silence for awhile and I felt the ache of her doubts. "I have an idea," I suggested. "There are some things that need doing around here. How about if I paid him to do some odd jobs?"

She gave me a kiss and said I was great. "That just leaves the other thing . . ."

"I don't think he's ashamed of you, Ali."

She shrugged. "Sometimes . . . I guess, maybe I'm a little ashamed of him. Like when he bends over to pick up a flat stone or something, you can tell he doesn't wear any underclothes."

I could tell that she was very embarrassed to tell me this. She was all coiled up inside. "He's a very clean boy and everything . . ."

"It's no sin not to have what you can't afford," I said.

"It's not fair, Dad," she said, her voice tight with the unfairness she wanted to explain. "It's not fair that I should know. He should have his secrets."

I put my arm around her shoulder and gave her a hug. Her skin was cool and soft, and it brought back indistinct memories of my own adolescence. Pain mostly, from that time before we learn how not to feel so keenly. "I'm proud of you," I told her. "Your friend has good taste in girls."

"Then you think it's all right to like him. I won't if you don't want me to."

I said I thought it was fine and I could tell that made her happy.

Susan was already in bed when I came in, and she wasn't mad at me any more. Like many people who got angry quickly, it never took her long to simmer down. When I crawled in beside her, she snuggled. "I listened in on your conversation with our daughter," she said. "I love you all over again."

"Have you talked with her about things?"

"Yes. She's very well educated."

"Good. I worry about boys who don't wear underpants. There's no way to tell how many unwanted pregnancies have been avoided by the wearing of that particular garment."

"Not as many as have been avoided by scruples and good loving fathers."

We kissed and I slipped out of my own undershorts. Susan stopped our natural progress only once. "You know those times when you haven't been able to?" she said.

"Have there been so many?"

"Of course not. But was it me? Because I was unattractive to you?"

"Don't be an idiot."

We made love very successfully, the way two people can sometimes when it really matters.

The end of July was hot. So hot the sea breeze didn't do much good. Neither did the condo's window unit air conditioners, which rattled like hell and blew furiously, signifying nothing. It was so muggy that after Maria washed the tiled floors in the morning they would still be wet when we gathered for lunch. It was too hot to lie on the beach, too hot to go for excursions in the car. I continued to work in the morning, but the hotel terraces were intolerable in the afternoon, even if you followed the shade, so my afternoon sessions got axed. I could have made it through by drinking plenty of cold beer, but then the work wouldn't have been any good.

Only Ali did not seem affected by the heat. She bounced in and out in her bathing suit, practically the only article of clothing we ever saw her in. Under Maria's tutelage her Spanish was improving and she practiced by talking back to a local radio station that blared raucous Mexican rock and frantic dj's. "Juan Travolta!" they screamed. "El Fevré de Sabado Noché!"

"Good lord," Susan said. "Is that just getting here?"

Every day after lunch Dan Henderson headed up the beach toward the hotels. He always leaned forward, as if the trek were up hill. I never caught even a glimpse of Alice's Mexican lover. He either sneaked in through the patio door on the other side of the condo or was waiting for the heat wave to break. It was far too hot to screw. Certainly too hot to screw Alice. Even Susan's wandering around semi-nude, trying to keep cool, failed to give me ideas. The bed sheets were always damp, like sweating skin.

Ali's Raul never came by except in the evening. When his uncle's boat went out, just about every day in season, he crewed. I did as I promised and put him to work a few times, but while he was grateful for the work, it didn't help Ali's dilemma, because the money disappeared and we figured that whatever he made must have gone into the family kitty. There was no money for him to see "El Fevré de Sabado Noché" unless he held back part of his earnings, and this the boy was apparently unwilling to do. He remained steadfast in his refusal to let Ali treat and never told her precisely where his family lived in Guaymas, perhaps for fear that she would want to meet them. The two of them just walked along the beach, night after night. I'd have given a lot to know what they found to talk about, or even if they talked. But at thirteen, of course, talking isn't strictly necessary. You can just walk and listen to the sound of your own hormones.

In August, Dan Henderson got into serious trouble. I learned about it third hand, from Susan, who heard about it from Alice, who wasn't there, so the details were pretty sketchy. Apparently, Dan had gotten very drunk at the Playa del Rey where he had savagely beaten one of the Mexican waiters. I had been on the terrace of the hotel next door, about a hundred yards down the beach, and seen the ambulance pull up, along with several police cars, but I didn't go see what the commotion was. It must have been awhile before anyone bothered to tell Alice Henderson that her husband was in jail, because she had just left our place after telling Susan when I returned several hours later. I went down to the Guaymas station where I got exactly nowhere with the policia, who wouldn't let me see Dan and looked as if they would have liked to tie me into the whole thing somehow. Eventually, I gave up and went home.

After dinner, against Susan's advice, I went next door to see Alice, who was inside and very drunk, lounging on the sofa. It was an utterly ridiculous pose to strike under the circumstances, like something out of a thirties b movie. She had been crying, but her mood right then was hard to place. She looked like she'd tried all the emotions she knew and couldn't settle on one. "S'my fault," she grinned at me pitifully. "That's what you think."

"Have you called anyone? A lawyer? The American consulate?"

She shook her head.

"Don't you think you should?"

"Why should I?"

I let that go. I didn't want to fight with her. "They wouldn't let me see him," I said. "I'll take you to the station in the morning. They can't refuse to let you in. At least, I don't think they can."

My doubt on that particular point triggered a genuine emotional response. At least as genuine as she was capable of, given her condition. She began to shake with fear, and drew herself upright on the sofa. "They hate Americans," she said. "They hate us, they all do. Just because we're Americans."

"What did the police tell you?"

"I don't know. I don't remember. They all hate us. You know they do. Because we're Americans."

"Alice . . ."

"I want to be in America," she whined, big tears welling up in her eyes. "I want to go home. Would you take me to Arizona?"

"No," I said.

She wiped her eyes and stopped crying. Just like that, which made me wonder if the response had been genuine after all.

"First thing in the morning you'd better call a lawyer here in town," I told her. "You can afford a good lawyer, can't you?"

She snorted, her eyes suddenly small and hard. "There's nothing in the whole country you can't buy for ten dollars." She smiled at the observation and it was so nasty and contemptuous that it seemed to encompass not just Mexico but the whole world and everyone in it. I'd had enough of her.

When I turned to leave she said, "I don't see where you're so hot."

She studied me openly, evaluating. "You may be all right, but you're not that hot."

She flashed me a smile then, and it occurred to me that she was making a pass. A strange one, by any standard, but a pass. I was supposed to show her that I *was* pretty hot. I felt like telling her that she wasn't so hot either, but I could tell by looking at her that she knew it already, and that made me feel a little sorry for her. Not carried away with sympathy maybe, but decently sorry.

In the morning I went back to the police station, but they still would not let me see Dan. I should have taken Alice with me, but I had not wanted to see her and was afraid she might cause trouble. After cooling my heels for awhile, I went through the phone book and selected a lawyer at random. He spoke some English and gave me some good free advice. I shouldn't have taken it, but I did.

The waiter that Dan had beaten up turned out to be the one who had served us that first afternoon on the hotel terrace. I had been there many times since then, and he knew who I was. I always tipped him well, and I hoped that would count for something. He had spent the night in the hospital, but by the time I got there, he had been released. I hoped that meant his injuries were not serious, but it didn't. He and his wife and children lived in a side street in Guaymas not far from the mercado. The neighborhood wasn't good, even by Guaymas standards. The square, stucco houses were crammed up against each other. The black-haired children in the narrow street stopped playing to see where I would go.

The man's wife took me to a dark room at the back of the house. It was very clean but there was little furniture except for the bed and just the obligatory Mexican Jesus on one wall. Dan Henderson had given the waiter a terrible beating. One eye was swollen shut and about the size of a tennis ball. I wondered why the man allowed it, since Dan, though larger, was soft and not very strong, even when sober. But then I'd seen drunks get strong, like frightened mothers are supposed to be when they lift cars to free pinned children. The waiter did not seem surprised to see me, and his wife left us alone. She knew, of course, why I had come.

"Do you hurt much?" I said.

"Yes, very much," the man said. "You can see."

"Yes, I do see. It was a terrible thing."

"Mr. Henderson is your friend?"

I shook my head. "No. He is not my friend."

He nodded almost imperceptibly. I'm not sure he believed me, but he may have.

"He has a bad wife," I explained. "It makes him very crazy."

Again the man nodded. He knew about bad women and that they made you crazy. That was our allegiance, and I took advantage.

"Mr. Henderson is very sorry," I told him. "He is not a bad man. He is crazy but not bad."

I gave money to the woman on the way out. In the street the children had resumed their game, and they paid me no attention.

The next morning Charley Stewart called from the States to find out how things were going. Susan talked to him for awhile before putting me on. They had been friends before, but she seemed just a little aloof now. She had never championed the idea of priestly celibacy, but then she'd spent a good part of her youth in confessionals, and that made her feel wronged.

"I hear you've had some excitement," Father Stewart said.

"The Hendersons."

"Ah, yes."

"Right."

He must have sensed my unease across the miles. "Things can be rough down there if you aren't the right sort," he said seriously. "How's your work coming?"

"Great," I said. "The work's great."

"You don't have to stay if you don't want to. Just lock the place up and come back."

"It's wonderful," I told him. "You can't beat it."

We steered clear of the Hendersons after Dan's release, but one night about a week after the waiter dropped the charges, Dan appeared on the patio. I was reading in the living room, Susan and Ali were someplace else. Dan seemed glad to find me alone, and we went out onto the patio. It was the first cool night in a long time. I offered him a beer, but he shook his head. "We're heading north," he said.

"Now? To the States?"

"The station wagon's packed."

"What about your belongings?"

"We'll rent the place furnished. Or sell it. The main thing is to get out."

"What is the status of things?"

"Who knows?" he said. "This is Mexico, remember? If the guy changes his mind tomorrow I'm back eating frijoles in the slammer." That was supposed to be humor, but he didn't bother to smile at it. "Who needs it?"

I resisted the temptation to say he did. I couldn't think of anyone I knew who needed as badly to sit still for a while and eat frijoles until they worked a vision.

"It's funny," he said with staged thoughtfulness. "Since getting out, things have never been better between Alice and me. I realize now that she'd loved me all along."

He watched for my reaction, half expecting me to contradict him, probably.

"Tell her goodbye for us," I said.

There was an awkward moment then. I could tell he was trying to decide whether I might object to shaking his hand. "I guess you probably don't think much of me any more . . ."

"You did a rotten thing."

"Hey," he said. "*I* know that."

"Then I guess it's all right."

He did not react to my sarcasm. "At least let me pay you back what I owe you," he said, taking a thick wad of bills out of his pants' pocket. I almost laughed. He was going to give me Mexican money.

I motioned for him to put the money away. "Forget it," I told him. "Everything's cheap in Mexico."

"I know," he agreed. "I'm sure going to miss that."

I walked with him as far as his driveway. At the other end Alice was in the loaded station wagon waiting. Dan resolved the handshake issue by thrusting his fists in his pockets. "Kiss that kid of yours for me," he said. Then he told me to kiss my wife. And when I drank tequila on the hotel terrace, I was to think of him. I said I would.

Their leaving made Susan and me very happy. We drank a bottle of Mexican wine that night before going to bed. "Did you ever tell Alice I was hot stuff?" I said.

"I may have mentioned it," Susan admitted. She was great when she drank wine.

In September, Ali's boyfriend stopped coming around and she went through a mild depression. I told her there would be other boys, and she believed me the way you believe someone who tells you something that doesn't matter. In the mornings she went into town with me to the mercado. It was pretty rough on her at first. She wanted very badly to give money to the beggars. Only when Maria told her that it was not a good idea did she become resigned.

The Hendersons left, owing Maria for more than a month's worth of service, but although the girl was crushed she would not allow us to make up the difference. The Henderson place remained shut up until one day the police came, along with a flatbed truck which backed up to the patio door. Then several sweating men that I'd seen lounging around the mercado loaded all the furniture on and drove away. I told Alice about it one day when she called, and she cursed the whole country. I couldn't speak to Dan because they weren't living together.

With the Hendersons and the humidity gone, things settled down. I worked during the day, and in the evenings Susan and I drank Kahlua and cream on the patio while the waves lapped against the shore. No horsemen ever rode up the beach after that first night, but the late September moon was lovely on the bay. One day Susan went into Guaymas and bought new towels and linens. We didn't really need them, but they were nice and cost very little. When my wife gathered the old ones together and asked Maria if she could use them, the girl broke down and cried, thanking Susan over and over. "Oh, Señora," she said. "Now I can be married."

SUSAN FROMBERG SCHAEFFER
1996

The Old Farmhouse and the Dog-wife

He sat at the table, his head in his hands, and thought about what, over the years, he had done to the house. He was wearing blue jeans and an old plaid shirt. The blue jeans had been washed so many times they were soft, like flannel, and faded almost to white over the knees and the crotch. The rim of the pant legs, where they brushed against his leather boots, were beginning to fray. He fingered the sleeve of his shirt, which was soft and thin, thinner than a summer shirt, and remembered how stiff it was when his wife bought it for him, how stiff and bright, although now it had faded until the red plaid design was barely discernible, and when he stood back from the mirror to take himself in, the shirt was rose-colored and vaguely patterned. As time passes, he thought, things become softer. Look at the shirt, look at the jeans, look at his skin, look at the clapboards on the porch, the wood so soft you could push a pencil point into them. At what point would he grow too old to make the repairs on this house himself?

The man who came in winter to plow the road to the house still called it the big white farmhouse, although of course now it was smaller, because in the years he had the house, he had torn down the barn and the screened-in porch that ran the length of the two front parlors. His wife had been against these demolitions. She would take out the pile of old photographs displaying the original owners of the house swinging from their hammocks on the small porch in front of the kitchen, or sitting on their fancy chairs in front of the large porch. She was particularly fond of one postcard that showed an automatic sprinkler, something the owners had evidently invented themselves. They were there in the background like shadows while in the foreground, water, caught in the act of falling, suspended itself in a rain of silver beads over the whirling metal arms attached, somehow, to the thick garden hose. *It works!* read the message on the back of the card. *Look at this handwriting, how spidery it is!*

his wife said. *And the ink, this color purple. I believe they made the ink themselves!*

The house was built in 1780, and for this reason his wife was against making any changes, as if, should the first owners come back, they would not recognize the place and begin to reproach her. He suspected her, moreover, of having a religious faith in the rightness of old things simply because they were old, and when he accused her of this, she had nothing to say in her own defense, and so he knew he was right, not that she liked to argue. When they first married, she would argue about everything, or so it had seemed to him, but after they had been married some years, she would shake her head when something saddened her and go about her business, humming. When she was displeased with him, she said nothing, but somehow, whenever he entered a room she had a task that took her somewhere else. If he came into the kitchen and she was baking, she had to attend to the clothes on the line outside. If he followed her behind the house to the clothesline, she remembered the pies in the oven, dropped her clothespins into the little twig basket, and hurried back inside. It was like pursuing a nervous cat, and eventually he stopped. He knew when he was forgiven because when he entered a room, she stayed where she was.

He was tearing boards away from the barn walls one day when his wife came out and stood behind him. "Don't stand there like a guilty conscience," he said to her. "Take up the old nails."

When he had stripped the planks from the walls, the barn stood there, its slate roof varnished with dew. Now that the clapboards were down, you could see through the barn to the hills in back of the house. "Someone coming along wouldn't know if it was going up or coming down," he said. His wife made an odd, choking noise and gathered up a handful of the old nails. They were long and thick, with oddly shaped heads. "I know you think if something's been standing a long time, that's reason for it to go on standing forever," he said. When he turned to look at his wife, she was gone. He saw her going through the kitchen door, back into the house.

In those days, he was fond of saying that life was a struggle. The weather was against you, the bank was against you, and your own children were against you. He felt genuine pity for the barn swallow who every year built her nest over the kitchen door, and in the late spring when he got up and went out and saw the nest filled with gaping, squawking beaks, he would shake his head in commiseration every time. It made sense to try and even the odds. If the barn came down, there would be no more climbing up on the roof to nail down loose shingles, no more climbing up there in the winter to shovel off the roof which, under the weight of fallen snow, was threatening to collapse. If the big porch came down, there would be no need to climb out the bedroom window and shovel off that roof, no need, in the spring and summer to jack up the porch roof and repair the rotted floorboards. *What you can get rid of, that you should get rid of,* he said, quoting his father.

Of course while they had a horse and a cow the barn had to stand. In exchange for two loads of gravel from the gravel pit up the road above the house, a man in the village gave him an old red cow and he took it, thinking it might give a little milk, and if not, he would slaughter it and cook it into stew. The cow, which promptly became his wife and children's pet, gave so much milk the sound of churning was heard day and night, the buttery overflowed with butter and cheese, and the children's cheeks rounded. In those days, they often paid bills with cheese and milk and fresh-baked bread. In those days, too, cars were less reliable than you would like them to be, and his children always arrived at the school in the horse drawn sleigh, and not only his children, either, but the children of other families who were stranded in cars stuck in snowdrifts along the roads. In those days, the barn was steamy with the breath of the cow and the horse and the pigs and the heat from the wood stove, and the smell of the bales of hay. In those days the barn had a use, but when it had no use, he began to tear it down. It seemed to him obvious that useless things ought to be torn down and it annoyed him that this was not only unclear to his wife, but was the source of discord between them.

He sat in the old kitchen in front of the old kitchen table and worked on his drawing of the house as it looked when he first saw it. They had been looking for a place for two years when he drove over the little bridge, turned right, and saw the big white farmhouse smack in the middle of its eight acres. "This is it," he said. From the porch of the house, there was no other house in sight. The thick trees on the bank of the creek hid the road from view, although in winter when the leaves fell, they would be able to see passing cars and the old white house across the road.

His wife observed that the house was a wreck, that its roof leaked, its walls were rotten, and you had to hop from floorboard to floorboard unless you wanted to wind up in the cellar, which was no more than a hole cut in the ground and lined with stones. Inside, the house was cut up into many tiny rooms, some not much larger than cupboards, but he said he could knock down the walls and install wood stoves and put up chimneys and in six months the house would be warm enough to live in while he continued to work on it. His wife stood on the porch, and the cool breeze blew the smell of fallen pine needles toward her, and an enormous stand of lilacs was in full, aromatic bloom.

"One thing," said his wife. "I want a nice bedroom. I don't want to sleep in a half-finished room." He promised her a nice bedroom and they bought the house outright. The owner was glad to get rid of it. There were sinkholes in back of the house, where the water ran off from the hills behind. Probably the previous owner saw the house as a responsibility he was happy to have off his hands.

His drawing of the house had progressed, was, in fact, almost finished, when he heard the sound of a car's motor outside the house. He got up, stiffly, and walked through the open kitchen door onto the screened-in porch. His old dog, Ruff, heard him get up, lifted his head, sniffed the air, and lay back down. "You are a useless animal," he said to the dog.

A brilliant green Dodge was idling on the curved drive that wound around the lilac bushes, its nose pointed at the house. The sun glared on the windshield so that he couldn't see the driver, but a white-shirted arm came through the open window and opened the car door from the outside. He stayed where he was, watching. The driver got out, reached down and rubbed his knee, then looked up at him, smiling. "I was hoping for a drink of water," he said. Still smiling, he held out a silver canteen. It glinted in the blinding sun.

The farmer stood on the porch and looked at the car, thinking, Once I had a car like that. It was a 1950 Dodge. Everything about it was familiar, its curved swelling shape, its rounded bottom, its divided windshield. "How does it run?" he asked the stranger.

"It runs fine, but it eats gas," the man said. Everything about him was thin. His gray hair was thinning. "Until I get where I'm going, I don't have a nickel to spare," he said. "Every penny goes for gas and oil."

"I'll get you some water," he said, walking down the steps and over to the car. The thin man was about to hand him the canteen when loud, frantic barking erupted from the back seat. "Got a dog?" he asked the thin man.

"Well, not exactly," the stranger said.

Before he could say anything, Ruff erupted into loud barks on the porch.

"My dog thinks it's a dog," the farmer said. He could feel the smile leaving his face, but the thin man was smiling more intensely than ever. His teeth, he saw, were bright white, the color of brand new kitchen sinks. If his wife were still here, he thought, she'd say, Why doesn't he just wear a sign saying, *I paid a lot for these teeth?* A man with teeth that white, he thought, has something to hide.

"I could use some cold water," the thin man said. "My name's Fred."

"Fred," he said. "What about your dog? You want some water for your dog?" He moved toward the back seat of the car, but the man moved in front of him. When the stranger turned back to him, he tripped over Ruff, a big old shepherd, and as he righted himself, the farmer moved quickly and looked through the window into the back seat of the car. "My God," he said. "That's no dog."

"Well, I never said it was a dog," Fred said.

In the back seat of the '50 Dodge was an unkempt woman, very thin, her bones showing everywhere, her gray hair long and wild. She was up on her hands and knees, crouched down, her nose almost against the glass, crouched and growling as if she were a dog.

He moved away from the car and a few steps away from Fred.

"What's this, now?" he asked him.

"Don't get excited," the thin man said, his eyes on him. "Nothing to get excited about."

He thought about his rifle, behind the kitchen door. If this man Fred had a gun in the glove compartment, he could take it out and shoot him in the back as he walked back to the house.

"She must be hot in that hot car," he said.

"Oh, she is hot," the man said edgily. "Hot and thirsty. How about that water?"

"I'll get it and come out," he said, and turned to walk into the house. When he got to the porch, he turned, expecting to see the thin man pointing a gun at his back, but the man's head and shoulders had been swallowed by the back window and the blackness inside the car. Ruff was sitting on the grass behind the thin man, his head tilted to the left, as if he were trying to hear better. He took down his rifle, walked to the kitchen sink, and filled the canteen. As he passed, he looked at the picture he had drawn of the house, but in the picture, the house looked deserted and unreal. Once it had been a stagecoach stop. He should try drawing the stagecoach in front of the house. The drawing needed something to bring it to life. He walked across the porch and back outside. The thin man was extricating himself from the back of the car, wiping sweat from his forehead.

"That gun isn't a real friendly thing," Fred said.

"It's got nothing to do with you," he said. "There's a woodchuck tearing up the shed floor."

"A woodchuck," said the thin man. "Well, a lot of people start seeing woodchucks after they look into that car."

"You kidnapping her or what?" he asked, the rifle still under his arm.

"A man doesn't have any call to kidnap his own wife," the thin man said.

"She's your wife?" he said. "She looks older."

"She always did look older," the thin man said, "but after she fell ill, she looked a lot older. The doctor said it happens. When they're sick that way, they hold their faces stiff, and their faces freeze that way."

"She's sick or she's crazy?" he asked, moving closer to the car. When he was near enough to the window to see his face reflected in it, the crouching woman rose up on all fours and began snarling, then barking ferociously.

"A little bit of both, I guess," the thin man said.

He looked over his shoulder at the thin man who felt edgy but not dangerous. The farmer had been a hunter all his life. He thought he knew when an animal, man or beast, was threatening. This man wasn't threatening, not this minute, although he knew he could be. The farmer turned away from him and thrust his head suddenly against the car window. At this, the crouching woman jumped up, pulled her teeth back, and began barking like a maddened, chained dog. He turned to the thin man.

"She knows who she is?" he asked the stranger.

"Well, I couldn't say," the man said. "She clearly thinks she's a dog and she clearly thinks it's her business to protect me. She always was a protective kind of woman."

He looked from the thin man who stood with his hands thrust deep and tight into his jeans pockets and back to the '50 Dodge. A hot wind picked up the elm branches and dropped them down. An elm in front of the house was diseased. "I want it to last as long as we do," his wife once said, and after that he paid the tree surgeon his exorbitant yearly fee. From the look of things, the tree was going to outlast him. He thought again of the old stagecoach that used to stop in front of the house, and for the first time thought about the original owner of the house and what misgivings he must have had each time the coach stopped and let out its load of strangers, any one of whom could be a thief, a murderer, or worse.

"Where do you sleep at night?" he asked the man. "In the car?" The thin man nodded. "I guess you don't want to answer questions," he said. The thin man smiled a tight, wry smile. He held tight to the silver canteen of water. "The streams around here are good and clean, you know," he told the stranger. "You can drink from them and not worry about anything."

"Yes, well," said the thin man. Now that he had his water, he seemed ready to go.

"At night it drops down very cold. Well, since last Monday it's been dropping down very cold. I came home last night and already there was smoke coming out of chimneys."

"It's a nice smell, that wood smoke," the thin man said.

"Not so nice when you're chopping the wood, though," he said. "Look. My hands are full of splinters."

"Your wood's all chopped?" the stranger asked.

He thought about the wood in the shed, stacked from floor to ceiling, stacked against all the walls, six or seven cords. Since his wife died, what did he have to do but chop wood?

"Look," he said to the thin man, "you could stay here the night, but you'd have to tie up—"

"Tie up the dog. Sure," the thin man said. "She likes being tied. You should see her, how she curls up and lies around my feet."

"Well, I wouldn't have gone so far as to call her a dog," he said.

"She's not yours," the thin man said flatly.

"Why don't you come in now and have a sandwich?" he said. He looked nervously at the car.

"Oh, she eats anything," the thin man said. "I'll put her on her leash."

"You put her on her leash and bring her in," he said.

They were sitting in the kitchen, eating buttered frankfurter rolls and drinking bottles of beer. He had quieted Ruff, who lay under his chair, his ears down, his nose pointed in the direction of the woman whose feet and arms were tied together. She lay peacefully on the floor next to her husband who, every now and then, reached down and handed her a piece of buttered roll. He fed her piece by small piece and she took each one gently and chewed it up. After she swallowed each piece, he said, "Good girl, Martha," and the woman would tilt her head of grayish blond hair and look gratefully up at him, although at times her eyes looked spiteful.

"This is a nice house you have here," the thin man said, looking around. "You did a lot of work on it?"

"It was rotting when we got it," he said. "But the original beams were good, under the floor and under the roof, so little by little, I did it over. Those wide planks on the floor? They're from the old barn. I sanded them down after I pulled the barn down. The beams in the ceiling? The original beams. Can you imagine the trees, how tall they were then? How many oxen it took to pull them back through the snow?"

"I know these old houses," the thin man said. "A jumble of tiny rooms. You can see clear from one end of the house to the other in here."

"That's my work," he said. "I told my wife, 'We have a wood stove, we have all the wood we need, if we get rid of the walls, we can heat the whole house with no trouble for no expense at all.'"

"I bet she didn't like it," the thin man said, handing down a bit of buttered roll. The wild-haired woman took it between her teeth, chewed it and swallowed it.

"She said, 'Who wants to sit on a couch and look at the kitchen sink,' but after a time she saw I was right. Easier to clean, easier to heat. Do things the easy way, that's my motto."

"She died long ago?" the thin man asked.

"Five years this April," he said. "She sat down on the couch, picked up a book, made a funny little noise, and then she sort of slid against the arm rest. She's buried out there in the back, way out back, under those two big willows."

"You changed anything in the house since then?" the thin man asked. The woman on the floor lifted her head and growled slightly.

"Well, I added a few more dirty dishes to the sink," he said.

They sat in silence. The thin man's index finger began tracing the geometric design which bordered the enamel-topped table. "This is a nice table," he said. "Real old-fashioned. When I was a boy, my father did sums on a table like this, right on the table with a black crayon, and when he was finished, he took a damp rag and wiped the table down."

"Two thousand and fifty little knife marks," the farmer said. "All the times she cut up vegetables or meat or dough on this table top. Thousands of tiny scratches, but you have to look to see them." He saw it was getting dark and got up to turn on the light over the table.

"It's wicked dark outside for five o'clock," the thin man said.

"It's going to storm," the farmer told him. "I always feel it along my skin, the way it lies there, like a knife blade you took out in the sun."

"I hope it doesn't storm," the thin man said. "It frightens the dog. Once she broke a table, trying to hide herself under it. Some dogs are afraid of thunder, you know. They don't flinch at guns, but thunder, that's something else."

"She's not a real dog," the farmer said and then was sorry he said it.

"If it storms, I'll have to tie her up hand and foot and put a blanket over her," the thin man said. "It's for her own good." He looked around the kitchen and from it to the parlor where a gray couch and two gray velvet chairs surrounded a pink flowered rug. "Sometimes when a person dies and you don't change a thing, you're keeping the house like a monument to them. Sometimes it means you really loved that person. Sometimes it means the opposite altogether. 'This was your house, this was how you wanted it, now you're gone, I'm never going to be bothered with it again,' that's what you're saying."

"If it's going to storm, maybe you should take her out to the bathroom," he said. "Before the lightning starts."

"Oh, she can use the indoor plumbing," the thin man said. "She remembers how to do that."

"Sometimes I wonder how well the house is grounded," he said. "I don't like to sit on a toilet in a thunderstorm."

"I'll take her now," said the thin man. He untied the woman's feet and led her off. Before they entered, the woman turned, looked at him and growled.

I can think of one hundred good reasons why I shouldn't have let him in the door, he said to himself. Outside the trees sighed, just as his wife would have sighed if she were there.

When he returned, they began to talk. The thin man talked mainly about his wife, how one day she had begun to grow forgetful. For instance, she would put down her pocketbook and search the house for it when all she had to do was stop and think what she had been doing when she first came back in. Then it got worse. He would come home and find her going from room to room, looking for the pocketbook, and there it was, swaying from her wrist. Of course, he said, all that wasn't too bad, but when she forgot to turn off the burners on the stove, or when she put a pot on and forgot to turn down the fire and the stew boiled over and the grease caught fire, well, then she was a plain hazard. The doctor said, hire a helper, and he hired one, but she got away from her and they found her trying to wade across a river in the middle of December and when they got her out of the ice water, she had a three-inch gash in her foot, so the doctor said it was time to put her away, and he was thinking about putting her away when she got it into her head that she was a dog, and she'd been a dog ever since. But he didn't have the heart to put her in some asylum, so he took her with him in the car, and when it was warm enough, they went from place to place sleeping in the Dodge, and when it was cold, they headed out to the little island on Maine where she grew up and where they still had a little house. In the winter they were the only ones there so no one came out and asked questions. You know how it is in these small towns, he said. If you want to be left alone, they leave you alone. Every so often, he said, he sat Martha up in a chair at the window when the postman went by, so the man saw her sitting there. Half the people in the shore villages were recluses for one reason or another, so they thought nothing of it. Probably they thought she didn't come out because at her age she was afraid of the ice, slipping on it and breaking her hip. The towns were full of old people who only came out when the ground was smooth and dry and otherwise stayed inside playing solitaire and watching television. You only need one experience going out for wood and falling and lying there and waiting all day hoping someone will find you and then you don't want to go out anymore. You move the woodpile indoors, you don't care what it looks like. Everyone up there has a TV dish, he said. They have to. They have nothing else to do. And the funny part is, he said, it seemed to him that every other house had a member of the opposite sex: first a widow, then a widower, then a widow, and so on down to the last house on the street, and it didn't seem to occur to any of them to double up. A whole line of sad arks, he said, just one of a kind in each one and the name of each animal out there on the front stoop or the mailbox, like the name of the particular kind of animal it was. If he were a free man, he said, he wouldn't waste time moving in with someone else.

"I never gave it much thought," he told the thin man.

"Well, Martha here, she used to say that a happy widower wasn't much of a compliment to his dead wife, because, if he'd been happily married, he'd want to be married again. You did say that, didn't you, Martha?" He reached down and patted the woman's head. Just then, thunder crashed and shook the house, Martha raised her head toward the ceiling and began howling. "She'll never eat her franks and beans now," the thin man said.

"Well, you must have had one of those happy marriages, that's obvious," he said. "To go to so much trouble to keep her with you."

"Oh, we weren't happy at all. Never were. Always snapping at each other, always disagreeing. I was restless, always wanted to go back out to sea, and she'd say, 'Then go!' and throw a shoe after me, well, it got to the point that the children knew if they heard something hitting the wall and then falling down that I wanted to go back out and she was against it, so I never did go, but I never did stop complaining and she never did stop trying to prevent me. So that's how it went on, until this happened. 'I am your cross to bear.' She used to say that. 'I am your cross to bear.'"

"But how do you know she's sick?" he asked the thin man. "Maybe she's plain crazy and a doctor in one of those places could do something for her."

"I took her to doctors," the thin man said. "They said she had that aging disease, but whatever she had, there was nothing they could do for it, so I thought, well, we stuck together this long, she was a faithful wife, I owe her this much."

He shook his head.

The thin man saw it and said, "I know what you're thinking. You don't know if you could do it. That's right. You don't know. If anyone had asked me, four, five years ago, what would I be doing now, I'd have told them I'd lock her up and throw away the key and live the life of Riley. Well, maybe I am living it. Anyway, I can't do otherwise."

The storm was right over their heads now and the lightning flashed and crackled and lit up the kitchen appliances, once white, but spray-painted yellow when his wife, looking through homemaking magazines, decided her kitchen looked too much like a hospital. He hated yellow. Yellow was the color he liked least in the world, but he knew better than to suggest painting the cabinets and refrigerator blue. "Blue is a terrible color," she used to say. "When you have it indoors, what can it look like but a poor imitation of the sky?"

Now when the skies rumbled and crashed, the walls of the house shook. He was not afraid. The house had stood this long. It would continue to stand after he was long gone.

The thin man was covering his howling wife with a blanket. Ruff stood up, his big paws on his knees. The dog was frightened by the woman on the floor, howling like an animal. Ruff was not frightened by storms.

The night wore on in this way, the two of them drinking beer, eating franks and beans, or bacon and eggs, or buttered rolls, the thin man untying his wife when the storm died down to take her to the bathroom, then tying her up again. Finally, by morning, the sky was clear and he said, "You must be worn out. Up over the shed there's a bedroom at the head of the stairs on the right. Go get some sleep." The thin man untied his wife's legs and led her, yelping and growling, up the shed stairs after him.

By morning the sky had cleared and the storm was over. He went out into the shed and started up the mower and began mowing the three acres he and his wife had kept cleared in front of the house. The triangular stretch between the road and the bank of the creek, which his wife had claimed as a flower garden, had long ago overgrown itself with weeds and small scrub trees and he never started up the mower without casting a guilty look at that unattended patch. The grass was still wet and it was slow going, but at least he'd made a start. The neat swath he carved out in front of the lily beds under the house windows would taunt him until he brought the rest of the lawn to the same state of grace. He had just cut the motor when the man came out of the house.

"The wife's tied up upstairs," he said. "She can't do harm."

The two of them stood still, looking at one another, then out across the meadow to the mountains, soft and green in the still misty light, breathing in the smell of wet, cut grass and taking in through their skin the cool glassy feel of the freshly washed air.

"Have some breakfast?" he asked the thin man, who said, "I don't mind if I do."

He cooked bacon and eggs and toasted bread on the oven grill because after their third toaster had broken down, his wife said the best bread didn't fit in them anyway; she was tired of pulling bread out piece by piece and finally turning the toaster upside down to shake out the last broken pieces and crumbs, and why waste money on a toaster when they could make toast just as well in their wood cook stove which was always on anyway. He himself liked bread crisped in a toaster, where it came out having a purer taste than bread from the oven, which inevitably tasted smoked and redolent of whatever meal had last been baked inside that black cavity, but he had respected his wife's wishes while she was alive, and he supposed he was respecting them still. When she was alive it had always been a question of money, where the next two cents was coming from, but now that she'd died and the price of land had gone so astronomically high, all he had to do was sell off part of his acreage, and he'd never miss it. He never even saw it anymore, it was too much trouble to borrow a horse and ride up there, and he'd lost his nerve for the snowmobile ever since his neighbor took his up a mountain trail, ran out of gas, and was clawed by a cougar, probably after he froze. Probably he never knew he was clawed by a cougar, but still. Well, if he sold off even a small part of his land he'd be a rich man and wasn't that something, that he'd finally gotten to a place where he had no need for money at all?

As he toasted the bread, he spoke of this to the thin man, although he omitted any mention of how much land he had, and how, if he sold it, he could be a rich man, because he could hear his wife saying, "Don't talk about money to people unless you want them to cut your throat." She had strong opinions on everything, his wife, and whenever possible, she enforced them on everyone else, a strong woman altogether, although not strong enough to last as long in this world as he had.

The thin man said he'd better go up to get his wife. "She'll be ready for her visit to the water closet and in the morning she's always hungry as a horse," he said, and disappeared upstairs.

He took out the butter, put it on the counter in the square of sunlight to let it soften, and turned over the bread on the baking tray in the oven. Some things were nice about women as they aged, he thought. For one thing, you could take them for drives without stopping at every gas station and asking the attendant for the key to the washroom because they were never so frantic about anything as they were about getting blood on their skirts. He stood there, smiling, thinking of the high excitement on the highway while everyone in the car strained for the sight of a gas station or a rest stop while his wife sat next to him, white and immobile and panic-stricken. For their children, these panics were funny, but not for his wife, a member of what their oldest girl called The Clean Generation. "You think this is funny, but it is not," his wife told their daughter. "Wait until it happens to you." And this would strike them as the funniest thing of all, and while he hunted for the next garage with bitten lips, the children whispered to one another in the back and roared with laughter. "From now on," said his wife, "when it comes to those days of the month, I stay home."

The thin man tied a rope on his wife's ankle and then to a leg of the table. "She won't run off now that she's familiar. She won't cause trouble at all," he said.

He set out three plates and dished out the scrambled eggs, the bacon and the toast. He had a large container of homemade applesauce left him by the woman across the creek, and filled a large blue and pink-striped ceramic bowl, and set that down in the center along with the two-gallon bottle of milk. He had to lift that bottle with two hands because of the arthritis in his wrists.

"I guess once she was a good housekeeper," he said, looking down at the woman on the floor, who was growling up at the table. The thin man lowered a full plate to the floor, whereupon the growling stopped.

"She was terrible, the worst," the thin man said. "My mother, when she came, used to say, 'You look before you let anyone in here because if that person is from the Board of Health, they will condemn this house surely as I'm standing here.' I went into our bedroom one day looking for her and I didn't see her anywhere and I searched the house and I was about to go call the police when she came walking out the bedroom door. The bed was so heaped up with things I never saw her sleeping there. And once she picked up a load of laundry and threw it over the railing from the second floor and it let out a yowl and what did she do? She'd thrown down the laundry and the family cat. Well, she never knew the cat was in there, of course, it was such a mess. Of course you think I'm exaggerating.

I'm not embroidering a thing. When the boys moved out, we had to close off their rooms. They were filled from floor to ceiling with trash. Not just used clothes and toys. Dishes, cups, forks, everything. When I tried to clean it out, she'd get upset and start ranting. The boys, when they called up, they'd ask, 'How many rooms you got left now?' We had this beautiful greenhouse-sun porch combination I built with my own hands, but we couldn't use it, it was so filled with trash, and then she had two dress racks set up in the living room so she could sort out her things, but she never did, so they stayed there permanent, until I sold the house. We didn't get much for it, neither, because how could we? Most people opened the front door and beat it back to their cars."

"So she was a good mother," he said, buttering a piece of toast and turning it this way and that, as if it mattered which corner he bit into first.

"Terrible," the thin man said. "She had no patience at all, not in the early years when they woke up crying at night, and then, when they got bigger and got into bigger troubles, she had so much patience you wanted to kill her. They'd come home at one in the morning, two in the morning, and I'd be out driving around, and she'd say, 'They have to take care of themselves sooner or later,' and go back to her painting. After the youngest was four years old, she said, 'That's enough cooking,' and she never cooked a meal again. She was a real trial in the house, I can tell you."

Painting! Then she was an artist! So that was why he had put up with her! He'd said as much.

"Oh, she was real talented," the thin man said, "but even then I should have known there was something not right. All she painted was dogs. If she saw a nice dog in the village, she'd go plead with the owner as nice as you please, her hair all washed, wearing her best dress, until they'd let the dog stay with us until she finished the picture. I don't know how many rugs we ruined because of those dogs, since, naturally, they wanted to go home and didn't like it in a strange house with this woman who was always hollering at them to sit still."

"You have any of those paintings?" he asked the thin man, who said, Yes, he had a few folded up in the trunk of the car. "Folded up?" he asked, and the thin man said yes, the best thing about them was how easy they were to transport because they were painted on the best quality velvet. Well, the thin man said, they used to look upon the paintings as an investment, because after all they did bring in money.

"People bought them?" he asked the thin man, who said, Oh, yes, she sold most of the portraits. You'd be amazed at how sentimental people were about their pets. For years they made a pretty good living off those paintings, but then things began to go wrong. Well, first they went wrong in the paintings, and then they went wrong in real life. But it was a shame about the paintings, because while they were going well, there was always money for fixing the roof or getting a rebuilt engine for that Dodge out there.

The farmer wanted to know what had gone wrong with the paintings.

First of all, the thin man told him, she gave up velvet and began painting on wood. And not just any wood. It had to be wood with lots of cracks in it, and the planks he cut down for her had to be wide planks, so he was always looking for a barn about to come down. And then the dogs! Well, you could recognize who the dog was supposed to be, at least for a while, but sometimes the dogs' flanks were covered with fish scales, and sometimes the dogs had wings springing from their dog collars and even bigger wings springing from their sides, and sometimes their tails were curved and curled and ended in snake heads. And that was just the beginning, the thin man said, picking up another piece of toast. After she started ruining the dogs, she couldn't stop and she'd paint a wingless dog with the face of the postmaster or the owner of the general store or the local minister, and then there were dogs with saints' faces and halos over their pointed ears, and dogs with horns and devils' tails, but always with faces of people in town. "So," said the thin man, "everyone was insulted, and everyone said it wasn't very neighborly of her, and if that's what she thought of them, then she could just go shop in another store, and then I had all the shopping to do and everything else as well, and it wasn't long after that she forgot to turn off the gas and went off wandering into town and getting on buses and when the bus came to its last stop, she just sat there because she didn't know what she was doing on the bus or who had put her on. So," he said, taking another bite of his toast, and picking up his mug of milk, "that's how we got from here to there."

"You have any of the paintings she did on wood?" he asked the thin man.

"Some idiot from the city came and took them all off," the thin man said. "He said, 'I'll give you a hundred dollars for a hundred paintings. That's fair enough,' and I said 'Done,' because how could we take them in the Dodge anyway and whoever bought the house, he'd only use them for firewood. He seemed happy to get them. A New Yorker probably. My cousin, he runs an antique shop, he says you can always recognize them. When they see something they want, they pick it up and carry it around the shop with them as if some big bluejay would fly in the window and make off with it, but country folk, they put the thing back down and walk far away from it so you won't think they're interested. But I saved some of the nice ones on velvet, to remind me, because I guess one of these days I'll miss that house. I have one on burgundy velvet—that one's a dalmatian—and one on black—that one's a French poodle. They're the most artistic."

"I saw an article somewhere about paintings of dogs with human faces," he said. "In a paper in here somewhere. Maybe I burned it up. But if I didn't it's in that basket."

"It's something I don't need to see," the thin man said. "It will only remind me."

"Dogs with people's faces in some museum," he said.

"You're fixing over that bedroom at the top of the stairs?" the thin man asked. "You need any help? To tell you the truth, wouldn't mind another night in a warm bed. I can't stretch out these legs in the back seat of that car."

He said he wouldn't mind the company and he could use someone to help with the sheetrock for the ceiling and besides that, he was opening up the wall near the door and he knew his wife put things in there behind the wall the last time he paneled the room, souvenirs, things to let the next owner know who lived here, like a time capsule, that's how she thought of it.

Shortly thereafter, he was prying loose the sheetrock from that wall. The thin man crouched behind him. His wife lay in the middle of the room, her head resting on her thin arm. When a car or truck passed by on the road on the far side of the creek, she would raise her head and growl slightly, look first at her husband, then at him, and lie back down. "Well," he said, sitting back on his heels, "this is it."

On the other side of the sheetrock was a flat, oblong box. He took it out, opened it, and saw it was filled with photographs. The topmost were snapshots of his children and of the house. Beneath were copies of the first photographs of the house, when it still had its barn and its two front porches. He handed these back to the thin man, who looked through them.

"Houses are full of ghosts," the thin man said.

"Not this house," he said. "I never felt this house was haunted."

"That's because your wife kept these pictures and gave them a place," he said. "She did them an honor."

Probably he is crazy as a bedbug too, he thought, traveling as he does with this—and then he hesitated because he didn't know how to say it—*dog-wife?*

Still, he could see it, he could see it happening. Already he was used to the woman lying on the ground, growling like a dog. Already he liked feeding her bits of buttered bread from the table. He liked filling the plate for her and watching her eat as if she'd never seen food before. This wasn't affection. This was growing used to something. You grew used to it, you grew fond of it, pretty soon you thought you loved it. He saw clearly, saw it so fast and so vividly, it was as if it had already happened, that if the man and his growling dog-wife stayed on, the two men would compete for the attention of the mindless woman on the floor. They would push one another at the table, hustling to see who could get her plate ready first. In a few weeks, in a month, whoever was first to stroke her wild hair would be glared at by whoever was still sitting with his hands on the table. Proximity was everything. Whoever said that familiarity bred contempt, that person had never lived in an empty house, alone except for the creaking of the floorboards and the walls, contracting and expanding in the heat, sighing and squeaking like something half-alive, night after night. No, what familiarity bred was familiarity, the biggest part of love.

He took out another box: three pairs of tiny shoes, the first pair each child owned. The leather had discolored and cracked and the laces looked brittle. His fingers moved slowly over these shoes before he handed them behind him to the thin man. A small doll, what the children used to call a Grandmother Moses doll, an old black typewriter whose keys stood up in the shape of a fan. She had used that typewriter, but what had she ever written? Some letters back to the family in Ohio. But maybe she'd written other things, things he didn't know about, letters to other people. "Well," he said, "I guess that's it," thinking, not much to show for fifty years of married life, when his eye caught sight of something farther in. He edged carefully in between the strips of molding toward the thing farther back, and finally his shoulders and then his body were through, but when he pushed back behind the wall of the house, his body shut out the light. His hands retained the memory of the object and closed on it and he knew immediately that his hand had closed on something once made of skin and bone. He carefully lifted the object and began working his way back out through the hole in the wall.

"Well, look at that," said the thin man. "A cat skeleton." On the floor, his wife growled but did not stir.

"That's Daisy," he said. He held the cat in both hands like a precious object. The thin man watched him, saying nothing. A great silence fell over the house, and present time slid away like a decal washed from a wet window and outside it was thirty years ago and his wife, slender in her rose-printed house dress, seemed to drift above the mowed meadow grass, her hands to her mouth, calling *Daisy! Daisy! Come on, Daisy! Time to eat, Daisy!* Then she would stop, stand stock-still, and lower her hands, place her hands on her hips and stare out into the meadow, looking for the cat. He watched from the kitchen where it was cool and hopeless, knowing she would not find the cat. Probably, he thought, the cat had been caught by raccoons and never made it back. He saw his wife turn back toward the house, wave helplessly in the direction of the kitchen window, her hand moving up and down with an odd, floaty motion, as if it were made of fabric, as if it had become a surrendering flag. She began drifting, rose pattern and all, under the floating clouds, in sight of the brook in which clouds floated, back toward the white house, floating in the middle of the green green sea of the meadow.

"She is gone," said his wife.

"The raccoons," he said again.

"I don't believe it was the raccoons," she said. "I don't believe she is really and truly gone."

"Well, eat something," he said.

"Eat something. That's your answer to everything," said his wife. Still, she chewed absently on a piece of leftover doughnut. After awhile, she stood up and looked out the window, where, of course, there was no sign of the cat. "Sometimes, when you lose something, you're relieved," she said. "Other times, you say to yourself, 'I've lost a little piece of my soul.' And you tell yourself, 'It's just a little piece.' But one little piece and then another and then another and one day there's nothing left."

"It's only a cat," he said.

"Yes. Well," said his wife, fixing him with a look that always frightened him, as if to say, If you were a piece of wood, you'd have more reason to exist on this planet, on this part of the planet where I myself exist.

"My wife loved this cat," he said to the thin man. "When it was gone she never really believed it went away."

"They're always right," the thin man said. "Always. They speak in riddles like the Sphinx."

"She didn't know where the cat was," he said. "If she'd known, she'd have torn down the walls."

"What are you going to do with that cat?" the thin man asked him, and he said he guessed he'd put it back where it was. Or maybe he'd take it out and bury it next to his wife, deep, deep, so that nothing could come along and dig it up.

"Which is it?" the thin man asked. He said he didn't know. He supposed it would depend on how much energy he had when he got around to it.

"You kept this house up real well," the thin man said, and he told him he had no choice: his wife was always after him to fix this and that.

"When we first came here," he said, "people used to call this the house with the pink walls, because of the insulation, you know. Once I got the insulation in—in those days it came in pink rolls—then I felt finished. We were warm enough, there was a lot to do out in the barn and all around, so I forgot about the walls. But she said she was tired of these pink filaments all over everything, and besides, she'd long ago picked out wallpaper and why couldn't she have walls like everyone else? So eventually I got it done. But you look around, you'll see there's always something left undone, like the floorboards where you slept last night. They're mostly painted, but then there are stretches of unpainted wood because a bureau used to stand there and I thought, Why move the bureau? So she used to say, that was my signature, something left undone. And usually she'd follow after me and finish the thing up, but not always.

They stopped talking then and began to work on the room. When they were finished, they looked like ghosts, so thoroughly were they covered in plaster dust, and then they went down to the creek, leading the man's wife on her rope, and the three of them bathed until they were clean. They sat on the bank of the creek and let the sun dry them out.

"I guess you loved her," he said to the thin man, who looked at his dog-wife, and said, "No, I didn't love her in the old days, but I love her now." He began beheading the purple clover near his left hand. "But you," the thin man said, "you must have loved her."

"She always made me feel I was in the wrong," he said.

"But you loved her," the thin man insisted.

"I guess I did," he said. "But at night, I had this habit. I used to like to come out and look at the stars and see if they'd moved any since I last looked at them, dropped down the sky, or whatever they do. And she'd always say, 'Shut that door. The heat is escaping.' And I used to laugh at her. 'The heat is escaping!' When it was always too hot in that house, even in the coldest, open winters because of those wood stoves! And the idea of the heat *escaping*! As if it were something alive that spent its time plotting to get out! So you know what happened. After awhile, I stopped going out to look at the stars and the heat couldn't escape. I used to think about the heat, locked up in the house with no hope until spring. I used to laugh at her about it. But she'd just look at me and think what an impractical man I was. A male flibbertygibbert, that's what her mother called me, whatever that meant."

"Well," said the thin man, "I guess I'd better be getting on if I want to get to Maine tomorrow night." He jiggled the rope and his wife got up on all fours and began crawling to the house. "Stand up," he said, and the dog-wife got up and walked stiffly toward the old Dodge. "It was a nice break in the journey," he said. "We're much obliged to you."

After the man and his wife had gone, he went in and cleared up the kitchen. Then he went up to the room over the shed and put the skeleton of the cat back where he found it. He replaced the other objects where he had found them. This was a simple matter because the dust had settled around them and when he disturbed them, they left their outline on the unpainted wooden floor. Then he sat back and proceeded to talk to his wife, who, for one reason or another, seemed at that moment to be inhabiting the house.

"Helen," he said, "this life is a mysterious thing. Can you tell me why he is traveling the countryside with that dog-woman?" Outside, the wind sighed in the trees and he took this for an answer. "And you, after all these years of dissatisfactions, you weren't really dissatisfied with me, nor was I with you. 'You can't let them know how important they are to you.' I heard you telling that to Emily the night before she married and I thought, 'Shut up, woman! That is the worst advice I ever heard!' But of course Emily is happy with her husband.

"Still, I want to know why that man sticks with that dog-wife. Why is it no one can know the most important things? Was it accommodating and accommodating that led to love, or was it love that gave you the patience to adjust and shift until you hardly recognized the person you became? Poor Daisy here, dying inside the wall, trying to get back to you and you're out there, scouring the countryside, nailing up reward notices to trees and stores! I want to know: we felt so much for one another. Was it love? We spent a life together. We were married longer than some people live, but that's not the same thing. Or is it the same thing? Tell me. I want to know."

Nothing disturbed the silence in the house. He picked up the piece of sheetrock, cut to fit over the section of wall behind which his wife had hidden the objects precious to her. There was no photograph of him, none of her. Perhaps she thought those photographs belonged to him, that they would keep him company for the rest of his life in this empty house. But what should he do with the skeleton of the cat? He put the sheetrock down and decided to work on another wall. There was no reason he couldn't leave this task for last. Besides, he wasn't ready to nail in the three small pairs of shoes.

He thought that he had loved his wife best when they were first married, least when their children began to grow, and most when the children left home and she had little use about the house. Of course she cooked and cleaned for him, but she was no longer a mother, could no longer be a mother—she was too old. He loved her most when she was least necessary.

Outside, he could hear the wind lifting and dropping the great elm branches, stirring with a low moan through the pines they had dug up in the forest. Once they were only seedlings they had dug up in the forest and seen disappear beneath the first, shallow snow. Now the pines were so tall their shadows covered the meadow in the afternoon and licked at the wooden steps leading up the screened-in porch. The white birches shook their shimmery leaves in the late afternoon light like spangles, like sequins on his wife's dress when she dolled herself up for weddings and christenings, and he looked at the wall and could see the birch leaves as clearly as if he were looking at them through a window, as if the walls and the lathing and the beams had suddenly become utterly transparent. And he saw the dust around the curved roadway blown up into the air by a brisk wind, an autumn wind, although sometimes you got winds like that early in August, it all depended, and if the wind blew the dust just right, it hung in the air for an instant and caught the light, and each dust particle shown like pure gold. And then he saw himself carrying the lawn furniture out from the shed and setting it up in front of the house even though there was still snow on the ground, because in country where the winters lasted so long, you wanted to take advantage of every second of summer, and then, when the leaves began blowing across the meadow from the bordering trees, he saw himself carrying the furniture back into the shed, hosing down the plastic cushions and leaning them against the house walls to dry. These must be the things that mattered, he told himself, carrying the furniture out every season, carrying it back in as the season changed, his wife standing on the porch steps watching and smiling, saying nothing, or watching from the kitchen window, smiling and not even waving, but there was no need for a wave. And he stood still, looking through the wall, and there was his wife, kneeling on the grass, holding her trowel, planting tulip bulbs and crocuses and irises and lilies, and every year when she came back in, she would brush off her skirt and say, "That is my act of faith," because who without faith would plant bulbs in the winter that did not come up until spring? And he would lean against the barn door and watch her and smile even when he didn't know he was smiling, but when she dug her lily beds she was the sun that reaches you in the deep pine woods when you believe no light can ever reach down to that deep place where you are.

Lilies and weeping willows, she was so partial to them that he used to tease her and say there was nowhere on the property you couldn't lie down and fold your hands over your chest and call the photographer to take a picture of you beginning your last, deep sleep. These, he thought, were the things that signified something to human beings. These were the things you remembered, not what you thought, at the time, you would remember, all those things you squirreled away into albums and keepsake boxes, so that now when you looked at them, all you could ask yourself was why on earth you had kept them. Even the children, who were now gone: how rarely he thought of them. And when he did, he remembered them as the small, bright beings they were when the first arrived home, wrapped in their flannel baskets, set safely in their bassinets. Then years had passed and what had they become? Just three more grown-ups. It was a mystery, what you remembered and what you did not, what mattered to you and what did not.

All his life he had tried to get things down to their simplest, easiest forms and so he had torn down the barn and the long front porch. He thought, now, he had been foolish. Now he wished there were unnecessary things for him to look after. It occurred to him that the unnecessary things might be the things one truly loved.

In the distance, a dog howled, and another took up the cry, and then another, until you would think every house in the valley had someone breaking in through the back door. Perhaps, he thought, he should get a new dog, a big dog—he liked big dogs—that would last as long as he did. Well, he didn't want to ask for more than that. You had to be reasonable.

The wind, as if it were getting the last word, as if it were his wife's voice, sighed and sighed again in the many, great trees.

LYNNE SHARON SCHWARTZ

1987

What I Did for Love

Together with Carl I used to dream of changing the power structure and making the world a better place. Never that I could end up watching the ten o'clock news with a small rodent on my lap.

He was the fourth. Percy, the first, was a bullet-shaped, dark brown guinea pig, short-haired as distinct from the long-haired kind, and from the moment he arrived he tried to hide, making tunnels out of the newspapers in his cage until Martine, who was just eight then, cut the narrow ends off a shoebox and made him a real tunnel, where he stayed except when food appeared. I guess she would have preferred a more sociable pet, but Carl and I couldn't walk a dog four times a day, and the cat we tried chewed at the plants and watched us in bed, which made us self-conscious, and finally got locked in the refrigerator as the magnetic door was closing, so after we found it chilled and traumatized we gave it to a friend who appreciated cats.

Percy had been living his hermit life for about a year when Martine noticed he was hardly eating and being unusually quiet, no rustling of paper in the tunnel. I made an appointment with a vet someone recommended. On the morning of the appointment, after I got Martine on the school bus, I saw Percy lying very still outside the tunnel. I called the vet before I left for work to say I thought his patient might be dead.

"Might be?"

"Well . . . how can I tell for sure?"

He clears his throat and with this patronizing air doctors have, even vets, says, "Why not go and flick your finger near the animal's neck and see if he responds?"

Since I work for a doctor I'm not intimidated by this attitude, it just rolls off me. "Okay, hold on a minute . . . He doesn't seem to respond, but still . . . I just don't feel sure."

"Raise one of his legs," he says slowly, as if he's talking to a severely retarded person, "wiggle it around and see if it feels stiff." He never heard of denial, this guy. What am I going to tell Martine?

"Hang on . . . It feels stiff," I admitted.

"I think it's safe to assume," he says, "that the animal is dead."

"I guess we won't be keeping the appointment, then?" I'm not retarded. I said it on purpose, to kind of rile him and see what he'd say.

"That will hardly be necessary."

We buried Percy at sea. I put him in a shoebox (a new one, not the tunnel one), wrapped the tissue paper from the shoes around him and added some flowers I bought on the way home from work, then sealed it up with masking tape. Carl and I kept the coffin in our room that night so Martine wouldn't have to be alone in the dark with it. She didn't cry much, at least in front of us. She keeps her feelings to herself, more like me in that way than Carl. But I knew she was very attached to Percy, hermit that he was. The next morning, a Saturday, the three of us set out carrying the box and a spade and shovel we borrowed from the super of the building. Carl's plan was to bury him in the park, but it was the dead of winter, February, and the ground was so frozen the spade could barely break it.

"This isn't going to work," he said.

Martine looked tragic. She's always been a very beautiful child, with a creamy-skinned face and an expression of serene tragic beauty that, depending on the situation, can make you want to laugh or cry. At that moment I could have done either. We were huddled together, our eyes and noses running from the cold, Martine clutching the shoebox in her blue down mittens.

"I know what," Carl said. "We'll bury him at sea."

Martine's face got even more tragic and I gave him a funny look too. What sea? It was more than an hour's drive to Coney Island and I had a million things to do that day.

"The river. It's a very old and dignified tradition," he told her. "For people who die on ships, when it would take too long to reach land. In a way it's nicer than an earth burial—in the course of time Percy's body will drift to the depths and mingle with coral and anemone instead of being confined in—"

"Okay," she said.

So we walked up to the Hundred Twenty-fifth Street pier on the Hudson River. This is a desolate place just off an exit of the West Side Highway, where the only buildings are meat processing plants and where in the daytime a few lone people come to wash their cars, hauling water up in buckets, and even to fish, believe it or not, and at night people come to buy and sell drugs. I looked at Martine. She handed me the box like she couldn't bear to do it herself, so I knelt down and placed it in the river as gently as I could. I was hoping it would float for a while, at least till we could get her away, but Carl was saying something poetic and sentimental about death and it began to sink, about four feet from where we stood. It was headed south, though, towards the Statue of Liberty and the open sea, I pointed out to her. Free at last.

We got her another guinea pig, a chubby buff-colored one who did not hide and was intelligent and interested in its surroundings, as much as a guinea pig can be. We must have had it—Mooney, it was called—for around a year and a half when Carl began talking about changing his life, finding a new direction. He was one of those people—we both were—who dropped out of school because it seemed there was so much we should be doing in the world. I was afraid he would be drafted, and we had long searching talks, the way you do when you're twenty, about whether he should be a conscientious objector, but at the last minute the army didn't want him because he had flat feet and was partially deaf in one ear. Those same flat feet led all those marches and demonstrations. Anyhow, he never managed to drop back in later on when things changed. Not that there was any less to do, but somehow no way of doing it anymore and hardly anyone left to do it with, not to mention money. You have to take care of your own life, we discovered. And if you have a kid . . . You find yourself doing things you never planned on.

He started driving a cab when Martine was born and had been ever since. It's exhausting, driving a cab. He spent less and less time organizing demonstrations and drawing maps of the locations of nuclear stockpiles. Now he spent his spare time playing ball with the guys he used to go to meetings with, or reading or puttering with his plants, which after me, he used to say, were his great passion. It was not a terrible life, he was not harming anyone, and as I often told him, driving a cab where you come in contact with people who are going places was more varied than what I do all day as an x-ray technician, which you could hardly call upbeat. Most of the time, you find the patients either have cancer or not, and while you naturally hope for the best each time, you get to feel less and less, because a certain percentage are always doomed regardless of your feelings. Well, Carl was not satisfied, he was bored, so I said, "Okay, what would you do if you had a totally free choice?"

"I would like to practice the art of topiary."

"What's that?"

"Topiary is the shaping of shrubberies and trees into certain forms. You know, when you drive past rich towns in Westchester, you sometimes see bushes on the lawns trimmed to spell a word or the initials of a corporation? You can make all sorts of shapes—animals, statues. Have you ever seen it?"

"Yes." I was a little surprised by this. You think you know all about a person and then, topiary. "Well, maybe there's someplace you can learn. Take a course in, what is it, landscape gardening?"

"It's not very practical. You said totally free choice. I don't think there could be much of a demand for it in Manhattan."

"We could move."

"Where, Chris?" He smiled, sad and sweet and sexy. That was his kind of appeal. "Beverly Hills?"

"Well, maybe there's something related that you can do. You know those men who drive around in green trucks and get hoisted into the trees in little metal seats? I think they trim branches off the ones with Dutch Elm disease. Or a tree surgeon?"

This didn't grab him. We talked about plants and trees, and ambition, and doing something you cared about that also provided a living. Finally he said it was a little embarrassing but what he really might like, in practical terms, was to have a plant store, a big one, like the ones he browsed in down in the Twenties.

"Why should that be embarrassing?"

"When you first met me I was going to alter the power structure of society and now I'm telling you I want to have a plant store. Are you laughing at me, Chris? Tell the truth."

"I haven't heard you say anything laughable yet. I didn't really expect you to change the world, Carl."

"No?"

"I mean, I believed you meant it, and I believed in you, but that's not why I married you." It struck me that I had never truly expected to change the power structure but that I liked hanging out with people who thought they could. It was, I would have to say, inspiring.

"Do you think I'm having a mid-life crisis?"

"No. You're only thirty-three. I think you want to change jobs."

So we decided he should try it. He could start by getting a job in a plant store and learning about it, and drive the cab at night. That way we could save some money for a small store to begin with. He would have less time with me and Martine but it would be worth it in the long run. Except he didn't do it right away. He liked to sit on things for awhile, like a hen.

That summer we scraped together the money to send Martine to a camp run by some people we used to hang out with in the old days, and since it was a camp with animals, sort of a farm camp, she took Mooney along. Her third night away she called collect from Vermont and said she had something very sad to tell us. From her tragic voice, for an instant I thought they might have discovered she had a terminal disease like leukemia, and how could they be so stupid as to tell her—they were progressive types, maybe they thought it was therapeutic to confront your own mortality—but the news was that Mooney was dead. Someone had left the door of the guinea pigs' cage open the night before and he got out and was discovered in the morning in a nearby field, most likely mauled by a larger animal. At first I sounded relieved and not tragic enough, but fortunately Carl had the right tone throughout. At the age of eleven she understood a little about the brutalities of nature and the survival of the fittest and so on, but it was still hard for her to accept.

Martine is a peacefully inclined, intuitive type. She would have felt at home in our day, when peace and love were respectable attitudes. We named her after Martin Luther King, which nowadays seems a faraway thing to have done. Not that my estimation of him has changed or that I don't like the name, only it isn't the sort of thing people do anymore. Just as, once we stayed up nights thinking of how to transform the world and now I'm glad I have a job, no matter how boring, and can send her to camp for a few weeks.

Anyway, the people running the camp being the way they were, they immediately bought her a new guinea pig. Aside from her tragedy she had a terrific time, and she came home with a female pig named Elf, who strangely enough looked exactly like Mooney. In fact if I hadn't known Mooney was dead I would have taken Elf for Mooney. I remembered remarking to Carl that if things were reversed, if Mooney had been left at home with us and died and we had managed to find an identical bullet-shaped replacement, I might have tried to pass it off as Mooney, in the way mothers instinctively try to protect their children from the harsher facts of life. But Carl said he wouldn't have, he would have told her the truth, not out of harsh realism or any notion of confronting mortality but because Martine would be able to tell the difference, as mothers can with twins, and he wouldn't want her catching him in a lie. "You know she has such high standards," he said.

In the dead of winter, even colder than in Percy's era, Martine told us Elf wasn't eating. Oh no, I thought. *Déja vu.* The stillness, then the stiffness, wrapping it in the shoebox, burial at sea . . . Nevertheless, what can you do, so I made an appointment with the vet, the same old arrogant vet—I didn't have the energy to look for a new one. I was feeling sick when the day arrived so Carl took off from work and went with Martine and Elf.

"There's good news and bad news," he said when they got home. "The good news is that she doesn't have a dread disease. What's wrong with her is her teeth."

I was lying in bed, trying to sleep. "Her teeth?"

"You've got it. Her top and bottom teeth are growing together so she can't eat. She can't separate them to chew." He gave me a demonstration of Elf's problem, stretching his lips and straining his molars.

"Please, this is no time to make me laugh. My stomach is killing me."

"What is it? Your period?"

"No. I don't know what."

"Well, listen, the bad news is that she needs surgery. Oral surgery. It's a hundred twenty-five including the anesthetic."

"This is not the least bit funny. What are we going to do?" Martine was putting Elf back in her cage, otherwise we would have discussed this with more sensitivity.

"Is there a choice? You know how Martine feels—Albert Schweitzer Junior. I made an appointment for tomorrow. She'll have to stay overnight."

"I presume you mean Elf, not Martine."

"Of course I mean Elf. Maybe I should call a doctor for you too."

"No, I'll be okay. What's a stomach-ache compared to oral surgery?"

"I don't want you getting all worked up over this, Chris." He joined me on the bed and started fooling around. "Thousands of people each year have successful oral surgery. It's nothing to be alarmed about."

"I'll try to deal with it. Ow, you're leaning right where it hurts." Martine came into the room and Carl sat up quickly.

"She's looking very wan," she said.

"Two days from now she'll be a new person," Carl said.

"She's never been a person before, how could she be one in two days?"

"Medical science is amazing."

"I have no luck with guinea pigs." She plopped into a chair, stretched out her legs and sat gazing at her sneakers. I noticed how tall she was growing. She was nearly twelve and beginning to get breasts. But she wasn't awkward like most girls at that stage, she was stunning, willowy and auburn-haired with green eyes. There was sometimes a faint emerald light in the whites of her eyes that would take me by surprise, and I would stare and think, what a lucky accident.

"Maybe none of them live long," I said. "I doubt if yours are being singled out."

"They have a four-to-six-year life span. I looked it up in the encyclopedia. But in four years I've gone through almost three."

That night I had such terrible pains in my stomach that Carl took me to the emergency room, where after a lot of fussing around—they tried to send me home, they tried to get me to sleep—they found it was my appendix and it had to come out right away. It was quite a few days before I felt like anything resembling normal, and I forgot completely about Elf's oral surgery.

"Chris, before we go inside, I'd better tell you something." Carl switched off the engine and reached into the back seat for my overnight bag. He was avoiding my eyes.

"What happened? I spoke to her on the phone last night!" I was about to leap out of the car but he grabbed my arm.

"Hold it a minute, will you? You're supposed to take it easy."

"Well what's wrong, for Chrissake?"

He looked at me. "Not Martine. Jesus! Elf."

"Elf." I thought I would pass out. I was still pretty drugged.

"She got through the surgery all right. We brought her home the next day. But . . . I don't know whether she was too weak from not eating or what, but she never started eating again. And so . . ."

"I never liked that doctor. How did Martine take it this time?"

"Sad but philosophical. I think she's used to it by now. Besides, she was more concerned about you."

"I'm glad to hear that. So where is the corpse? At sea again?"

"Well, no, actually. That's why I wanted to tell you before you went in the apartment. The temperature has been near zero. The river is frozen."

"Just give it to me straight, Carl."

"She's wrapped in some plastic bags on the bathroom window sill. Outside. The iron grating is holding her in place. I was going to put her in the freezer with the meat but I thought you might not care for that."

"Couldn't you find a shoebox?"

"No. I guess nobody's gotten new shoes lately."

"And how long is she going to stay there?"

"They're predicting a thaw. It's supposed to get warm, unseasonably warm, so in a few days we'll take her out to the park. Anyway, welcome home. Oh, there's another thing."

"I hope this is good."

It was. He had found a job working in the greenhouse at the Botanical Gardens.

Since Martine never brought the subject up again after the thaw and the park burial, I assumed the guinea pig phase of her life was over. Two weeks after she returned from camp that summer, the super who had loaned us the spade and shovel for Percy came up to say there was a family in the next building with a new guinea pig, but their baby was allergic to it and couldn't stop sneezing. Maybe we wanted to do them a favor and take it off their hands?

Martine and I turned to each other. "What do you think?" I said.

"I'm not sure. They're a lot of expense, aren't they?"

"Not so bad. I mean, what's a little lettuce, carrots . . ."

"The medical expenses. And you don't like them too much, do you, Mom?"

I tried to shrug it off with a blank smile. I looked at Mr. Coates — what I expected I'll never know, since he stood there as if he had seen and heard everything in his lifetime and was content to wait for this discussion to be over. I wondered how much of a tip he would get for the deal. Nothing from us, I vowed.

"I've noticed," Martine said, "You don't like to handle them. You don't like small rodents."

"Not a whole lot, frankly." They looked to me like rats, fat tailless rats. For Martine's sake I had wished them good health and long life, but I tried not to get too close. When she was out with her friends and I had to feed them, I used to toss the lettuce in and step back as they lunged for it. I didn't like the eager squeaks they let out when they smelled the food coming, or the crunching sounds they made eating it. And when I held them — at the beginning, when she would offer them to me to stroke, before she noticed how I felt about small rodents — I didn't like the nervous fluttery softness of them, their darting squirmy little movements, the sniffing and nipping and the beat of the fragile heart so close to the surface I could feel it in my palms. "But they don't bother me so long as they're in the cage in your room." Which was true.

"You could go over and take a look," said Mr. Coates finally. "I'll take you over there if you want."

"Maybe I'll do that, Mom. Do you want to come too?"

"No. I know what guinea pigs look like by now."

"What color is it?" Martine was asking him on the way out.

"I don't know the color. I ain't seen it myself yet."

I didn't pay any more attention to Rusty, named for his color, than I had to the others. I made sure to be in another room while Martine and Carl cut his nails, one holding him down, the other clipping—they took turns. Martine started junior high and got even more beautiful, breasts, hips, the works, with a kind of slow way of turning her head and moving her eyes. She also started expressing intelligent opinions on every subject in the news, test tube babies, airplane hijackings, chemicals in packaged foods, while Carl and I listened and marveled, with this peculiar guilty relief that she was turning out so well—I guess because we were not living out our former ideals, not changing the world or on the other hand being particularly upwardly mobile either. Carl was happier working in the greenhouse, but we still hadn't managed to save enough to rent a store or qualify for a bank loan.

At Martine's thirteenth birthday party in May, we got to talking in the kitchen with one of the mothers who came to pick up her kid. I liked her. She was about our age, small and blonde, and she had dropped out of school too but had gone back to finish and was even doing graduate work.

"What field?" I asked. I was scraping pizza crusts into the garbage while Carl washed out soda cans—he was very big on recycling. In the living room the kids were dancing to a reggae song called "Free Nelson Mandela," and the three of us had been remarking, first of all, that Nelson Mandela had been in prison since we were about their age and in the meantime we had grown up and were raising children and feeling vaguely disappointed with ourselves, and secondly, that dancing to a record like that wouldn't have been our style even if there had been one back then, which was unlikely. Singing was more our style. And the fact that teenagers today were dancing to this "Free Nelson Mandela" record at parties made their generation seem less serious, yet at this point who were we to judge styles of being serious? The man was still in prison, after all.

"Romance languages," she said. She was playing with the plastic magnetic letters on the refrigerator. They had been there since Martine was two. Sometimes we would use them to write things like Merry Xmas or, as tonight, Happy Birthday, and sometimes to leave real messages, like Skating Back at 7 M. The messages would stay up for the longest time, eroding little by little because we knocked the letters off accidentally and stuck them back any old place, or because we needed a letter for a new message, so that Happy Birthday could come to read Hapy Birda, and at some point they would lose their meaning altogether, like Hay irda, which amused Martine no end. This woman wrote, "*Nel mezzo del cammin di nostra vita.*"

"What does that mean?" Carl asked her.

" 'In the middle of the journey of our life.' It's the opening of *The Divine Comedy*. What it means is, here I am thirty-five years old and I'm a graduate student."

"There's nothing wrong with that," said Carl. "I admire your determination. I'm driving a cab but one day before I die I'm going to learn to do topiary, for the simple reason that I want to."

She said what I knew she would. "What's topiary?"

He stopped rinsing cans to tell her.

I never read *The Divine Comedy* but I do know Dante goes through Hell and Purgatory and eventually gets to Paradise. All the parts you ever hear about, though, seem to take place in Hell, and so a small shiver ran up my spine, seeing that message on the refrigerator above Happy Birthday. Then I forgot about it.

In bed that night I asked Carl if he was serious about learning topiary. He said he had been thinking it over again. Since he had gotten a raise at the greenhouse, maybe he might give up the cab altogether, he was so sick of it, and use the money we'd saved for the store to study landscape gardening.

"Well, okay. That sounds good. I can work a half-day Saturdays, maybe."

"No, I don't want you to lose the little free time you have. We'll manage. Maybe there's something you want to go back and study too."

"I'm not ambitious. Why, would I be more attractive, like . . . if I went to graduate school?"

"Ha! Did I hear you right?" He let out a comic whoop. "I don't even remember her name, Chris. Listen, you want me to prove my love?"

That was the last time. The next day he came down with the flu, then Martine and I got it, and just when we were beginning to come back to life he had a heart attack driving the cab. He might have made it, the doctor said, except he was alone and lost control of the wheel and the car wrapped around a lamppost. All through those next insane days I kept seeing in my mind a scene on the Long Island Expressway when Martine was a baby and we were going to Jones Beach. About three cars ahead of us over in the right lane a car started to veer, and as we got closer we could see the driver slumping down in his seat. Before we could even think what to do, a state trooper appeared out of nowhere and jumped in on the driver's side to grab the wheel. Sirens started up, I guess they took him to the hospital, and a huge pile-up was averted. Watching it, I felt bad about how we used to call cops pigs. That sounds a little simple-minded, I know, but so was calling them pigs. And now I wondered how come a miracle in the form of a cop happened for that person and not for Carl, which is a question a retarded person might ask, I mean, an out-of-the-way street in Queens at eleven at night . . . Anyhow, it happened the way it happened. A loss to all those who might have enjoyed his topiary. I do think he would have done it in his own good time. If only we had had a little more time, I could have taken care of him. I wouldn't have been a miracle but I would have done a good job. The way he vanished, though, I couldn't do a thing, not even say goodbye or hold his hand in the hospital or whatever it is old couples do—maybe the wife whispers that she'll be joining him soon, but I have no illusions that I'll ever be joining him, soon or late. I just got a lot less of him than I expected. Another thing is that the last time we made love I was slightly distracted because of the graduate student he admired for her determination, not that anything transpired between them except some ordinary conversation, but it started me wondering in general. Stupid, because I know very well how he felt, he told me every night.

So I did end up working half-days on Saturdays. In July Martine was supposed to go back to the camp run by the progressives and pacifists where she had always had such a great time except for her tragedy with Mooney, and I didn't want to begin my life alone by asking for help.

"I don't have to go," she said. "If we don't have the money it's all right. I don't think I even feel like going anymore." My beautiful child with the tragic face. Now she had something worthy of that face.

"You should go however you feel. When you get there you'll be glad."

"Except there's a slight problem," she said.

"What's that?"

"Rusty. I'm not taking him. Not after what happened to Mooney."

"No," I agreed.

"Which means . . ."

"Oh God! All right, I can do it. How bad can it be? A little lettuce, cabbage, right? A few handfuls of pellets . . ."

"There's the cage to clean too."

"The cage. Okay."

It was hard, her going off on the bus, with the typical scene of cheery mothers and fathers crowding around waving brown lunch-bags, but I forced myself through it and so did she. I would force myself through the rest of my life if I had to.

First thing every morning and before I went to bed I put a handful of pellets in Rusty's bowl and fresh water in his bottle, and when I left for work and came home I dropped a few leaves of something green into the cage. Since I never really looked at him I was shocked, the fourth night after Martine left, when Mr. Coates, who had come up to fix the window lock in her room, said in his usual unexcited way, "Your pig's eye's popping out."

The right eye was protruding half an inch out of the socket and the cylindrical part behind it was yellow with gummy pus, a disgusting sight. "Jesus F. Christ," I said.

"He won't be no help to you. You need a vet."

The thought of going back to that arrogant vet who I always suspected screwed up Elf was more than I could take, so I searched the Yellow Pages till I found a woman vet in the neighborhood. When I walked in the next day carrying Rusty in a carton I knew I had lucked out. She had curly hair like a mop, she wore jeans and a white sweatshirt, and she seemed young, maybe twenty-nine or thirty. Her name was Doctor Dunn. Very good, Doctor Dunn, so there won't be all that other shit to cope with.

To get him on the examining table I had to lift him up by his middle and feel all the squirminess and the beat of the scared delicate heart between my palms.

"It looks like either a growth of some kind pushing it forward, or maybe an abscess. But in either case I'm afraid the eye will have to go. It's badly infected and unless it's removed it'll dry up and the infection will spread and, uh . . ."

"He'll die?"

"Right."

Seventy-five dollars, she said, including his overnight stay, plus twenty-five for the biopsy. Terrific, I thought, just what I need. It was lower than the other vet's rates, though.

"I want to explain something about the surgery. He's a very small animal, two or three pounds, and any prolonged anesthetic is going to be risky. What this means is, I can't make any guarantees. I'd say his chances are . . . seventy thirty, depending on his general condition. Of course we'll do everything we can . . ."

"And if I don't do it he'll die anyhow?"

"Right."

Squirming there on the table was this orange rat whose fate I was deciding. I felt very out of sync with reality, as if I was in a science fiction movie and how did I ever arrive at this place. "Okay. I guess we'd better do it."

The receptionist I left him with told me to call around four the next day to see how he came through the surgery. If, was what she meant. That evening out of habit I almost went in to toss him some celery, then I remembered the cage was empty. There was no reason to go into Martine's room. But I decided to take the opportunity to clean the cage and the room both. I had found that the more I moved around the more numb I felt, which was what I wanted.

On the dot of four, I called from work. Doctor Dunn answered herself.

"He's fine! What a trouper, that Rusty! We had him hooked up to the EKG the whole time and monitored him, and he was terrific. I'm really pleased."

"Thank you," I managed to say. "Thank you very much." In one day she had established a closer relationship with him than I had in a year. That was an interesting thought. I mean, it didn't make me feel emotionally inadequate, I simply realized that's why she went through years of veterinary school, because she really cared, the way Carl could have about topiary, I guess.

"Can you come in and pick him up before seven? Then I can tell you about the post-op care."

Post-op care? I had never thought of that. I had never even thought of how the eye would look. Would it be a hole, or just a blank patch of fur? Would there be a bandage on it, or maybe she could fix him up with a special little eye patch?

I found Rusty in his carton on the front desk with the receptionist petting him and calling him a good boy. "We're all crazy about him," she said. "He's quite a fella, aren't you, Rusty-baby?"

Where his right eye used to be, there was a row of five black stitches, and the area around it was shaved. Below the bottom stitch, a plastic tube the diameter of a straw and about an inch long stuck out. That was a drain for the wound, Doctor Dunn explained. He had a black plastic collar around his neck that looked like a ruff, the kind you see in old portraits of royalty. To keep him from poking himself, she said.

"Was he in good condition otherwise?" I thought I should sound concerned, in this world for animal-lovers.

"Oh, fine. Now, the post-operative care is a little complicated so I wrote it down." She handed me a list of instructions:

1. Cold compresses tonight, 5–10 minutes.
2. Oral antibiotics, 3x a day for at least 7 days.
3. Keep collar on at all times.
4. Feed as usual.

5. Call if any excessive redness, swelling, or discharge develops.

6. Come in 3–4 days from now to have drain pulled.

7. Call early next week for biopsy results.

8. Make appointment for suture removal, 10–14 days.

9. Starting tomorrow, apply warm compresses 5–10 minutes, 2x a day for 10 days.

"Here's a sample bottle of antibiotics. Maybe I'd better do the first dose to show you how." She held him to her chest with one hand, while with the other she nudged his mouth open using the medicine dropper and squeezed the drops in, murmuring, "Come on now, that's a good boy, there you go." As she wiped the drips off his face and her sweatshirt with a tissue, I thought, Never. This is not happening to me. But I knew it was, and that I would have to do it.

When I went to get some ice water for the cold compress that night, I saw the message the graduate student mother had left on the refrigerator near Happy Birthday, which was now Happ Brhday. "Ne mezz 1 camn di nstr vita," it read. I knew some letters were missing though not which ones, and those that were left were crooked, but I remembered well enough what it meant. I sat down to watch the ten o'clock news with Rusty on my lap and put the compress on his eye, or the place his eye used to be, but he squirmed around wildly, clawing at my pants. Ice water oozed onto my legs. I told him to cut it out, he had no choice. Finally I tried patting him and talking to him like a baby, to quiet him. Don't worry, kiddo, you're going to be all right—stuff like that, the way Carl would have done without feeling idiotic. It worked. Only hearing those words loosened me a little out of my numbness and I had this terrible sensation of walking a tightrope in pitch darkness, though in fact I was whispering sweet nothings to a guinea pig. I even thought of telling him what I'd been through with my appendix, a fellow-sufferer, and God knows what next, but I controlled myself. If I freaked out who would take care of Martine?

I figured seven and a half minutes for the compress was fair enough— Doctor Dunn had written down 5–10. Then I changed my mind and held it there for another minute so if anything happened I would have a clear conscience when I told Martine. I held him to my chest with a towel over my shirt, feeling the heart pulsing against me, and squirted in the antibiotic. I lost a good bit but I'd have plenty of chances to improve.

In the morning I found the collar lying in the mess of shit and cedar chips in the cage. I washed it and tried to get it back on him, but he fought back with his whole body—each time I fitted it around his neck he managed to squirm and jerk his way out till beyond being repelled I was practically weeping with frustration. Two people could have done it easily. Carl, I thought, if ever I needed you . . . Finally after a great struggle I got it fastened in back with masking tape so he couldn't undo it. But when I came home from work it was off again and we wrestled again. The next morning I rebelled. The drops, the compresses, okay, but there was no way I was going to literally collar a rodent morning and night for ten days. There are limits to everything, especially on a tightrope in the dark. I called Doctor Dunn from work.

"Is he poking himself around the eye?" she asked. "Any bleeding or discharge? Good. Then forget it. You can throw the collar away."

I was so relieved.

"How is he otherwise? Is he eating?"

"Yes. He seems okay. Except he's shedding." I told her how when I lifted him up, orange hairs fluttered down into his cage like leaves from a tree. When leaves fell off Carl's plants, which I was also trying to keep alive though that project wasn't as dramatic, it usually meant they were on their way out. I had already lost three—I didn't have his green thumb. It seemed my life had become one huge effort to keep things alive, with death hot on my trail. I even had nightmares about what could be happening to Martine at camp. When I wrote to her, though, I tried to sound casual, as if I was fine, and I wrote that Rusty was fine too. Maybe Carl would have given her all the gory details but I didn't mind lying. He was going to be fine. I was determined that pig would live if it was over my dead body. Luckily I wasn't so far gone as to say all this to Doctor Dunn. "Is that a bad sign?"

"Shedding doesn't mean anything," she said. "He doesn't feel well, so he's not grooming himself as usual. It'll stop as he gets better."

I also noticed, those first few days, he would do this weird dance when I put the food in his cage. It dawned on me that he could smell it but not see it. While he scurried around in circles, I kept trying to shove it towards his good side—kind of a Bugs Bunny routine. Then after a while he developed a funny motion, turning his head to spot it, and soon he was finding it pretty well with his one eye. I told Doctor Dunn when I brought him in to have the drain removed. She said yes, they adapt quickly. They compensate. She talked about evolution and why eyes were located where they were. Predators, she said, have close-set eyes in the front of their heads to see the prey, and the prey have eyes at the side, to watch out for the predators. How clever, I thought, the way nature matched up the teams. You couldn't change your destiny, but you had certain traits that kept the game going and gave you the illusion of having a fighting chance. We talked about it for a good while. She was interesting, that Doctor Dunn.

A few days later she plucked out the stitches with tweezers while I held him down.

"I have to tell you," she said, "not many people would take such pains with a guinea pig. Some people don't even bother with dogs and cats, you'd be amazed. They'd rather have them put away. You did a terrific job. You must really love animals."

I didn't have the heart to tell her that although it didn't turn my stomach anymore to hold him on my lap and stroke him for the compresses, he was still just a fat rat as far as I was concerned, but a fat rat which fate had arranged I had to keep alive. So I did.

"Well, you could say I did it for love."

She laughed. "Keep applying the warm compresses for another day or two, to be on the safe side. Then that's it. Case closed."

"What about the biopsy?"

"Oh, yes, the lab report. It's not in yet, but I have a feeling it wasn't malignant. He doesn't look sick to me. Call me on it next week."

In eleven days Martine will be back. Beautiful Martine, with her suntan making her almost the color of Rusty. I'll warn her about the eye before she sees him. It doesn't look too gruesome now, with the stitches out and the hair growing back—soon it'll be a smooth blank space. In fact if not for the missing eye she would never have to know what he went through. The house will feel strange to her all over again without Carl, because whenever you're away for a while you expect to come home to some pure and perfect condition. She'll be daydreaming on the bus that maybe it was all a nightmare and the both of us are here waiting for her. But it'll be an altogether different life, and the worst thing is—knowing us, sensible, adaptable types—that one remote day we'll wake up and it'll seem normal this way, and in years to come Carl will turn into the man I had in my youth instead of what he is now, my life. I even envy her—he'll always be her one father.

So I'm applying the warm compresses for the last time, sitting here with a one-eyed guinea pig who is going to live out his four-to-six-year life span no matter what it takes, in the middle of the journey of my life, stroking him as if I really loved animals.

ELIZABETH ALEXANDER
1989

Boston Year

My first week in Cambridge a car full of white boys
tried to run me off the road, and spit through the window,
open to ask directions. I was always asking directions
and always driving: to an Armenian market
in Watertown to buy figs and string cheese, apricots,
dark spices and olives from barrels, tubes of paste
with unreadable Arabic labels. I ate
stuffed grape leaves and watched my lips swell in the mirror.
The Wonderland subway went to Logan Airport
for sixty cents! "If I were a younger man,"
my Super would sigh at six a.m. when I'd fetch
the newspaper from the stoop. I'd read, eat breakfast,
and return to sleep. I took four rickety flights
of stairs three times a day waiting for mail.
Winter of course set in and I lived in black wool.
The floors of my apartment would never come clean.
Whenever I saw other colored people
in book shops, or museums, or cafeterias, I'd gasp,
smile shyly, but they'd disappear before I spoke.
What would I have said to them? Come with me? Take
me home? Are you my mother? No. I sat alone
in countless Chinese restaurants eating almond
cookies, sipping tea with spoons and spoons of sugar.
Popcorn and coffee was dinner. When I fainted
from migraine in the grocery store, a Portuguese
man above me mouthed: "No breakfast." He gave me
orange juice and chocolate bars. The color red
sprang into relief singing Wagner's *Walküre*.
Entire tribes gyrated and drummed in my head.
I learned the samba from a Brazilian man

so tiny, so festooned with glitter I was certain
that he slept inside a filigreed, Fabergé egg.
No one at the door: no salesmen, Mormons, meter-
readers, exterminators, no Harriet Tubman,
no one. Red notes sounding in a gray trolley town.

SHERMAN ALEXIE
1997

Wake

I don't know about death,
but am learning to bury my own kind.
—Ralph Angel

We sift this flour and offer you bread.
At every wake, are we mourning ourselves?
We are learning how to bury our dead.

The mourners are all waiting to be fed.
What we have we give. We empty our shelves.
We sift this flour and offer you bread.

Stories must be told. We cannot forget
to give away our blankets, books, and shells.
We are learning how to bury our dead.

We pull our men from predictable wrecks
and then collect their blood from where it fell.
We sift this flour and offer you bread.

We light fires. The smoke becomes our breath.
Our lungs fill with ash we cannot expel.
We are learning how to bury our dead.

We listen to what the women have said.
Our Indian women have taught us well.
They sift this flour and offer us bread.
They are teaching us how to bury our dead.

SHERMAN ALEXIE
1997

Toward Conception

for Diane

we kneel in this stream
as mother, as father

cup our hands
and drink from this water

because we believe the salmon
who were spawned in this bed

will someday return
tattered, exhausted, alive

oh, the glorious things
we do to survive

A. R. AMMONS
1988

Commissary

What sort of person in
drought puts a saucer of water out
for hornets: maybe
their placid pulsing
at drink
allures and dreams him:
maybe he needs to appease bees, too,

or wasps or
those glimmery little fellows
too small to name:
or he's seen a hornet
snip a silk-hung worm
from the air under a bough
and liked the address:

I'd as lief
watch a day lily sway:
I don't have a thing for
porcelain or stings:
but it's okay with me:
anything you starve is food,
anything you feed kills.

DAVID BAKER
1983

Poison

The summer Sally Millsap fell from the graceful
perch we shared on the split-rail fence
that divided bobbing necks of iris and jonquil
from the dusty, wilder ivy
we knew only to avoid, like the dead
animals we found in spring stinking up the cellar,

was the first time they tried to keep us apart.
That fast and she was gone, knees
kicked up and over, and me just laughing there
looking at her on the ground.

Her mother came flying at us from the house
and grabbed her up still breathless,
then looked at me hard. She was mad all right
and I felt my young skin grow
hot right there, and heard only a few words
as they trotted across the grass,
her mother saying *soap, soap,* saying *dirty girl.*

I played alone for days. Each morning my father
told me Sally was sick and I was one
lucky boy this time, and had to stay away.
So when I waited beneath her
window one afternoon, in a slow rain
that fell more like long hair, I was surprised
to see her up and walking in her room,

though when I tapped, and when she raised
the window, I finally saw

the price of our first sin. Her arms were chapped,
red as burns, her eyes, even
in that dry house, wet as mine,

and when she smiled at me and spoke,
her whole face seemed swollen with the awful touch
our parents had told us once,
and would tell us so often after that, to avoid
no matter what it took.

CHARLES BAXTER
1981

Astrological Guide

This morning, I read about myself in the paper.
A wealthy astrologist is analyzing my character.
Oh Taurus, you stubborn homebody—learn to avoid

personal contacts. Stop being suggestive.
How comforting to see
bears and saucepans in the sky's random light.

Representational art still lives, out there in the darkness.
The stars have determined this poem: they touch
my fingers touching the typewriter keys.

This astrologist makes everyone feel like a star.
Orion, with his glittering belt, makes us feel special.
All the same,

there are gaps
between stars, those enlarging black spaces
that have their own influence. But they are empty and black.

ROBIN BECKER
1997

In the Days of Awe

for Abbe, Sally, and Joseph

I *Amidah*

Hear my personal prayer, *the words of my mouth and the meditation
of my heart*, that I may find a way back through love
In the hospital room, packed in blood-soaked cotton, the new mother lay
animal-exhausted technicians whisked the child away   in the first
hours there was fear o teach me to withhold judgment

of the one who took my place who said *yes* when I said *no*
whose days opened to the child when my days foreclosed
she who conceived of joy where I imagined the crossbar
against my chest, subjugation of family life, the double
harness, the neverending tasks, the clamp and vise

II *Shofar*

The *shofar* blasts birthday of the world of our dominion
over nature in the Kingdom of the Lord our God Ruler
of the Universe   Then why am I weeping into this tissue?
What is this child to me who refused to stay and raise him?
What is this broken covenant, this yoke?

III *Tashlikh*

By a small stream, as is customary,
we cast into the water with its drift
of leaves our quarrels like stones, our envies
and resentments *O Lord, You do not maintain anger
but delight in forgiveness*

IV *Aleinu*

You take me down to the nursery to see
Joseph in his little cap of many colors
with his jaundice and his brisk efficient keepers
Will you be kind?   *Cleanse my mind of wickedness*
Teach me to attain a heart of wisdom

In the synagogue the families praise *all fruitbearing trees*
and cedars, all wild beasts and cattle   I watch a woman
and her teenage daughter confer, lean into each other
They hold the *mahzor* between them, their mouths shape the beautiful
Hebrew I do not know how to read except in transliteration

V *Teshuvah*

Turn from evil and do good, the Psalmist says, turning
Round the turn, turn the key, clock the turn, turn in time,
time to turn words into footsteps, to lead the young colt to the field
to turn from the old year, the old self   You are ready
to turn and be healed only face only begin

VI *Amidah*

Inscribe him in the Book of Life, for Your sake, living God
She opened up the book of her body again and again
She would not stop trying though I mocked her   a year
ended and a year began   I had no imagination for family life
inhabiting sadly that place for years

inhabiting sadly that place for years   with me   who chose
to keep my faith with those who sleep in dust   she chose
against the quiet house and noiseless rooms she chose
to bear her mortal woman's share and split her life in two
or three or four   she said *I know what you want I want more*

VII *Avinu malkeinu*

Avinu malkeinu inscribe us in the Book of Deliverance
Avinu malkeinu inscribe us in the Book of Merit
Avinu malkeinu inscribe us in the Book of Forgiveness

162

Sarah beseeched God for a child and brought forth Isaac
And Sally brought forth Joseph   *Amen*

A voice commands the lightning that cleaves stones
A voice shatters stately cedars
A voice twists the trees and strips the forest bare
The devout say *In your love for your neighbor will you find God*
They say *Days are scrolls Write only what you want remembered*

VIII *Kedushah*

We believe that God abides in mystery   in a diaspora of dust
in the control-freaks and the disordered in the lonely
in the bosses in the unendurable in the technological
and pharmaceutical failures in the very old
in the newborn in memory in kindness in acts of lovingkindness

We belive that God abides in the unfit, in those unshielded
by luck or faith and by bad luck made abject by the unctuous
I believe in the uncomputerized and the demoralized
the belittled and benumbed gazing like dumb beasts
like my sister groping mid-seizure back to speech

IX *Mourner's Kaddish*

Bless my sister who could not endure, bless her failure to thrive
and bless my parents in their magnificent witness
Sanctify this *Day of Remembrance   Grant them peace*
from the clichéd language of condolence cards Be merciful to those
who passed *Your blessed days* in a curtained room of shame

An enormous concordance of grief indexes human sorrow, a Book of
    Death
ghosts the Book of Life   We must enact our sadness, repeat the prayers
by rote, take comfort or not, execute the verses in proper order,
confront our losses by rising to praise God whose *word is performance*
Then may we say *Relent, O Lord! How long must we suffer?*

In the public place, in the hall outfitted with a simple ark
the mourners stand *Whom shall I dread?* we ask with our private

dreads on our civic faces   We are an assembly of stunned
children called to recite *Yit-gadal ve-yit kadash shmei raba*
There is always someone to mourn   Look around

X *The Fast of Yom Kippur*

Look around   the congregation atones   we certify regret
we recall our transgressions and those who transgressed against us
Where is my milk?   Joseph cries and she feeds him The Torah
teaches repentance.   I remember my *zayde*, a shrunken man
at the front of the *shul*, fasting   By the last *Aleinu* he could not stand

My father brought smelling salts, the son who did not know
the prayers sat with his father   *His life was one long prayer*
to the hereness of God   On the maternity floor food and flowers
Choose life! shouts baby Joseph tightly bound in a cotton blanket
I'm afraid it's time to go says the kind nurse after visiting hours

XI *Selihot*

The days of women and men are as grass
They flourish as flowers in the field
The wind passes over them and is gone
and no one can recognize where they grew

XII *Amidah*

Inscribe for me a childless life   O lift me
to the Book of Many Forms that I might find another way
to honor my father and mother   their agony of bereavement
Let me understand the girlchild I was, beloved as Joseph in his coat
of many colors, favored by his father, hated by his brothers

And by his brothers thrown into the pit. Then to live among strangers
in Egypt far from family   Bind me to these friends and to this child
that I may learn my true relation to the people of this story
Sanctify difference and refusal, acknowledge the faggot and his lover,
the lesbians, the child with two mothers   *Amen*

RUTH BEHAR
1997

Shaken After Receiving a Letter from a Miami Poet with a Mean Tongue Who Doesn't Want a Bridge to Cuba

The letter arrived on heavy linen bond,
the kind where the tree is still breathing.
It was three pages long and typed on a laser
printer in ink so sharp it wanted to bite.
The poet said he had received my invitation
for the special volume about bridges to Cuba
and without even saying please or thank you
to cross him off my list immediately
to cross all his friends and enemies off too
and never again to write to him for anything.
Was I crazy or stupid or was my head stuck
in one of those academic Michigan clouds,
to think there's anything left in Cuba
except hunger and jails and mulatas
with half-peach tits like you'll never have?
And to hurt where it really hurts, he said,
Tell me, would you have stretched a hand
toward Hitler? Tell me, do you like Nazis?
I was never able to answer his letter. . . .
Europe, green from the bones of six million.
I tell you my femur is there, trying to walk.
A poet cruel to history is cruel to poetry.

SANDRA BERRIS
1996

The Clock Shoe

Mother can't remember who I am,
talks in riddles, shifts place
and time mid-sentence.

Her body looks the same, her face
under a tent of tidy gray hair,
sweet, alert, yet wild-eyed.

Of the memories we shared
and used to laugh about
I have my half only.

She thinks she's in trouble
with *her* mother for staying out too late
with a girlfriend, both long dead.

Today when I visit Mother
she opens the door a crack.
She calls me aside to ask,

"*Who* is that man?
He's very nice, and I don't
want to hurt his feelings,"

as she points toward my father,
"but I really *must* have him leave now."
They've been wed for fifty years.

I give her that simple Alzheimer's test, the task
of drawing a clock face with paper and pencil,
but she ponders, "Hmm, a clock?"

and stalls. "I could draw a violin."
A clock sits on the table in front of her
and she deftly draws a shoe. "A clock shoe,"

we laugh and begin a new set of memories
that will last her only for minutes.

MICHAEL J. BUGEJA
1995

Love Talk

No more lines of Shakespeare *wherefore art thous*
No more *shall compare* or *how I love thees*

But now a spouse or partner parts the lips
To ear or lobe and then espouses slips

The analysts attribute to the tongue
Like pen pet nick names advertisements songs

After which a man and woman mimic parts
TV bleating in the bedroom as it starts

She's his animated Winnie he her Pooh
He's Mister Rogers she his Miss McGoo

She likens him to network anchorites
He loves her till the end of *Guiding Light*

She can melt the iceman as he cometh
As he taketh her in Nikes just doeth

Just dialeth 1-900 Hotline darling
Just keepeth going and going and going

CHARLES BUKOWSKI
1993

the laughing heart

your life is your life.
don't let it be clubbed into dank
submission.
be on the watch.
there are ways out.
there is light somewhere.
it may not be much light but
it beats the
darkness.
be on the watch.
the gods will offer you
chances.
know them, take them.
you can't beat death but
you can beat death
in life,
sometimes.
and the more often you
learn to do it,
the more light there will
be.
your life is your life.
know it while you have
it.
you are marvelous.
the gods wait to delight
in
you.

SCOTT CAIRNS
1996

Musée

The old masters? Seldom wrong about *anything,*
never quite able to admit it when they were.

> *Notice, please, the execution of the wretched figure*

That, I suppose, is the most fraught disadvantage
in *being* master, especially an old one.

> *all but veiled by chiaroscuro and the prominence*

Still, when it came to suffering, they had the most
reliable perspective, compelling credentials.

> *of the winged tormentors whose features nearly radiate*

They came to it, as they came to everything else—
practice, repetition, unwavering habit.

> *with pleasure taken in such consummate facility*

O, long before they seemed anything like masters
they had come to observe every human torment

> *with the hooks, with which they daub the matter near the*
> *signature.*

as the fortunate occasion (they *were* masters)
for their most passionate renderings.

RAFAEL CAMPO
1993

Cuban Poetry

My grandfather loved my grandmother.
My uncle is an alcoholic. My aunt
Looks so much like my father, I can't
Understand why they never speak. My mother
Is from New Jersey. She hates the heat.
Her skin is whiter than my other aunt's,
Who was killed by a drunk driver. I can't
Understand why they never hate, why they speak
Spanish like it was butter knives, not plates
Hurled at the children. My cousin married Joy,
Who is blonde. My aunt was raped by a boy
Wearing camouflage, in the parking lot by Ames.
My mother cried for her. She is white, so white
I keep expecting her to melt, or faint.
My father holds his briefcase, like a saint
Who can't save anyone. Grandpa died last night.

RAFAEL CAMPO
1994

The 10,000th AIDS Death in San Francisco

January 1993

A woman hurried past me in the street
Today, reminding me it's not a dream:
While eating an expensive lunch in some
Expensive Caribbean restaurant
I keep imagining is Cuban-owned,
I notice that I keep imagining
The AIDS ward where I saw a man my age
Die yesterday. I can't say why, but when
He looked at me I wanted him to kiss
My face. I wanted him to live with me
And tell me stories, stories seventeen
Or eighteen hours long, involving sex
Beneath the stars, or with celebrities
Beneath some perfect, countless stars, about
The days before the epidemic killed
So many thousand people. Wanting him
To live, I stood erect beside the bed,
Wanting him. The sex itself was great,
I'm sure, but what I'd really like to know
Was how it felt to know that after lunch
In some expensive restaurant, your friends
Would be alive. Your friends would be alive—
To know no friend would die like that,
Of cryptococcal meningitis, or
Another kind of meningitis, or
A lung infection so severe it makes
A kiss impossible because the need

To breathe is even greater. Hurriedly,
I pay the bill, because I need to breathe
And suddenly I'm seeing stars, I see
Myself outside some Cuban restaurant.
A woman hurries past me, frowning, far.

AMY CLAMPITT
1982

Botanical Nomenclature

Down East people, not being botanists,
call it "that pink-and-blue flower
you find along the shore." Wildflower
guides, their minds elsewhere, mumble
"sea lungwort or oysterleaf" as a label
for these recumbent roundels, foliage
blued to a driftwood patina
growing outward, sometimes to the
size of a cathedral window,
stemrib grisaille edge-tasseled
with opening goblets, with bugles
in miniature, mauve through cerulean,
toggled into a seawall scree,
these tuffets of skyweed
neighbored by a climbing tideline,
by the holdfasts, the gargantuan lariats
of kelp, a landfall of seaweed:

Mertensia, the learned Latin handle,
proving the uses of taxonomy,
shifts everything abruptly inland,
childhoodward, to what we called then
(though not properly) bluebells:
spring-bottomland glades standing upright,
their lake-evoking sky color
a trapdoor, a window letting in distances
all the way to the ocean—
reaching out, nolens volens,
as one day everything breathing
will reach out, with just such

bells on its fingers, to touch
without yet quite having seen
the unlikelihood, the ramifying
happenstance, the mirroring
marryings of all likeness.

JUDITH ORTIZ COFER
1992

The Changeling

As a young girl
vying for my father's attention,
I invented a game that made him look up
from his reading and shake his head
as if both baffled and amused.

In my brother's closet, I'd change
into his dungarees—the rough material
molding me into boy-shape; hide
my long hair under an army helmet
he'd been given by Father, and emerge
transformed into the legendary Ché
of grown-up talk.

Strutting around the room,
I'd tell of life in the mountains,
of carnage and rivers of blood,
and of manly feasts with rum and music
to celebrate victories *para la libertad*.
He would listen with a smile
to my tales of battles and brotherhood
until Mother called us to dinner.

She was not amused
by my transformations, sternly forbidding me
from sitting down with them as a man.
She'd order me back to the dark cubicle
that smelled of adventure, to shed

my costume, to braid my hair furiously
with blind hands, and to return invisible,
as myself,
to the real world of her kitchen.

JUDITH ORTIZ COFER
1985

Claims

Last time I saw her, Grandmother
had grown seamed as a Bedouin tent.
She had claimed the right
to sleep alone, to own
her nights, to never bear
the weight of sex again nor to accept
its gift of comfort, for the luxury
of stretching her bones.
She'd carried eight children,
three had sunk in her belly, *naufragos*,
she called them, shipwrecked babies
drowned in her black waters.
Children are made in the night and
steal your days
for the rest of your life, amen. She said this
to each of her daughters in turn. Once she made a pact
with man and nature and kept it. Now like the sea,
she is claiming back her territory.

JUDITH ORTIZ COFER
1985

The Woman Who Was Left at the Altar

She calls her shadow Juan,
looking back often as she walks.
She has grown fat, her breasts huge
as reservoirs. She once opened her blouse
in church to show the silent town
what a plentiful mother she could be.
Since her old mother died, buried in black,
she lives alone.
Out of the lace she made curtains for her room,
doilies out of the veil. They are now
yellow as malaria.
She hangs live chickens from her waist to sell,
walks to the town swinging her skirts of flesh.
She doesn't speak to anyone. Dogs follow
the scent of blood to be shed. In their hungry,
yellow eyes she sees his face. She takes him
to the knife time after time.

MARTHA COLLINS
1984

Running

People with two dogs run in the yard with their two dogs.

When I started to run, I ran around
a three-mile pond, meeting, sometimes, the priest
before morning mass, and the old woman, who looked contempt
at my blue shoes:
                   'In my time,' she said once,
'women got their exercise at home.'

A still pond: reflection as clear as its source.

Straits Pond: an ocean across the way.

Last night in the film the man became
the woman and then the man for the woman he loved:
for her, the whole old story at once,
the best parts of its plots.

Between the patterns
the terriers make,
                   the upright creature,
coated in bright cloth, starts
and stops and starts and stops and claps her hands.

PETER COOLEY
1990

Husband and Wife

Gods to him, the father and the mother.
They grip a hand at either side
supporting the toddler as he starts out
the sidewalk a river to be foraged.
From my position on the wind
whoever you think I am, reader,
I assure you he's fine, treading
the blue momentum they have set in motion.
Yes, gods. Even as the infant burbles
to see trees, lawns, a green mirage
widening before him, they are at each other
javelin and spear, disappearing in clouds
or martial epithets. They yank, they tug,
and he is mortal, to be divided limb from limb.

JIM DANIELS
1997

Letting the Grounds Settle

Neven, killed in a car accident
in Zagreb last month. Blind in one eye
he thought it funny he drove so poorly —
just like how he thought Tito was funny.

I met him in '85, my wife's cousin
pricking an abscessed tooth with a pin
numbing it with shots of slivovitza
in a dreary train station under
the everpresent Tito portrait
he drew a moustache on with words.

He laughed when I sputtered out
the grounds of my Turkish coffee.
You must wait, he said,
let it settle. He was an expert
in waiting — for a train, a decent job,
an apartment, the end of Tito.

We were headed to the movies
when we got the call. Still,
we went, the babysitter pushing
us stunned out the door.

Boom, boom, boom, my baby's heart
pounds away, in joy, in hunger,
boom and a boom.

They're both asleep, my wife, my child,
when weeks later I creak up to the attic

and take out the shirt I traded Neven
for—baggy, striped. I cry into it,
poor mourning cloth. I've been waiting

for the grounds to settle:
He smoked a cigarette like it was oxygen.
On the coast, he took me to a grocery store
in a nudist camp. Buying meat from a naked
butcher—his kind of joke. He took me
to a cafe-bar where we jolted
shots of brandy, then coffee, then brandy,
then coffee till we slurred our syllables
into a common tongue/
                            oh, I don't know, I mean
he was my age, and liked to fish
he gave up his bed for us
he cooked us a horrible meal
proud in his first apartment—
holes punctuating the walls—
he said he was lucky, lucky to have.

He lived to see Tito die, then
Yugoslavia. The civil war, he'd predicted
years, years ago. He tried to turn
every ticking bomb into a bitter
metronome of laughs.

I can't send tears, so I write a check
for his widow and baby—yes, a baby too.
I look through pictures. I want to take
one out and frame it, but I don't. I slam
the album shut, I lick the envelope,
I fold the shirt up and go downstairs
to watch my child sleep. The movie,
it was just okay. We'd hoped for more.
We always do. We all do.

HELENE DAVIS
1987

I Visit the Prosthesis Lady

She is cold and gray and properly dressed, buttoned
right up to her chin in a crisp blue shirt and sensible
shoes. She stands like a soldier and stares at me.
Instantly I know I've been a bad girl. Somehow I've
gone and lost a breast or given myself cancer; and
worse, far worse, I haven't been wearing my wonderful,
humanlike prosthesis, although no one has told me I
must.

She stands me in front of a mirror and points out that
my right shoulder is lower than my left, strong evidence
that my body has been missing the weight of a left
breast. How much can it weigh, I asked myself, having
always been an A minus or less. Couldn't it be the thirty
pounds of books I carry? I ask. I'm bad. Not only am I
off-balance but I ask questions too. She marches out one
prosthesis after another but none fit. I keep stuffing
them in my bra and they are cold and warm at the same
time, sweet and squishy; and I want to sail them across
the room and drop them out the window on the heads
of women who have hair and breasts. Finally, inevitably,
we find a fit. Size zero. I am a zero. It was meant to be.

I'm a zero and bad. I'm getting worse. I tell her I don't
really need the box it comes in. "Yes, yes; it will lose its
shape if you don't use it. You must put it to bed at night
after carefully washing and rinsing and drying it." "The
care and feeding," she says. My baby. Which will never
grow, ask questions. Which will never die. "You need
pockets in your bras," she tells me. "Can't I make do

without them?" "What if one falls out and lands on the floor?" she asks.

I always think on my feet. Little squishy baby falls on the floor in the middle of my teaching a class. "Silly putty," I will say. "I never have been able to kick the habit." I give in, have pockets made—pink and lavender and black buntings for my baby girl. I picture the prosthesis lady in heaven with the wig lady, both serene in the knowledge that they have set bad girls straight.

TOI DERRICOTTE
1994

For My First Grade Teacher and Her Special Messenger

I thought you were without genitals, that nothing cracked you open and
    made you insatiable.
I thought the blood ran clear out of you like out of the side of Christ.
I thought your whole body was made of chalk dust, flaking ash.
Without children, your body burning in a yellow godlight.
Your brain, a seamless garment buried beneath your eyes.

Maybe it was God who taught you cruelty —
the black boy you made sit in his shit until it dried
had to stand up and say pardon me sister pardon me class
for the rest of eternity.

You could make a child stutter at her book.
You could make a child recognize his rot.
Perhaps you did it by ignoring, by letting be what had already happened.
A girl carried your words on paper,
walking past the huge stone statues.

What was she but a poor Irish factory worker's daughter
disappearing inside
the harrowing cleanliness and bright light?

TOI DERRICOTTE
1994

Family Secrets

They told my cousin Rowena not to marry
Calvin—she was too young, just eighteen,
& he was too dark, too too dark, as if he
had been washed in what we wanted
to wipe off our hands. Besides he didn't come
from a good family. He said he was going
to be a lawyer, but we didn't quite believe.
The night they eloped to the Gotham Hotel,
the whole house whispered—as if we were ashamed
to tell it to ourselves. My aunt and uncle
rushed down to the Gotham to plead—
we couldn't imagine his hands on her!
Families are conceived in many ways.
That night when my cousin Calvin lay
down on her, that idol with its gold skin
broke, & many of the gods we loved
in secret were freed.

TOM DISCH
1980

What to Accept

The fact of mountains. The actuality
Of any stone—by kicking, if necessary.
The need to ignore stupid people,
While restraining one's natural impulse
To murder them. The change from your dollar,
Be it no more than a penny,
For without a pretense of universal penury
There can be no honor between rich and poor,
Love, unconditionally, or until proven false.
The inevitability of cancer and/or
Heart disease. The dialogue as written,
Once you've taken the role. Failure,
Gracefully. Any hospitality
You're willing to return. The air
Each city offers you to breathe.
The latest hit. Assistance.
All accidents. The end.

RITA DOVE
1988

The Other Side of the House

But it wasn't a dream; it was a
place! And you . . . and you . . .
and you . . . and you were there!
—*Dorothy,* The Wizard of Oz

I walk out the kitchen door
trailing extension cords into the open
gaze of the southwest—

the green surreptitious,
dusty like a trenchcoat.

From the beautiful lawnmower
float curls of evaporated gasoline;
the hinged ax of the butterfly pauses.

Where am I in the stingy
desert broom, where
in the blank soul of the olive?
I hear the sand preparing to flee . . .

Many still moments,
aligned, repair
the thin split of an afternoon—
its orange fiction, the dim
aggression of my daughter on the terrace drawing
her idea of a home. Somewhere

I learned to walk out of a thought
and not snap back the way
railroad cars telescope into a train.

The sand flies so fast, it leaves no shadow.

STEPHEN DUNN
1988

Father, Mother, Robert Henley Who Hanged Himself in the Ninth Grade, *Et. Al.*

I've sensed ghosts more than once,
     their presence
a kind of plucking from the memorious air.

Always they reveal themselves as lost,
     surviving
on what's loose in me, some last words

I never said, some I did. I've heard
     they can't live
if fully embraced, if taken fully in,

yet I do nothing but listen to their
     wingless hovering,
the everything they never say.

If only I could give them what they need,
     no, if only
I could convince myself these things

must die as naturally as apples
     on the apple tree . . .
but that's in Nature, which is never

wrong, just thoughtless and without shame.

CORNELIUS EADY
1993

Walt Whitman Mall

Weren't it been wonderful, if on his death-bed
The world had opened up for poor Walt Whitman,
Poor white beard,
The future guessed, but too slow
To do him any good.

This is the drawback of clairvoyance,
If you have the misfortune
To imagine a future
Only a part of you will inhabit.
What would it have hurt to let the old duffer
Know

A few of his hunches were on the money.
Weren't it been the height of kindness
If, on his way out
Some force—an angel, say or a muse
Pulled a bit of mischief
In the name of what-does-it-matter
And sloppy American genius,

Showed Walt a few seconds of evidence
—Say, a teenage boy, seeking out
    his book in a mall,
—Say, the religion of commerce
    and distribution,
And his name lit up on the highway.

CORNELIUS EADY
1993

Anger

I am trying to calm down. Again. I am forcing myself to think of the plants in my wife's garden. I am trying to avoid confrontations. I am living in fear of nuance.

It has been a very difficult few weeks, these days after the verdict and the L.A. riots. Last night, after watching some spin doctors do their stuff, I reached for my pen. I was going to write a letter to the op-ed page when I stopped and thought about it.

It would be difficult to stuff my anger into an envelope, harder still, even dangerous, to send it through the us Postal System.

I have an anger that could, as they say, lay waste to planets. I have an anger that could converse only with volcanos. It is surly and diffident and doesn't care to talk about it.

O haughty anger, O dark sunglassed angel repository, O unreasonable man, all that would spill onto the mail room floor would amount to an inarticulate sputter. That's what I told myself, but now as I sit in the backyard, dark beer in my hand, a sun shining on flowers I would have called normal last month, I hear a voice.

LYNN EMANUEL
1980

Dracula

How he unworks the iron latch she'll never know.
He comes by transformation: a wolf,
each eye a red harvest moon,
suddenly there, in the pendulous drapery.
The bed is a landscape of heavy pillows,
her hair, a dark wing, among them
and he moves lightly, a current of smoke
eddying at the window
as if somewhere a city burns
and he is coming, assembling,
reassembling, like a column
of immigrants, his nation of women moving
beyond help for the hundredth time.

LYNN EMANUEL
1980

What I Know About The End
Of The Second World War

In L.A. someone is kissing Veronica Lake
and here, outside the window, the neon says *Hotel Clover.*
Trains haul copper all night through the quiet state,
snakes hunt across the old nests in the town dump.
In the hotel kitchen, my grandmother lays out knives
and down the dark hall guests, their skirts and trousers
on the chairs, rock slowly across each other.
It is raining. My mother comes into the room
and I can hear the slight noise of buttons and see
my mother's hands on her breasts, how they follow
one another. And now she is all white and shadow,
waltzing slowly in the little room, hands on her forehead
like a fainter, the light outside murmuring
Clover, Clover, Clover.

JOHN ENGMAN
1996

A Bird Flies into the Room and Then Flies Out Again

Just as one of those simple people
Who believe the world will end next Tuesday
Drives through my neighborhood shouting "Repent!"
Through a megaphone thrust from his black van,
I throw my window open for a gulp of winter air
And he begins shouting directly at me:
The government is falling and my brain
Has been damaged by the blue light of television,
The last war is coming
And unless I do some quick work on my soul,
My stay in eternity will be mighty unpleasant.

He's crazy, but what he's saying is true:
Scientists agree the earth is losing momentum,
That eventually the old 9-to-5 with two weeks vacation,
Poor working slob at the wheel, kids in back with Ruffy,
Sally beside him, "sweetest li'l gal in the world,"
On their way to the lake for fishing,
Will fall into the sun. Do I care?
I have no kids, no Sally, no Ruffy.
The room I rent is small and unpleasantly cold.
I don't even have a job—let it all fall into the sun!
I'm taking off my shirt now, unzipping my trousers,
Climbing back on the bed to nurse my grudge
Into full-blown depression when something stupid happens:
A bird flies into the room and then flies out again!
It scares me, the way that investigating angel
Must have scared St. John when she came to judge,
Grading him down for lack of grace and lack of lust,

"Dear John, you can do better. c plus, c plus."
So I'm standing here in my winter underwear
And my room feels cold but suddenly good—
If this is the way the world ends, that's okay,
It's winter, and my window is wide open.

LOUISE ERDRICH
1989

The Return

The scarred trees twisted and the locked garage
held all my secrets, and my father's hunting bows
unstrung, my mother's empty canning bottles.
Once a mouse slipped in and tipped the glass
straight up so that it starved dead
at the bottom of a clear well.
I found a husk, a smear of grease, and a calm
odor of the ancient.

All winter, I dug tunnels in the snow
that mounted, mounted to the eaves and blew
like dry foam off the ridgepole. In my den
the air was warm and supernatural.
The quiet hung around me like a bell
and I could hear my own heart jump
like a frog in my chest. The crushing weight

of church was up above. I hid and waited
while God crossed over like the Hindenburg
and roared, like my grandfather to his men
and traced the ground with his binocular vision
but never saw me, as I was blue
as the shadow in a chunk of snow,
as a glass horse in a glass stall.

Down here my breath iced the walls.
The snow fell deeper than I could crawl.
I was sealed back into the zero
and then at last the world went dark.

My body hummed itself to sleep
and her heart was my heart,
filling the close air,
slowing in the empty jar.

JANE FLANDERS
1988

Two Sisters

Maybe they're old and live together —
tease each other, sport tatty
wigs that match the Pekingese —
in a drafty house their father built
ninety years ago. Nobody (certainly not
the antique maid) bothers to clean. Still,
the chairs are comfy, worn linoleum's
easy on the feet.
                But maybe they're young
with skin like satin and wispy hair
that's never been trimmed. One sits
on the sofa, holding the other and holding
her breath. They will share baths and
clothes, sleep side by side, grow up loving
the same dogged fellow. "Give me sons!"
cries Rachel to Jacob, "as you have given
my sister, or I die!"
             Listen!
Two sisters are singing a Brahms song.
("We are sisters, lovely we are . . .")
They are your daughters, aunts, nieces,
your next-door neighbors, shelling peas
on the back porch. Like pairs of matched bays
Maude and Ada, Kate and Nell, Helen and
Clytemnestra step along the avenue, joined
by something pliable, intricate as lace.

CAROL FROST
1989

Apple Rind

Someone else was afraid and spoke to me
and I couldn't answer . . . swallowing oxygen
from a tube. And then? The cool blade
freeing rind from an apple,
like the first touch of day. How long
I'd been in someone's still life—the blade
hidden, dividing—and was helpless.

Perfectly drugged, I lay just shy of winter
in my own mind. My cut chest felt nothing,
no terror, no pain. And there were morphine's sweet-
and-fruit boxes piled on the white terrain
like reasons for lives and death.
The orchard was weathered to admonitory bareness
except for a few frozen apples
above a disturbance of snow—the hoof prints
of deer coming by several routes to this late harvest,
the dim haunches and various limbs
afloat on movement that can break
or double back into the gray calm of woods.

How to explain directions a mind takes
or why I told no one how much I wanted
to come back to this beautiful, stupid world.

PATRICIA GOEDICKE
1987

Cathay

for Margaret Fox Schmidt

Even after the chemotherapy I said o you
Perfect roundness of celestial fruit
I'm nuts about you.

Your cupcake face sits
In the middle of the gold star of your hair
Like a child's picture of the sun smiling

You fly over our heads such a bright snappy flag
Fuzzy with peach bloom but crisp,
Jaunty as a pirate,

What's in your hold is a mystery,
But cutting through the deep blue seas of your eyes
The tart juices spurt up, delicious

As candied ginger from Cathay
And I'd load you into my market basket
Any day: there you'd roll around

Like a pale yellow grapefruit rubbing cheeks
With lesser creatures; dull turnips, potatoes
For you're not only the cream, you're the citrus in my cargo,

Just listening to you tell stories makes me want to jump up,
Hearing about all those swashbuckling ladies,
Your heroic chuckle like the rough chunk of waves

Keeps slapping at my sides with such encouraging spanks
I just wanted to tell you, for a kewpie doll you're some dame,
For a gun moll you're some sweet seagoing daisy;

With your round face waving to me from the bridge
If just being around you for two minutes turns me into a brandied apricot
All dippy and dizzy and brave as a gangster bee

With one arm and a broken leg
All you'd have to do is say *Vamonos!*
And I'd follow you anywhere, honey.

ALBERT GOLDBARTH
1993

"Jeff" of "Mutt and Jeff" Leans on Air

The very earliest animators
were literalists. Their pleasure was a woman
walking, a man rising out of a chair,
obeying gravity. Their pleasure was a line
displaying the laws of Newtonian physics,
a study of bodies and forces.

Maybe at dusk he'd come home, close
the door against the moon and river, talk about it
all night with his wife: the reels, the cels.
The kettle was boiling. The baby was learning
to make a fist and focus her eyes, was
learning to work the limits of musculature.

It wasn't until around 1917, and then it was
accidental: shooting some art, a photographer
left a cel out, with the drawing of a railing
on it. "Jeff" was left leaning on air. They saw
a man could lean on air. That year, every
woman, man, and mouse in the nation's cartoons was floating.

Outside, the moonlight on the water was
miraculous. He stood on the porch, in the quiet.
Although, he thought, if we really believed it
was miraculous, we wouldn't require fairy tales.
A stone would be enough. He breathed some darkness
in, so deep, it might come from the stars. On nights

like this sometimes he thought of his daughter,
wherever she was . . . LA? Morocco? Maybe another
suburb not 30 minutes away. And when his hand
had slapped her face for goodbye . . . hard. Now
he only wanted to say it was ok, he understood:
sometimes he also wanted slipping from the bindings,

and though he'd never once gone, he knew the night
was ink that could absorb and then reshape us.
The river came out of the dark, and flowed back to the dark,
while here for a moment the moon was a white arm up
to its elbow in this world's water. He looks at his hand . . .
Our hands; and what they do; and how impossible.

ALBERT GOLDBARTH
1993

Repeated Sightings

of the rock star we thought buried in his diamondwear
ten years ago, but here he is, wearing a worn and
comforting flannel-like face, with the drifters
huddled under the trestle at night; and here he is,
standing with a nightingale perched on his shoulder,
rumbling out a series of opaque parables
in the desert (or was it a lark, or was it an owl?);
and here he is, buying his beer in line like
anyone else, except for the anthracite-black
sunglasses; here; and then here; and then here. And

Nessie's reported raising her humpy bridge in the water
a dozen times this season alone, I read it in last
week's *National Insister*, and then a swallow flew
through my living room, in one window and straight
out the other, and when I returned to the page, the Virgin Mary
was weeping from an Idaho potato and the same day floating
as elegantly as a jellyfish, in the air, outside of Rome.
(Or was it a cardinal, or was it an indigo bunting?)
Anyway, Bigfoot. All the time, FELON ESCAPED. For
sure, those glowing pieplate flying saucers. And

so we come to see we need these repetitions, these
confirmings: our most singular of lunacies
are really communal, validated in Sydney and Bangkok
and Squalid Corners, stamped like a diplomat's papers
with innumerable approval. Sunspots.
Yeti. Messiahs. Shooting stars. Amelia Earhart.
Vampire outbreaks. Idiot savants who glance
at acoustic panels and tell you the number of dots.

All of these happen in lavish grabs
of overoccurrence, they won't stay home alone. And

that bird?—you can open the Norton anthology where
it's reported flown, lines earlier, into sombody else's poem.

MARILYN HACKER
1984

from Open Windows

for Sára Karig

On the back of a letter in French applying
for a place at a bilingual school for my daughter
I put words that will not contain the slaughter
of somebody's twenty-year-old. She is dying
under a modern airport where the roar
of takeoffs flattens screams and retching to blurred
industrial noise around the torturer.
Below the tiled floor is the dirt floor.
A woman is living whose name I say like a charm
because she acknowledged choice in the dulled eyes
of somebody's son who, needled to recognize
a congruent soul in the law student or farm
child he is reducing to an integer
of shamed pain, would be stripped and killed with her.
"How come, here, you see so many Black
people working in other people's houses?"
Does she notice, every other friend of ours is
ambiguous two generations back?
Like Bedouin for *sand,* or Eskimo
for *snow,* mixed races swell the lexicon,
peach-cream through copper to obsidian:
Preta, negrinho, mulata, moreno.
Her café-au-lait father, olive mother
made her *rubia,* gold on lion-gold
like the naked sungilt three-year-old
who, crouched near a bloat sewer, ferreted
his hillside of the disinherited
looking enough like her to be her brother.

RACHEL HADAS
1983

To a Youngish Professor Who Has
Waxed Eloquent Over Certain Students

Amanda. Julia. Celia. Marjorie.
Posies in a madrigal they might be.
Terrific, every one of them, you say.

Every flower in the garden blushes and blows for you.
But they are also orchids blooming blackly,
do you not understand, unfolding at your touch.

Steadfast gardeners stick to their husbandry
tilling the soil in Michigan or Maine
night after night next to their velvet beauties.

They fumble silent brides whose backs are turned,
who face the wallpaper. Those art nouveau
trellises entangling everything. . . .

They may have been fine students. It's not easy.
You put them in your file and they take root.
You are in theirs for better, worse, long winter

of being alone with the loved one.
Is there no less painful way to do it?
You taught them poetry was just for that—

dark lace of word-webs darning, darning, damning
the festering sore that's finally no one's fault.
Put it in black and white and call it art.

LINDA HOGAN
1983

Friday Night

Sometimes the light from her kitchen
almost touches mine
and her shadow falls
through trees and peppermint
to lie down at my door
like it wants to come in.

Never mind that on Friday nights
she slumps out her own torn screen
to cry on the stoop.
And don't ask about the reasons.
She pays her penalties for weeping.
Emergency Room:
Eighty dollars to knock a woman out.
And there are laughing red-faced neighbor men
who lay down their hammers
to phone the county.
Her crying tries them all.
Don't ask for reasons
why they do not collapse
outside their own tight jawbones
or the rooms they built
a tooth and nail at a time.

Never mind she's Mexican
and I'm Indian
and we have both replaced the words
to the National Anthem with our own,
or that her house smells of fried tortillas
and mine of Itchko and sassafras.

Tonight she was weeping in the safety of moonlight
and red maples.
I took her a cup of peppermint tea,
and honey,
it was fine blue china
with marigolds growing inside the curves.
In the dark, under the praying mimosa
we sat smoking little caves of tobacco light,
me and the *Señora of Hysteria*, who said
Peppermint is every bit as good as the ambulance.
And I said, Yes. It is home grown.

JONATHAN HOLDEN
1996

Such Beauty

It has long been known
that the ideal mortar positions
are pine groves and dappled sunlight,
ski slopes rated "Expert" —
the prettiest places in the world
above the quaintest towns.
How can we talk of such beauty
as the landscape above Sarajevo
without lapsing into easy
semi-automatic irony.
A bored American boy
with my family's woods to hide in,
I owned the largest collection
of cap guns on Pleasantville Road.
Like a flinty-eyed U.S. Marshal,
my idol, Randolph Scott,
I would routinely evaluate
every quarry or cluster of boulders
as a potential position
from which to ambush a posse.
Most grown-up American boys
know how the Bosnian Serbs
must delight in their hilltop positions
like spectators with the choicest seats.
They have the best view of the action —
puffs blossoming, sprouting tendrils
of phosphorus, frosty pistils
in the village below.
As I watch on TV, in Technicolor
the soldiers busying themselves

212

like Boy Scouts earning merit badges,
like squirrels in films by Walt Disney,
I remember my friend Irma
recalling her experiences
in the French Resistance:
plots, bombs, disguises,
tales more fascinating than the movies.
It's not for beauty that we do it.
Just as one's hand may return
compulsively to a bruise
again pawing at its pain,
I think that we humans
find pain interesting, that's all,
and warfare by far the most
interesting activity
that we have ever devised.

DAVID IGNATOW
1997

For Johannes Edfelt

I once had a religion to turn to.
I listen to a singer singing
the prayer I once sang.

What I have now is myself,
the skeptic,
looking at trees and grass
that live out their lives
never in doubt.

My childhood is in that song.
In contentment with my childhood,
I look skyward with curiosity.

DAVID IGNATOW
1997

For Rose

1913–1995

I have a name
a substitute
for the word
infinity

When my name is called
it is not me
you are calling.

RICHARD JACKSON
1988

Hope

I am going to talk about hope.
—Cesar Vallejo

. . . fogged in with hope.
—Paul Celan

When I give the few dinars to the little pharaohs,
if we call these two Gypsies by their right name,
when the boy tries to pull his sister away so that she
stares wide-eyed at me, I cannot help thinking of
those photos of the poor Gypsies the Nazis hung in the hills
just east of here. I imagine a young man, maybe
the grandfather of these two who has been directing them
from a few yards away, I imagine him hiding with the Partisans
in Marjin Pass, fingering by candlelight the worn
letter from his son. He must see in the steam that rises
from the winter's thin stew, by the light of a shot up
moon, a scene where some future daughter of his son is
playing Chopin on her piano, where the boy is kicking
a soccer ball against the side of a school, anything
but this scene which includes me, far from home, dreaming
the way he must have, wondering what has become of you.

You were right. The world slows down when you begin
to dream. Maybe it stops. The old pharaoh is
sitting on the 600-year-old bridge of abandoned hope
in Mostar, abandoned by the architect a few days before
he finished it, who was found weeping beside the grave
he would enter if it fell. He is sitting the way my father would,

flicking cigarettes the way he did, Chesterfields, without
moving his arm, *how did he do that,* I'd want to know,
into the Merrimack River in Lawrence, Mass. They were stars,
he'd say, or candles, dying to make the dusk a little
brighter, that we retrieve whenever we borrow
a little light against despair. Listen, I am borrowing
that light. I am watching my two pharaohs working
the street, how the boy keeps tugging at her dress to make
her look more desperate. I am looking beyond them,
towards the grave of the poet whose name I can't pronounce,
who fought for the poor. I am lighting this candle for him.
And I am looking towards our poet, towards Cesar Vallejo—
"Down the road my heart is walking on foot,"
he wrote, the poet who never lived where he was,
who knew, years before, how he'd die in Paris in the rain.
I see him as a child no older than these pharaohs, in Santiago
de Chuco, Peru, four days by horseback to the nearest
railbed, another day to the coast. One evening, he watches
a peasant being beaten for a few pesos, for a few words,
and knows, too, the future exile who will wander inside him.

Maybe it is impossible to live in one moment at a time.
Maybe Vallejo was right, that every moment we have is
a past we make into a future, or a future we must bless.
So maybe it is later, in another tense, in Sarajevo,
where you were startled for a moment by an old dream,
how the courtyard of the Serbian church became a hillside,
how as a child you used to dream of enormous animals
filling the windows. I think each dream is a hope we have
that we are not where we are. Each dream, my father
would say, is a dream of travel. Once by the Merrimack
we found the empty shells of beetles, dozens of them,
and he explained how they had been abandoned by horsehair
worms that grew three feet in their bellies, spiraling
like DNA until, almost becoming beetles themselves,
they abandoned one dream for another. To know anything,
he said, even love, is to know what lives inside it,
to know how we live inside each other, the terror
of any love. I did not understand that until this morning,
reading how Celan's poems grew smaller and smaller,

how he was afraid to talk directly because he feared
the Nazis were still listening, how his poems were codes
against despair. Certainly the pharaohs know that. I have
not forgotten these two, working their way back through
the crowd, handing the few coins to the grandfather,
handing over the years, the lives any moment holds.

I am handing this over to you, a little candle for the dark.
I am imagining the little pharaoh at her piano after all,
playing Chopin as her grandfather dreamed, I am thinking
of Chopin, beginning the second piano concerto, how
the piano seems to wait, awed by the orchestra's beauty,
or how the orchestra itself holds off what it knows will be
the plaintive entrance of the piano, how each gesture includes
the other. It was Chopin, like Vallejo, who would die
in Paris, in the rain, who was buried with a fistful of Polish
dirt, to stop, he hoped, his soul from wandering.

I am handing this over to you, a story for another time.
I no longer care what tense it is, what places we are
speaking from. What is any story but a form of hope?
Think even of the story of Osip Mandelstam, exiled
twice, tortured, how he asked in his last days only for
some candles and blankets. In one version he is thrown
out of the barracks by the other prisoners when he eats
their food, fearing the guards have poisoned his. His eyes
sink even deeper into his face than those haunting photos
of his early years, than the photos of Gypsies, than the eyes
of my little pharaohs. He is living near the camp refuse heap
as winter approaches, the long gray beard beginning
to stiffen with sorrow, the gypsy of Vladivostok, still
making the hopeful poems he says only to himself.
One day he will look out to see *mounds of human heads*
wandering into the distance, and then himself out there,
dwindling among them, unseen, but perhaps rising again
from the dead, from his own poems, to see the sun starting.
He is hoping to find out what it means to live. He is
dreaming of sleighs, the shy currents of boyhood streams,
knowing how the earth is always ready to take him back.

By now the little pharaohs have crossed over the bridge
of abandoned hope and have dissolved like Mandelstam into night.
They have dissolved like Vallejo who tried to love everyone,
whoever is crying for death, whoever is crying for water,
who would die, as he knew, from a pain that came from
everywhere that Good Friday, 1938, the way the world was.
I would make them appear again, maybe later, maybe Belgrade,
in the faces of the pharaohs who will run beside us, selling
flowers, jewelry, anything, in a city the Nazis tried
to steal. They will never be the pharaohs of Egypt though
they keep their secrets as closed as the hidden chambers
of pyramids. I am thinking of the small cave, the small room
outside the Church of St. Peter in Belgrade, of how I stood
beside my friend as he lit the candles for his parents, *one
for death*, placing it in the sand on the floor, *but two for life*,
he says, two hanging in the urn in the middle of the air,
between earth and sky, past and future, a candle for hope.

There are no pharaohs much later where I am sitting
in the cafe in Slovenia with a poet who is telling me
over the weakening table candle in its green, gaudy cup,
how as a child he would wander the Alps, how he could
name every bird, every tree, every thing that moved,
but now his voice breaks, he lights another cigarette,
another star, and he is telling me how he watched
the Germans pull his father from the house and shoot him
there in the street, how for years he felt, as Celan did,
that he had already died, that there was no word for hope.
We could be still sitting there, trying to separate the words
we have for fear and for hope. We could still be sitting there,
trying to find the secret codes Celan used in his poems,
even the bleakest, words that meant *we are still alive*.

Look, this is a moment that is not going to stop entering
your future, the way the boats of pharaohs were meant
to carry their dreams to whatever future the god had hoped,
beyond their deaths, beyond their suffering, gathering all
time around them,—as here in Mostar, Belgrade, Slovenia,—
as here in Venice where we will walk past Byron's mansion
near the old post office, where, when Teresa Guiccioli left,

he imagined her everywhere, sitting in the plush chair
in the corner, at the table with wine, along the canals.
I am standing there now. I am lighting a candle again
in the Church of St. Mark's for my little pharaohs, for Vallejo,
the gypsy poet who would walk brooding alone for hours,
for Mandelstam, who could find hope in the garbage of a prison
camp, for the sweet music of Chopin, I am lighting it
for all of us, handing it over to the memory of Celan,
and handing it over equally to the future of Celan, and to you,
the poet of slow dreams, I am lighting this candle for you,
a little light against despair, a little blessing for love,
a candle for death, a candle for life, a candle for hope.

PHYLLIS JANOWITZ
1982

Sardines

The baby is not exceedingly miserable.
Its bleat signifies, rather, a refusal.
It will not willingly accept betrayal.

What could it want? Does it have croup, catarrh?
It sings its sorrowful song from breakfast to supper
and vice versa. The frail notes convene and warble

from a vent above Letitia's self-cleaning oven.
She would like to complain, but no one can tell
her where an infant—possibly orphaned—

is roosting. Perhaps, in the wall, a cradle
is endlessly rocking a small, unblissful baby.
Perhaps it is merely a Platonic ideal,

the essential quintessence of infancy.
It might be the voice of the next generation.
There are other voices, Letitia insists.

When she wakes, she does not wake alone.
She looks around. She is the only one
in bed. Yet it's crowded, there is no room.

Covering her is a blanket of arguments,
demands, threats and regrets. This is existence
in a grand new complex. She doesn't know

what to do with the imps of exuberance
cavorting about her head, cartwheeling over
her stomach, the noise in the walls growing louder,

and no one to take a complaint, issue a citation,
and no one to say what is tangible, what is not—
no one with any substance or conviction.

MARK JARMAN
1992

Outside

God says to Adam and Eve, "This time nothing's forbidden.
You may have the garden and the fruit of every tree.
That tree's fruit will give you knowledge of good and evil.
The fruit of this tree, even better, will make you forget.
Eat all you want. Let bygones be bygones."
And so at once they go to find the wall
And the way out, eating as they go,
Burning as they go, going because just thinking
There is a wall makes them feel cramped. They cross
Rivers and mountains, seas, they find no wall.
They eat the fruit of knowledge and see the problem:
Without a wall, the world is all they have,
Crisscrossed by their progress, a vacant lot.
God reminds them, "Nothing is forbidden."
They eat the fruit of forgetfulness, and forget.

ALLISON JOSEPH
1997

Numbers

My father taught me to measure
the worth of any good thing
by the number of black people
involved. Without sufficient numbers,

he wouldn't root for a team,
wouldn't eat in a restaurant,
wouldn't turn on his television
to watch a local newscast

that didn't have a black anchor.
He wanted black people
to appear on *Masterpiece Theatre*
—he'd lived in England so he knew

black people lived there—
wanted us on *Evening at Pops*
and *Live from Wolf Trap*,
the orchestra's black musicians

conveniently placed up front
for his recognition, wanted
every diva who performed at the Met
to be brown, proud, beautiful—

an endless string of Jessye Normans
and Leontyne Prices. He'd rage
at commercials, at *The Brady Bunch*,
at soap operas, Broadway musicals,

at any bit of American culture
tossed before us as entertainment
that dared not have a black cast member.
So I grew up rooting against the then

all-white Mets, the Boston Red Sox,
(Jim Rice their only saving grace),
the Celtics, hell, the whole city of Boston,
the obscene snowy landscape of New England.

So he probably thought he'd failed
to instill his wisest lesson
when we drove to that college
in middle-of-nowhere Ohio

with its green clapboard shutters
on its white colonial cottages,
its manicured hedges
and windowboxes of tulips.

Resolute, he helped me hoist boxes
to my narrow, undecorated room,
watched glumly as Mom unpacked
suitcases, as my sister folded clothes.

Suspicious, he finally asked,
where are all the black people,
but I could show him only three faces
in the freshman picture book,

including my own photo booth snapshot.
He thought I was crazy to live
so close to them, the white people
who'd conspired so long against him,

the numbers on that campus
far too low for him, my scholarship
bleaching me, making me
less black, less daughter.

TED KOOSER
1983

As the President Spoke

As the President spoke, he raised a finger
to emphasize something he said. I've forgotten
just what he was saying, but as he spoke
he glanced at that finger as if it were
somebody else's, and his face went slack and gray,
and he folded his finger back into its hand
and put it down under the podium
along with whatever it meant, with whatever he'd seen
as it spun out and away from that bony axis.

MAXINE KUMIN
1996

The Riddle of Noah

You want to change your name. You're looking
for "something more suitable," words we can only guess
you've come by from television or teachers. All
your first-grade friends have names like Justin Mark
Caroline Emma or newly enrolled Xuan Loc
and yours, you sadly report, is Noah . . . nothing.

Noah *Hodges*, your middle name isn't nothing
your mother, named Hodges, reproves, but you go on looking.
Next day you are somebody else: Adam Stinger! The clock
turns back to my brother, Edward Elias, whose quest
to be named for his father (living names are death marks
on a Jewish child) was fulfilled by a City Hall

clerk. Peter Jr. went gladly to school all
unblessed. The names that we go by are nothing
compared to the names we are called. *Christ killer!* they mocked
and stoned me with quinces in my bland-looking
suburb. Why didn't I tattle, resist? I guessed
I was guilty, the only kid on my manicured block

who didn't know how to genuflect as we lock-
stepped to chapel at noontime. I was in thrall,
the one Jewish girl in my class at Holy Ghost
convent school. Xuan Loc, which translates as something
magical and tender—Spring Bud, a way of looking
at innocence—is awarded the gold bookmark

for reading more chapter-books than Justin Mark
or Noah, who now has tears in his eyes. No lack

of feeling here, a jealous Yahweh is looking
over his shoulder hissing, Be best of all.
What can be done to ease him? Nothing
makes up for losing, though love is a welcome guest.

Spared being burned at the stake, being starved or gassed,
like Xuan Loc, Noah is fated to make his mark,
suffer for grace through good works, aspire to something.
Half-Jewish, half-Christian, he will own his name, will unlock
the riddle of who he is: only child, in equal
measure blessed and damned to be inward-looking,

always slightly aslant the mark, like Xuan Loc.
Always playing for keeps, for all or nothing
in quest of his rightful self while the world looks on.

ALICE LEE
1993

A History Poem

a birth defect. a woman with a defect couldn't
go to school. she became her father's farmhand.
the days when she didn't work fast enough her
father would use the horsewhip. after the whipping
he would touch her shoulders.

a man wanted to marry her. a man wanted her. when
she saw him for the first time she felt a wet ache.
he gave her father a team of horses. her father
gave him her. her father gave him his old horsewhip.

after the whipping he would reach for her. then he
would love her.

the girl child is hers. from within her body. she
beats her. flesh stinging flesh.

someone has given the little girl a small black dog.
she hits it with a stick.

DAVID LEHMAN
1983

Exact Change

1.
Everything makes sense again:
Like a talmudic scholar you begin
With a crucial "if" and then
A new morning intervenes with yesterday's sorry conclusion:
You can't, and the timing is inscribed upon
The mistress of clocks, like the unseeing eyes of a rebus.

Can't sing, can't go home again, can't tell you how much,
Can't start the car or stop the war
Or alter the paths of the wandering planets,
Can't say no, can't wait for the wait to be over,
Can't take the shape of the wind
On a deserted beach along the New England coast.

And therefore the thief's ambivalence at the sight
Of the newsstand's blind proprietor.
And therefore the sinner's unfolded hands.

2.
For example, think of office buildings,
Think of the pressure, the elevator's rapid descent;
Think of the absence of snow in December,
Think of the absence of footprints in the snow

All of which lead to my doorstep. If, for example,
We could forget about the family, there would still be
Its nexus to contend with when, through lucky keyholes,
We catch a glimpse of enemy territory, the room
Full of sibling rivals, veteran sufferers of freeway phobia

Just like ourselves. And the first order of business is,
Should the negotiating table be round or square?
If we can agree on that, even peace becomes possible,
And we can move on to waves versus particles,
God in parking lots, the philosopher's brown shirt,
And how the war in Vietnam ended three separate times,
or never.

3.
But (and this is the strange part)
There was no forgetting the change
Or the sentiment that a change
(Other than a change in the weather) had taken place,

And if, one day, the faces seem friendly, the smiles unforced,
Wouldn't we still count the drops of blood on the snow
(We who had never truly loved the snow)
And wake up shocked by all the terrible noises of dawn?

CYNTHIA MACDONALD
1997

Singing Miriam's Lament

It is too late to have breakfast. Blue's Cafe serves from 6 to 8 A.M.
It is too late to touch you when you sleep beside me.
You are not there.
Considering my weak ankles and my middle age,
it is too late to become an Olympic-class skater.
It is too late to have lunch. Blue's Cafe serves from 12 to 3 P.M.
and the sushi is all gone and the halibut dried
till its bones stick out through its flesh.
It is too late to become a World War II spy, and in the next one
there will be no time to assemble spies.
It is too late to be on time for our wedding
which, for some reason even you could not explain,
you wanted in St. Patrick's Cathedral although
you are Jewish. I should have known then.
It is too late to have dinner. Blue's Cafe serves from 7 to 10 P.M.
and the food has become infected with toxins
so all the customers are dead in their seats.
The late Mr. and Mrs. Bixby still hold their wine glasses,
The late Mr. Porter is stiffening, his head resting in
the soup plate which makes a halo round it.
Perhaps being on time is not always a virtue,
as Opa and Oma found out on Kristallnacht.

WALTER MCDONALD
1994

Letting Go

Raised on the plains, we believe
in bald horizons where the sun burns
every crop. We cling to the myth
the world is flat under skies so dry

weeds wilt. Buzzards glide
always in sight, and rattlers coil
in our yard. Born in the Rockies,
our babies climbed before they could walk,

their eyes brimming with trees.
The steepest roofs were dwarfed,
and snakes draped above us on boulders.
The spoor of cougars tempted our children

to climb, to wander off. They scaled
mountain peaks, breathing thin air
they evolved to, believing that was the world,
that bears owned no more of the woods

than our children prowled
miles from the hearth where we stayed
stoking embers, sweeping,
oiling the locks.

JUDSON MITCHAM
1983

Noise and a Few Words

Tonight, when steam has risen from the bright streets
each vehicle must sizzle down, when the sun,
as sure as a man, has glanced off all it has caught,
fallen to the last green easing away,
aromas of fried corn, okra, and country steak
filling the damp air, and the old stray mongrel, ours,
has crawled still nameless under the back steps,
where the scraps come forth like stars, a man is called,
and still in a soiled T-shirt, wearing no shoes,
unaware, says grace for the last time.
He offers the few words we all know,
but before that soft amen, impatient, I raise my glass,
not hearing, when the hush gives, how the dark falls
loudly, hurries on, lawnmowers, jets, motorbikes,
trucks on a far highway, the radio's popping deep bass,
how the noise says too so be it.

JUDITH MOFFETT
1983

Will

The tamer, straining all his nerve and skill,
Keeps Panic hunkered on her pedestal,

Makes Jealousy the leopard leap through flame,
The panther Fury slope along the beam

Like any backfence tom with massive feet,
And Terror burst a paper hoop, and Hate

Rise supple in his gaudy stripes to beg
Then shoulder down, a rolled-up tiger rug.

Or not quite: if that fierce attention blinks
All spring. Beneath his shirt are scars like staves
His props—the whip, chair, pistolful of blanks—
Could not forestall, and ugliest are Love's.
Like stone his stare when Love's exploding din
Slams through the Big Top's shapely dome of bone.

PAT MORA
1994

Coatlicue's Rules: Advice from an Aztec Goddess

Rule 1: Beware of offers to make you famous.
I, a pious Aztec mother doing my own housework,
am now on a pedestal, "She of the Serpent Skirt,"
hands and hearts dangling from my necklace, a faceless
statue, two snake heads eye-to-eye on my shoulders,
goddess of earth, also, death which leads to

Rule 2: Retain control of your own publicity.
The past is the present. Women are women; balls, balls.

I'm not competitive and motherhood isn't
about numbers, but four hundred sons and a daughter
may be a record even without the baby.
There's something wrong in this world
if a woman isn't safe even when she sweeps
her own house, when any speck can enter even through
the eye, I'll bet, and become a stubborn tenant.

Rule 3: Protect your uterus. Conceptions, immaculate
and otherwise, happen. Women swallow sacred
stones that fill their bellies with elbows and knees.
In Guatemala, a skull dangling from a tree whispers,
"Touch me," to a young girl, and a clear drop
drips on her palm and disappears. The dew
drops in, if you know what I mean. The saliva moved
in her, the girl says. Moved in, I say,
settled into that empty space, and grew. Men know.
They stay full of themselves, keeps occupancy down.

Rule 4: Avoid housework. Remember, I was sweeping,
humming, actually, high on Coatepec, our Serpent
Mountain, humming loud so I wouldn't hear
all those sighs inside. I was sweeping slivers,
gold and jade, picking up after four hundred sons
who think they're gods, and their spoiled sister.

I was sweep-sweeping when feathers fell on me, brushed
my face, the first light touch in years, like in a dream.
At first, I just blew them away, but then I saw it,
the prettiest ball of tiny plumes, glowing green and gold.
Gently, I gathered it. Oh, it was soft as baby hair
and brought back mother shivers when I pressed it
to my skin. I nestled it like I used to nestle them,
here, when they finished nursing. Maybe I even stroked
the roundness. I have since heard that feathers
aren't that unusual at annunciations, but I was innocent.

After I finished sweeping, I looked in vain inside
my clothes, but the soft ball had vanished, well,
descended. I think I showed within the hour,
or so it seemed. They noticed first, of course.

Rule 5: Avoid housework. It bears repeating.
I was too busy washing, cooking corn, beans, squash,
sweeping again, worrying about my daughter,
Painted with Bells, when I began to bump into their frowns
and mutterings. They kept glancing at my stomach,
started pointing. I got so hurt and mad, I started crying.
Why is it they always get to us?
One wrong word or look from any one of them doubles me over,
and I've had four hundred and one without anesthetic.
Near them I'm like a snail with no shell on a sizzling day.
They started yelling, "Wicked, wicked," and my daughter,
right there with them, my wanna-be warrior boy.
And then I heard the whispers.

The yelling was easier than, "Kill. Kill. Kill. Kill."
Kill me? Their mother? One against four hundred and one?
All I'd done was press that softness into me.

Rule 6: Listen to inside voices. You mothers know
about the baby in a family, right? Even if he hadn't talked
to me from deep inside, he would have been special.
Maybe the best. But as my name is Coatlicue, he did.
That unborn child, that started as a ball of feathers all soft
green and gold, heard my woes, and spoke to me.
A thoughtful boy. And formal too. He said, "Do not be afraid,
I know what I must do." So I stopped shaking.

Rule 7: Verify that the inside voice is yours.
I'll spare you the part about the body hacking
and head rolling. But he was provoked remember.
All this talk of gods and goddesses distorts.

Though this planet wasn't big enough for all of us,
the whole family has done well for itself I think.
I'm the mother of stars. My daughter's white head rolls
the heavens each night, and my sons wink down at me.
What can I say—a family of high visibility.
The baby? Up there also, the sun, the real thing.
Such a god he is, of war unfortunately, and the boy
never stops, always racing across the sky,
every day of the year, a ball of fire since birth.
But I think he has forgotten me. You sense my ambivalence.
I'm blinded by his light.

Rule 8: Insist on personal interviews.
The past is the present, remember. Men carved me,
wrote my story, and Eve's, Malinche's, Guadalupe's,
Llorana's, snakes everywhere, even in our mouths.

Rule 9: Be selective about what you swallow.

Coatlicue: in Aztec mythology mother of Huitzilopochtli, the sun god, who is born
fully-armed and slays his sister Coyolxauqui, Painted with Bells, who becomes the
moon, and his four hundred brothers, Centzon Huitznahua, who become the stars.

LES A. MURRAY
1988

Hearing Impairment

Hearing loss? Yes, loss is what we hear
who are starting to go deaf. Loss
trails a lot of weird puns in its wake, viz.
Dad's a real prism of the Left—
you'd like me to repeat that?
THE SAD SURREALISM OF THE DEAF.

It's mind over mutter at work
guessing half what the munglers are saying
and society's worse. Punch lines elude to you
as Henry Lawson and other touchy drinkers
have claimed. Asides, too, go pasture.
It's particularly nasty with a wether.

First you crane at people, face them
while you can still face them. But grudgually
you give up dinner parties; you begin
to think about Beethoven. You Hanover
next visit here on silly Narda Fearing—I SAY
YOU CAN HAVE AN EXQUISITE EAR
AND STILL BE HARD OF HEARING.

It seems to be mainly speech, at first,
that escapes you—and that can be a rest,
the poor man's escape itch from Babel.
You can still hear a duck way upriver,
a lorry miles off on the highway. You
can still say boo to a goose and
read its curt yellow-lipped reply.
You can shout SING UP to a magpie,

but one day soon you must feel
the silent stopwatch chill your ear
in the doctor's rooms, and be wired
back into a slightly thinned world
with a faint plastic undertone to it
and, if the rumors are true, snatches
of static, music, police transmissions:
it's a BARF minor Car Fourteen prospect.

But maybe hearing aids are now perfect
and maybe it's not all that soon.
Sweet nothings in your ear are still sweet;
you've heard the human range by your age
and can follow most talk from memory;
the peace of the graveyard's well up
on that of the grave. And the world would
enjoy peace and birdsong for more moments

if you were head of government, enquiring
of an aide Why, Simpkins, do you tell me
a warrior is a ready flirt?
I might argue — and flowers keep blooming
as he swallows his larynx to shriek
our common mind-overloading sentence:
I'M SORRY, SIR, IT'S A RED ALERT!

LEONARD NATHAN
1981

Cold Snap

When the ice next comes down
over the taigas, the lakes, the northern cities,
the yellow shag of the wheat fields,
our eyes will open very wide
after thousands of years of sleep
to see the world again.

A smoky fire. On the cave wall
bisons stampeding south with spears in their sides,
taking with them the lost purpose
of our lives, leaving behind
a small pile of cold ashes
and a few cracked bones.

No one will have to ask—Who
am I? The stars will again shine down
on thin, clever, desperate companions,
reverent killers, moving wary
through the chill shadows and home will be
the word for anywhere.

HOWARD NEMEROV
1987

The Revised Version

The common curse forbidden to the young
When we were young—our grownups got it wrong,
Maybe from reading in a bad translation;

It wasn't so much a curse as an invitation
To the great world's permanent floating cocktail bash—
The scent, the smoke, the burning, and the ash.

A grownup in my turn I say the spell:
It isn't Go to Hell, it's Come to Hell.

KATHLEEN NORRIS
1989

The Sky Is Full of Blue
and Full of the Mind of God

for Odo Muggli, O.S.B.

A girl wrote that once
for me, in winter, in a school
at Minot Air Force Base.
A girl tall for her age,
with cornrows and a shy, gap-toothed smile.
She was lonely in North Dakota,
I think: for God, for trees,
warm weather, the soft cadences of Louisiana.
I think of her as the sky stretches tight
all around.

I'm at the Conoco on I-94, waiting for the eastbound bus.
Mass is not over: the towers of the monastery
give no sign that, deep in the church,
men in robes and chasubles
are playing at a serious game.

I feel like dancing on this
wooden porch: "Gotta get to you, baby,
been runnin' all over town."
The jukebox is wired to be heard outside
and I dance to keep warm,
my breath carried white on the breeze.

The sky stretches tight, a mandorla of cloud
around the sun. And now
Roy Orbison reaches for the stratosphere:
something about a blue angel.
It is the Sanctus; I know it; I'm ready.

NAOMI SHIHAB NYE
1984

No One Thinks of Tegucigalpa

No one thinks of Tegucigalpa, unless you are the man
at the Christmas party who sells weapons to Honduras
and smilingly bets on war. Or you have been there,
you wear the miles of markets like a cascading
undergarment beneath your calm white shirt, the slick
black tiles of the plazita, a girl coming early,
her little hum and bucket, to polish them. Near
the river, a toothless man kept parrots and monkeys
in his yard. *Por que?* He said, "Love."

No one wants to hear about Tegucigalpa because it
makes them feel like a catalogue of omissions.
Where is it? Now who? As if Houston were everything,
the sun comes up because Dallas exists—but if
you kept driving south, past Mexico's pointed peaks,
the grieving villages of Guatemala, you would reach
the city that climbs hills easily as mist, opening
its pink-lidded eye while the Peace Monument draws
a quiet breath. A boy stands all day skewering lean
squares of beef till the night hisses on his grill.
Where is it? At the end of the arm, so close I tap
the red roofs with my finger, the basket-seller
weaves a crib for my heart. Think of the countries
you have never seen, the cities of those countries,
start here, then ask: How bad is it to dress in a
cold room? How small your own wish for a parcel of
children? How remarkably invisible this tear?

ED OCHESTER
1994

Unreconstructed

When people talk about Form
distrust them.
These are the ones
who believe the starving
have themselves to blame
but that the sonnet
has a life of its own.
They believe in eagles,
two-headed kinds and
the one they've hunted
to near extinction.
They're headed for
a retirement villa
in the sky and don't
really want your kind
there, just as they didn't
want your kind here.
They believe in a human nature
which never changes (and don't
like ancient history either
since it's about different
human natures). Remember when
you were happiest? Remember
when you were first truly
sexually happy
(if you ever were)?
They say that's
just a pale reflection
of what's Real, they say
prepare yourself for death.

SHARON OLDS
1981

The Moment

When I saw the dark Egyptian stain,
I went down into the house to find you, Mother—
past the grandfather clock, with its huge
ochre moon, past the burnt
sienna woodwork, rubbed and glazed.
I went deeper and deeper down into the
body of the house, down below the
level of the earth. It must have been
the maid's day off, for I found you there
where I had never found you, by the wash tubs,
your hands thrust deep in soapy water,
and above your head, the blazing windows
at the surface of the ground.
You looked up from the iron sink,
a small haggard pretty woman
of 40, one week divorced.
"I've got my period, Mom," I said,
and saw your face abruptly break open and
glow with joy. "Baby," you said,
coming toward me, hands out and
covered with tiny delicate bubbles like seeds.

CAROLE SIMMONS OLES
1985

Maria Mitchell in the Great Beyond with Marilyn Monroe

What would my life have been with your face?
Once someone said I had good eyes. Mostly
on canvas, in photographs, I half turned away.
The camera, they say, was your most faithful lover.

  No one ever told me I was pretty when I was
  a little girl. All little girls should be told
  they're pretty, even if they aren't.

Little girls should hear the truth.
No one could make a beauty of me. I knew.
And Quaker Discipline decreed: "Be not conformed
to this world, but be ye transformed
by the renewing of your mind."
A child in my closet-size study, I hung a sign—
Maria is busy. Do not knock.

  When I was 8 my foster family made me wash
  every dish for 5 cents a month.

Dear child, how could fame repair such loss,
your mother's mind broken like her parents'
and brother's before. Though a woman, I
faltered when Mother's mind cast off from me.

  The same year, at the boardinghouse the nice
  man showed me a game, and when

248

I saw! They disbelieved, and you began to stammer.
What man on earth isn't selfish?
My sister died thankful never to have been naked
before her husband. I never married.
Come walk with me. Smell the ocean
and pick daphne, grapes, heart's ease.

Do you know how I got here? Three days before
at a party I wrote in the guest book
under Residence, *Nowhere.*

And now you live everywhere at once
whose ambition was to be men's earthly star.
Here are stars you can trust:
Sirius, Canopus, Arcturus, Vega, Capella,
Betelgeuse, Altair, Aldebaran.
Say these, Norma Jeane.
We are women learning together.

CAROLE SIMMONS OLES
1985

Maria's Ghost Addresses Hawthorne Concerning Chapter Five of *The Marble Faun*, in Which She Appears

"A needle is familiar to the fingers of them all. A queen, no doubt, plies it on occasion; the woman-poet can use it as adroitly as her pen; the woman's eyes, that has discovered a new star, turns from its glory to send the polished little instrument gleaming along the hem of her kerchief, or to darn a casual fray in her dress. The slender thread of silk or cotton keeps them united with the small, familiar, gentle interests of life, the continually operating influences of which do so much for the health of the character, and carry off what would otherwise be a dangerous accumulation of morbid sensibility.*** Methinks it is a token of healthy and gentle characteristics, when women of high thoughts and accomplishments love to sew; especially as they are never more at home with their own hearts than when so occupied."

Bosh, Mr. Hawthorne. The seam splits
and needs repair.
Yet I was honored to be present.
Amused, because I hate to sew.

But our "dangerous accumulation of morbid sensibility"?
Why did you sit before the fire,
volume of Thackeray open
in your lap, not reading it but
thereby keeping us from you?
In Rome your daughter Una
turned 16. We drank her health
(cold water) and you pronounced this
birthday wish: "May you live happily
and be ready to go when you must."

Why were you so inactive?
Always disappointed?—even
St. Peter's not grand enough.

Did you say "never more at home"
with our own hearts?
Better to ponder the spectroscope
than the pattern of a dress.
To crack geodes than match worsteds.
When I see a woman sew, I think of science.
When she puts an exquisite
fine needle exactly the same distance
from the last stitch as that
stands from the one before, I think
what capacity she has
for using a micrometer, graduating circles.
How she would be at home in stars.

You're right, it's academic
what with sewing machines,
machines to stitch the farthest sky
and even fabricate a novel.
But your attitude prevails
like mold that eats the Roman statues.
Please remember me to Mrs. Hawthorne.
I hope that her neuralgia's passed.

MARY OLIVER
1982

Howard

When the rescue trucks drove, red and clanging,
into our yard—*our* yard—
my grandmother leaned against the privet wailing:
What will the neighbors say? It was a bitter anger
squeaking out like that from a good woman who'd worked
all her life for the happiness of others—
and now, here was her youngest
daughter married to a pale and silent
disaster. My father
hauled him from the car and rode his ribs, hollering
for help, for God's mercy, for him to come back
and he didn't. My aunt
ran into the house weeping, and was forever altered.
I stood in the rain
frightened out of my wits. I could not look forward
into my life, to the year
I'd grow as old as he was then, though he wasn't
old, and holler
for him to come back. *Give us another chance!*
Let us ask you again, what's wrong? This time
we'll set it straight, we'll love you right, we'll
warm you! Once he drew for me
a picture of a band of Indians, thin
and muscular, on beautiful horses. I have it
still and it's still a letter in a strange language
I have no hope of learning, and I'm still
standing in the rain—the horizons
sucking inward upon the sorrow,

the inexplicable fact,
and nothing to hold them back
but an immense and universal pity
and the fury of the individual will.

ALICIA OSTRIKER
1986

Surviving

i
It is true that in this century
To survive is to be ashamed.
We want to lie down in the unmarked grave,
We want to feel the policeman's club that cracks
A person's head like a honey-melon, and lets
Human life spill like seeds, we want to go up
In milky smoke like a promise.
If we're women it's worse. The lost ones
Leach our strength even when we are dancing.
When we are working, there is that nameless
Weariness:
Lie down, lie down, a mule in a dusty ditch
The cart shattered into boards
Who can urge us to pull ourselves onward
How can the broken mothers teach us

It is true that when I encounter another
Story of a woman artist, a woman thinker
Who died in childbirth, I want to topple over
Sobbing, tearing my clothing.

ii
Soon the time will come when I don't
have to be ashamed and keep quiet
but feel with pride that I am a painter.
    —*Paula Modersöhn-Becker to her mother, July 1902*

A painting of a peasant woman's hands
As strong as planks, influenced by Cezanne

254

Who had struck her "like a thunderstorm, a great event,"
That first visit from Germany to Paris.
She was a raw girl, then,
But the thought was clear.
A coarse canvas of an orange, a lemon,
Local deep-red tomatoes, two fauve asters,
Globes and rays,
Designed like a reclining cross.
A naked woman and baby painted curled
On a mat, lacking a blanket, a portrait
Of what all skin remembers
And forgets.

I walked from painting to painting, I watched this woman's
Earth pigments growing thicker, more free,
More experimental,
Force augmented, it seemed, every year.
"The strength with which a subject
Is grasped, that's the beauty of art"
She wrote in her diary.
And she had resisted the marriage to Otto,
Had wished to remain in Paris
Painting like a Parisian, a modernist
But he had begged.
When they returned home, she knew herself
Already pregnant, delighted with pregnancy.

   iii
(*1876–1907*)
The little cards on the gallery wall
Explained the story.
Language is a form of malice.
Language declares: *Here is a dead thing.*
I cover it over with my thin blanket.
And here is another dead thing.
Please to notice, you soon can feel
Nothing. Not true: I feel beleaguered
Grief, in my chest and womb,
My throttled cry, nature is not our enemy,
Or the enemy is also the ally,

The father, the mother,
The powerful helpless hills
Where the pigment comes from.

I went from painting to painting, the photographs
Of my children in my wallet.
"I live the most intensely happy time of my life,"
She wrote her sister from Paris (1906).

iv

Only the paintings were not elegiac.
The paintings, survivors
Without malice—can it be?
Squeezed into me like a crowd
Into an elevator at 9 a.m. Pressing against each other,
Carrying their briefcases in one hand,
Pushing my buttons with the other,
Go ahead up, they said,
Carry us to our floors, our destinations,
Smoothly if you will, do not break down.
On the first floor
When the doors slid open
A child rested her chin on a city stoop
Among the giants.
There were many such scenes, viewed briefly.
At the forty-sixth floor, before
The doors could close, my mother
Rushed inside, carrying her shopping bags
And wearing her scuffed loafers.
Alone in the elevator
At the mercy of the elevator
So much space around her,
Four planes of polished aluminum,
Such indirect lighting,
Such clean and grinning chrome.
An entire blankness
And she was trusting it
To bear her down,
And she was talking, talking.

v
Today I got a big bargain
In chickens, she says, and a pretty big bargain
In skim milk. Skim milk's bluish
Like mother's milk. Did I ever tell you
I fought the doctors and nurses
The very day you were born. They said
"You'll stick a bottle in her mouth"
But I nursed you, I showed
Them. And did I tell you
When I was hungry because your father
Didn't have a job, I used to feed you
That beef puree, spoonful by spoonful
Until you would throw up.
Did I tell you that one.

Mother, a hundred times.

Did I tell you I was president
Of the literary society
When your father met me.
Did I tell you about the prize
I got for my poems.

Yes.

The checkout girl at the Shoprite
Tried to cheat me
Today but I caught her.
I told George but he was watching television.
He never pays attention, he pretends
He's deaf. Would you phone me
Saturday.

vi
So my mother should have been a writer. Her mother,
A Russian beauty, should have been a singer.
"She lost the bloom of her youth in the factories,"
My mother says, a formula sentence she often
Repeats, and her eyes fill up like paper cups.

It is seventy years later. Explain these tears.

No promise of help or safety, every promise of cruelty,
Impoverishment, that is our world. John Keats loved it,
Coughing bright red. Hart Crane, also, sank into it,
Like a penny the pig-white passenger throws
Into the oily water to watch the boys who will
Dive. Explain *St. Agnes' Eve*. Explain *The Bridge*.

Explain these tears.

   vii
We are running and skipping the blocks
To the Thomas Jefferson swimming pool
Where we'll both get in free
For the morning session,
You pretending to be my under-twelve
Elf-face sister, and when we've gone through
The echoing cavernous girls' locker rooms
Where underfed blondes shiver
Knock-kneed as skeletons, the waterdrops
Standing out on their skin like blisters,
And we're in the water
Green and chlorinous
Cool in the August day.
You hug me, mother, and we play
Diving under each other's legs
Until children collect around you like minnows
And you lead us in ring-a-rosy,

You get even the smallest ones to duck
Heads underwater, bubbling and giggling
Don't be afraid! Breathe out like this! Then we all sing
Songs against Hitler and the Japs.
I get to be closest. You're mine, I'm good.
We climb out, dripping on the tiles —
That bright day's faded. Today you are still running
As if you pushed a baby carriage
From a burning neighborhood.

viii
What woman doesn't die in childbirth
What child doesn't murder the mother
The stories are maps to nowhere

ix
A few flowers, two butterflies,
A screen of foliage green enough
To be purple, and herself,
Crude, nude to the waist
Fingers her amber beads, secretly
Smiling, like no man's wife.

x
Mother my poet, tiny harmless lady
Sad white-headed one
With your squirrel eyes
Your pleading love-me eyes
I have always loved you
And now you are nearly a doll
A little wind-up toy
That marches in a crooked circle
Emitting vibrations and clicks.
Mother, if what is lost
Is lost, there remains the duty
Proper to the survivor.
I ask the noble dead to strengthen me.
Mother, chatterer, I ask you also,
You who poured Tennyson
And Browning into my child ear, and you
Who threw a boxful of papers, your novel,
Down the incinerator
When you moved, when your new husband

Said to take only
What was necessary, and you took
Stacks of magazines, jars
Of buttons, trunks of raggy
Clothing, but not your writing.

Were you ashamed? Don't
Run away, tell me my duty,
I will try not to be deaf—
Tell me it is not merely the duty of grief.

ERIC PANKEY
1991

The Weekend Gardener

He stands in the garden and thinks as we all do
Of that first garden. The tumbled morning glories
Are shrouded, bound up, in a mess of spiderwebs.
The spider's nowhere to be found. The peonies
Sag a little, their leaves worn red at the edges.

He considers the word *misery*, the word *grief*
And wonders what deep-cut furrow separates them.
He is happy. He knows it. All his friends
Say of him, as if it were the truth, he's at home
In the garden, which he takes to mean the world.

LINDA PASTAN
1997

A Craving for Salt

Because I don't trust the future,
I look back over my shoulder
wherever I go, like one of those fish
with eyes at the back of its head, or an owl
who swivels its face around full circle.

And though the past is made up
of ordinary things, they smolder
in the heat of afterlight
until memory becomes longing,
as strong as a craving for salt.

Ask Lot's wife who knew
that what she left behind
was simply everything.

MICHAEL PETTIT
1992

Employment Alternatives

Zarco, L.A.'s Armenian king of garbage
is giving Watson a talking to,
a tongue lashing he'd better *by damn remember*,
curses cutting into smooth gray matter.
*No more accident! Keep you dumb brains
on business!* Watson wonders how.
Who could haul garbage without dreaming?
You've got to keep it distant,
like some little hostile village
the Air Force boys never see,
and no one else either when they're done.
So it was Flight Commander Watson
who rolled up lordly to them—
deep green dumpsters stamped HOLLYWOOD,
and sent them to oblivion.
And it was Grand Prix driver Watson
racing his big truck—steel arms out
to fend off this or that pastel wall,
this or that shredding eucalyptus,
flowering orange or lemon tree.
Motoring around the steep twisted hills,
Watson at the wheel is dangerous,
like, say, Bogart, had Bogie hit the skids
or never made it up. *This* isn't his
dream: this 5 A.M. coffee and donut,
this Armenian raving about Turks,
the high price of diesel fuel,
the long expensive scar Watson carved
into the black Jaguar on La Brea.
Zarco doesn't know he's talking to

a new talent, a huge talent, a talent
who lacks only recognition, the one break
that will slam the door for good
on this lousy, stinking life
you better by damn spend dreaming.

ALBERTO RÍOS
1988

Edith Piaf Dead

I have a young cousin who is fire.
Myself married, Edith
I would have given him to you.

I have seen the picture
The one always shown — she is
A glint in the pupil of an eye,
An eye, like this: we in the cheap seats
White, yellowish almost, garish
Lined against the blues and browns,
The evening wear of the monied.
Pupil, black center, the stage
Not yet lit.

Then she. A chip.
A nicking in the wood of a counter
Almost not worth the notice
So that one must see with full attention:
Stomach tightening, eyes getting hot
That way of a hard stare:
She is an imperfection
As a nick or a chip is a moment of pain:

Wood splinter caught under a nail,
A banged elbow, or a blouse caught
            By the hand of a man.

And then, you know. The pictures
Or the stories, you know:
That voice coming out like scarves

From a magician's sleeve
Finishing with the underwear, and laughs.
But then the hairs under that, and
The bone, the pubis, the mouth there
Singing too the same exact songs.
Loud.

I have dreams about you Edith Piaf.
How much I don't want to cry in my own life.
A voice comes out like scarves.

PATTIANN ROGERS
1986

Rolling Naked in the Morning Dew

Out among the wet grasses and wild barley-covered
Meadows, backside, frontside, through the white clover
And feather peabush, over spongy tussocks
And shaggy mane mushrooms, the abandoned nests
Of larks and bobolinks, face to face
With vole trails, snail niches, jelly
Slug eggs; or in a stone-walled garden, level
With the stemmed bulbs of orange and scarlet tulips,
Cricket carcasses, the bent blossoms of Sweet William,
Shoulder over shoulder, leg over leg, clear
To the ferny edge of the goldfish pond—some people
Believe in the rejuvenating powers of this act—naked
As a toad in the forest, belly and hips, thighs
And ankles drenched in the dew-filled gulches
Of oak leaves, in the soft fall beneath yellow birches,
All of the skin exposed directly to the *killy* cry
Of the kingbird, the buzzing of grasshopper sparrows,
Those calls merging with the dawn-red mists
Of crimson steeplebush, entering the bare body then
Not merely through the ears but through the skin
Of every naked person willing every event and potentiality
Of a damp transforming dawn to enter.

Lillie Langtry practiced it, when weather permitted,
Lying down naked every morning in the dew,
With all of her beauty believing the single petal
Of her white skin could absorb and assume
That radiating purity of liquid and light.
And I admit to believing myself, without question,
In the magical powers of dew on the cheeks

And breasts of Lilly Langtry believing devotedly
In the magical powers of early morning dew on the skin
Of her body lolling in purple beds of birdfoot violets,
Pink prairie mimosa. And I believe, without doubt,
In the mystery of the healing energy coming
From that wholehearted belief in the beneficent results
Of the good delights of the naked body rolling
And rolling through all the silked and sun-filled,
Dusky-winged, sheathed and sparkled, looped
And dizzied effluences of each dawn
Of the rolling earth.

Just consider how the mere idea of it alone
Has already caused me to sing and sing
This whole morning long.

LIZ ROSENBERG
1997

Crushed: Chapter Nine

Call it the Middlemarch syndrome. Certain young women fall in love with their professors. Perhaps we think it is the only way to gain knowledge. Perhaps we want to conquer knowledge itself; it may be the closest we can come to God. We don't realize what we are selling; we don't think we are selling anything. We are hungry for something, but is isn't sex, it isn't even romance. It may be that we have been trained too well; after all, we are bright and attentive. We are shiny, and like mirrors what we do best is to reflect. Perhaps the professor's brilliance will enter into us; like the moon, we will glow with his light. We forget that the male professor is human, that he has his vulnerabilities. We forget that talking about ideas is sexy. We are addicted to the intimacy of the closed office door. We are so tired of being the smartest person in the room, with no one to talk to, and nothing to do about it. We are greedy. We keep falling into the same trap over and over; we keep coming back for more. We are flattered and appalled when the man at last makes his move. We protest our innocence, and perhaps in a sense we are innocent—which is not the same thing, one finally learns, as ignorant.

We tell ourselves to stop, to be alert. We only become childlike again, convince ourselves that this time it *is* innocent. And there is no end to this misery, this desire, this humiliation, this grandiosity, this way of believing that we only matter because we are young and pretty.

HILLEL SCHWARTZ
1987

All Be Riders

Lummox, I was the first to call him lummox, lummox,
savoring the word. Some words you savor
for themselves, some for the moment they were shaped for.
I loved his being there for the right word as I
was there to name him for what he was,
so his hunch and stoop, his ponderousness were so
perfect that I could not help but perfect
him by shouting down the schoolhall at him
lummox, lummox, lummox.

Balance: what was missing of course was balance.
Rising from seats he would topple as if rising
had no business with the human, as if he had
wanted concessions from gravity but was found wanting,
large but undisclosed, a body with too many larger
desires, appetites. Stumbling, constantly bruised, he desired
anonymity, which I could not abide, the anonymous
too close to infancy and death for me to warm to.
I'd seen the huge worn Portuguese tombs of children, and I
knew their weight was less mass than will. He knew
that however he moved, things moved against him, like *that*,
instantly, while others seemed so adept and able, instance
after instance, to elude the crush and fumble of things.

                                              After
one solid month, the name caught on and someone
somewhere would always be chanting lummox wherever
he was, laughing lummox, giggling lummox, he he he
you old lummox. He would nod, agreeing with you,
trying on the word one more time like a young child trying

hard to please in new clothing in the hard
light of dressing rooms, mother testing for lightness
of material, for fit at cuff and crotch. What are you made of,
lummox? my friends asked. How'd you get to be such a lummox?

Years later, going through those junior high school years
at a reunion of sorts, asking where people were at,
I learned that he'd been in a crash, lost both eyes,
could no longer hear well but was happy. Could
you believe it? an old friend asked. What if you
were blind and deaf and a born lummox to boot?

                                                        Were
this story over, I'd know something polite to say about this,
or how to avoid saying anything much at all, or
where to look for an apt allusion, a turn of phrase. Where
he is now, I bump against him at every turn, and he
thumps at my shoulders in the bath, in the hall, in bed, thumping
there and there the leather saddle I had not known was there,
and pulls himself heavily up onto my shoulders and
rides me from the Algarve to Los Angeles, rides
me across braille canyons, coaxing and calling me
Oxeye, his white mount with the yellow mane: Oxeye,
my little one, *meu padrinho*, my godfather, my
good friend, keep moving, keep moving, it is all to the good.

MAUREEN SEATON & DENISE DUHAMEL
1997

Exquisite Incumbent

I'm here like a wife you've grown used to—
you like her casseroles, her dumb blonde jokes.
I'll never forget the secret entrance to the wine cellars,
how all along the way were footprints of past presidents.
Remember when Richard Nixon wore black socks
on the beach? Big mistake. I try to avoid caffeine and weak handshakes,
but I'm often lulled by my hopeless popularity,
the time it takes to call my limo to meet me at the back door.
I've held so many babies I feel like a nanny who wants to retire.
My smile is measured not to show too much gum.
Every tooth I've kept is a memorial to every unselfish political act,
every time I've asked myself: What about my country?
Then I feel bad about hearing the word "cunt"
inside country. I'm a pimp of my own people,
a ghostly duplicate of G.W. as he crossed the Delaware
in search of one more vote, one more chance to win.
I'm Henry VIII waiting for his own beheading.
Fix me a good stiff drink—I'll need it
as I study the graphs, the big chunk of voters
leaning towards the new kid on the block,
the new boy from California with his sun-drenched hair,
his cool three-wheeler and the tribal tattoo.
As an incumbent, it's not a good idea for me to endorse anything
though there'll be the book deal and speaking tour
if this doesn't work out. Like Stephen King I'll only read
at independent bookstores. Or I'll sell stuff on TV
like Joe Namath or Joe Garagiola. I'd like to open my own restaurant
and serve all the foods they made fun of me for eating—

seaweed, ovaltine, beef marrow sucked right from the bone.
Que sera sera, my fellow Americans.
When I was just a little boy, I asked my mother nothing
and went ahead, up ladders, over rooftops, and look where I am.

DAVE SMITH
1980

The Pornography Box

At eighteen, the U.S. Navy eye-chart
memorized, reciting what was unseen,
my father enlisted for the duration.
At nineteen he caught a casual wave
wrong off Norfolk, our home, called
Hell by sailors. The landing craft
cast him loose and burst his knee.
He lived, and wore his rigid brace
without complaint, and never in his
life showed anyone his Purple Heart.
I stumbled into that brace and more
when I climbed to our sealed attic
the year a drunk blindsided him
to death in a ditch, and me to worse.

Today I watch my ten-year-old son race
over the slick pages of *Playboy*,
ashamed I brought it home, imagining
his unasked questions have answers.
I remember the chairs I stacked
and climbed, the brace I put on
to see how it felt and, buried
deep in his sea chest, the livid
shapes shoved so far in a slit
of darkness a man could reach them
only hunched, on all fours. I clawed
through families of discharged clothes,
ornaments for Christmas, to feel
the spooky silk of webs slickly
part on my face where blood rushed.

Trussed on their wide bed, my mother lay
surviving wreckage, stitched back
beyond the secrets I knew he kept.
I shimmied through a dark hole
in the ceiling and listened to pine
rake the roof like a man's shuffle.
But he was dead and the box unlocked.
His flashlight pulsed through my body,
each glossy pose burning my eyes
that knew only air-brush innocence.
Sex rose in me like a first beard.
A woman with painted nails peeled
a foreskin, another held a man
kingly rigid at her tongue's tip.
I could not catch my breath.

I blinked at one spread on a table covered
by lace grandmotherly clean and white.
Here might have been service for tea,
dainty cups, bread, a butter dish
except she was in their place, clearly
young in middy suit. Behind her a vase
of daisies loomed, the parlor wall
held *Home, Sweet Home* in needlepoint,
and curtains were luminous at a window.
I remember the eyes, direct and flat,
as if she had died. Girlish stockings
knuckled at her knees, her plain skirt
neatly rolled. The man, in Victorian
suit, cradled her calves in furred hands,
and looked at the window, placid as
a navigator. He cut her like a knife.

After school, at night, weekend afternoons,
I raced to see them do it, legs cramped
in that freezing slot of darkness, gone
wobbly as a sailor into the country.
I came and went in the black tube,
ashamed, rooting like a hog to see.
In one sequence a black man held a pool

cue to a white woman, a black woman
held in both hands white and black balls.
The uniforms of sailors were scattered,
wadded everywhere I looked. I smelled
the mothballs from my father's chest
when late at night I woke to vomit
and stare at a clock's one-eyed glow.

How long does it go on, the throbbing dream,
waking obsessed with a hole in the air?
In Norfolk, from loaded cars, we spilled
at sailors passing alleys, asking where
we'd find some girls, beer, a good time.
All answers were sucker punched. *By-bye,
Seafood*, we screamed, then headed down
toward the Gaiety Theater and whores
bright as moths. We spit at mothers who
yelled *Fuck you, kid!* They never would.
The secrets of our fathers, we cruised
the hopeless streets blank as razors,
remembering nothing but naked images
whose neon flavored like pus. Seeing now
my son bent to see I imagine at last

my father climbing before me in blackness,
with the tiny light a man carries, bent
on pained knees where I will kneel also
at nameless images we each live to love
and fear. One is a young Spanish dancer
whose crinolines flare out around her
hidden rose. Another cooks in highheels.
Among these are angels, blonde sisters,
classmates suddenly gone from our towns,
one on a piano reclined, her long leg
crooked in invitation. She does not hide
the shorter leg. Each grins and burns
into our memory, speaking in shy whispers,
who are born to teach us violations.
At eighteen what fathers teach is wrong,

for the world is wrong, and only women
know why, their eyes dark and flat.

It isn't eyes that sons remember, blinded
by what never lies or leaves, but
sun's glint on that raw breast, that
thigh where face should not be but is,
and is the curve of the world's flesh
radiant in its rottenness, the secret
that leaves finally apart and other
all who walk on the earth. In memory
I see how each breast, each leg, each
face hissed our shame. By accident
I became the boy-father of the house,
owner of obscenities and a family
of creeps who fingered me as one.
What else is the world but a box,
false-bottomed, where the ugly truths
wait sailing in the skins of ancestors?

Escaping them at last I left for college.
But first climbed to what he left me,
carted that box and brace to grave,
and spilled those mild faces down
under the looming Baptist spire.
I spread gasoline where he lay, then
with his Navy Zippo snapped it off.
Quick bodies coiled and flamed, ash
flecks disappearing in sun forever.
I gouged the remains in a trench
of churchly dirt, tried once to spit,
then turned in the dark to catch a bus.
His pea-coat was black as the sea
at midnight but I took it and wore it
sweating against the cold to come.
Women smiled at me as if I'd been flush
with cash from months at sea. *Welcome,
Swabby*, one said, *You can sit by me.*
I was free, I thought, discharged from

Hell into the world that, for Christ's
sake, waited. I left home in a wink.
And would not go back at Christmas,
being after all busy, being holed up
with the nameless girl, the long blade
of her body even now slicing memory,
that darling who took my coat. But
by Easter was ready, went. House sold,
mother gone, maybe married, maybe Florida,
they said. I wandered in a cold sea-wind,
almost on shore leave, until I came
cast up where my father lay. Posters

of the nailed Jesus littered the grass,
announcing our inexplicable life. I saw
the crones kneeled there in sunbursts,
faceless, soft, as if to serve the sun
dying in the background. I shivered,
then rose up, hearing traffic hiss,
and walked until I found the old road.
I wished I had our goddamn stolen coat.
Boys yelled at me, but no one stopped.
Freed, I was myself. Who understands?
I walked hours in hard places, into night,
my first beard tingling, dreaming what
fathers know. I came to a seedy house.
Among sailors I, a man, heard the siren
call us forward to sit with the darkness
under reels of lighted, loving women.
At love's edge, braced, we were nineteen.

So we did.

GARY SOTO
1994

Chisme at Rivera's Studio

Siqueiros used a machine gun on Rivera's studio,
And Diego, I guess, ran his hands through his hair.
He didn't eat for two days.
He trudged his elephant weight around the patio
And waited for Frida,
Busy primping her eyebrow,
Busy wiggling her underwear into place,
Busy with a stiff brush and her bluish wounds,
Busy blowing smoke into the face of her clapping monkey.

And Rivera, I guess, tightened his belt.
He scolded Trotsky,
Poor guy who in the end crumpled under a knife,
Just as he was sitting down to lunch
Or was it a long letter to Russia?
Imagine this:
Rivera with his bad back,
Trotsky with his bleeding fountain pen,
These two greats, and now me, little piss ant,
Crawling through the studio in San Angel.

This was Mexico in the '30s,
With rain pelting the bellies of frolicking dogs,
With the president toasting dead colonels,
With Fords squashing the juicy life out of fruitstands.

This is me in the '90s.
Me and a buddy touching the walls
Where Frida leaned and said, Fuck off, America.
Maybe she laughed with smoke in both nostrils.

Maybe she touched her one eyebrow,
Maybe she went outside, cigarette lit,
And watched pine trees bleed the moon with their needles.
They were beautifully crazy as they howled
At each other from various beds.

I've never known anyone famous.
I've never known a singer
Or an actress with tears twisted into her handkerchief.
I've never known anyone on television,
Or even a barber humming "Dos Arbolitos."
I've only known my famous aunt,
Who could cha-cha-cha with a glass of water
On her head.
I'm wild crawling through Diego and Frida's studio.
Art happened here, and love, I guess.
I sneeze the dust of years, swallowing
My chewing gum when I look up at the skylight.

I drink water and crush my paper cup.
I remember the Spanish verb "to touch."
I touch the rope that keeps me
From the wheelchair where Frida sat,
A lasso of cigarette smoke in her hair,
Dead of light for thirty years.
The floor creaks. Voices carry to the second floor,
And I have nothing to carry home but two postcards.
I'm going to lean against the wall,
And rub fame and dirt into my peasant shoulders.

MARCIA SOUTHWICK
1993

Agatha's Butterfly

based on Agatha Christie's autobiography

Mosquitos slept on the mauve walls
of our hotel bedroom, and my brother said,
"Chimneys in Paris are quite different

from chimneys in England."
I was homesick for our raspberry garden
and the cake with sugar icing and four candles:

a red spider scurrying across my plate,
and mother saying, "It's a lucky spider, Agatha,
a lucky spider for your birthday."

We moved and I practiced my French:
un chien, une maison,
un gendarme, le boulanger,

and my brother told me that French babies
come in a doctor's black bag
whereas English babies are brought by the angels.

At first I was bored.
I cut pictures out of old magazines and pasted them
into scrapbooks of brown paper.

Then I bit my brother's finger
and realized I'd never have what I wanted most:
naturally curly hair, brown eyes, and the title of Lady Agatha.

We played the game of schoolmaster,
and I'd shout: "What year was the needle invented?
Who was Henry VIII's third wife? What are the diseases of wheat?"

One day the horses arrived and we zigzagged
up a path as the guide picked daisies
for me to put in my hatband. He caught a butterfly

and pinned it to my hat. *"Pour la petite mademoiselle,"*
he said. Oh the horror of that moment!
The wings still fluttered. I wept and couldn't stop.

I'd been thinking all day about the dollhouse furniture,
left at home, and the miniature family
with porcelain heads and sawdust limbs.

Mother had fixed with glue
a small black beard and mustache
to the face of the father, but none of that mattered now.

I wanted to disappear—
just like the cat I'd seen that morning:
it walked between wine glasses on a cafe table,

and without breaking a thing, curled up
and fell asleep, suddenly invisible, its white fur
blending into the white linen cloth.

It's the way sometimes, walking in the woods,
I'll say, "This is Agatha talking to herself."
Then I'll see a story unfolding.

I'll know exactly what Maud will say to Aylwin,
just where the stranger will be standing,
and how the dead pheasant figures in, causing Maud

to think of an incident long forgotten.
I'll rush home to the empty page, feeling almost invisible,
like the white cat. And the words will all be *there.*

It started that day as I wept and wept. I said to myself:
"This is Agatha riding a horse, a flapping butterfly pinned to her hat" —
as if Agatha were someone else. And the weeping stopped.

RUTH STONE
1997

Yes, Think

Mother, said a small tomato caterpillar to a wasp,
why are you kissing me so hard on my back?
You'll see, said the industrious wasp, deftly inserting
a package of her eggs under the small caterpillar's skin.
Every day the small caterpillar ate and ate the delicious
tomato leaves. I am surely getting larger, it said to itself.
This was a sad miscalculation. The ravenous hatched
wasp worms were getting larger. o world, the small
caterpillar said, you were so beautiful. I am only a small
tomato caterpillar, made to eat the good tomato leaves.
Now I am so tired. And I am getting even smaller. Nature
smiled. Never mind, dear, she said. You are a lovely link
in the great chain of being. Think how lucky it is to be born.

STEPHANIE STRICKLAND
1987

On First Looking into Diringer's *The Alphabet: A Key to the History of Mankind*

I wanted . . . a *Guneaform*—a woman's form—of writing
and thought, perhaps, Cuneiform it, so tactile that script, palpable
wedges pressed in wet clay: writing "at once," as a fresco

is painted. But in this book, in the pictographs
that underlie Cuneiform, there is only one sign for woman,
pudendum. Slavegirl and male servant, also

given by genital description.
Man is head, with mouth in it, plus beard.
I thought apart from Diringer's claim, *origin* of alphabets,

this script is just one instance. Hieroglyphic
determinatives for man and woman in Egypt look more
matched, both stickfigure-like, both kneeling on one shin—Except

the woman has longer hair, no arms, no *difference* between
first- and second-person-singular. How quietly here ancient grammar
     states
what our marital law, or canon teaching on abortion, legislates:

"I am—not only yours—but you."
I began to wonder whether, somewhere in the world, different
thinking existed. Flipping through the book,

I was struck by Chinese trigrams, their elegant
abstraction: just three lines
above each other meant, the footnote said, sky and dry and prime

and creative: grandfather-life. Slashed, into six
little lines, the sign meant secondarily
and destruction, and foreboding, and grandmother, and earth.

Later Chinese for man, an upright stroke, hook rising to the left.
For woman, a buckling crook, large bundle at the shoulder.
Woman, next to woman, meaning quarrel—

and man, next to word, meaning *true*.
I did find toward the end one group of people, the Yao
or Miao, or Miao-tzu tribe, called

by the Chinese "wild Southern barbarians."
Fifty thousand in Vietnam and Laos before our war.
The Yao had, I found nowhere else, four

different signs of *equal* complication:
mother, father, person, heart
—but as I said, wiped out.

TERESE SVOBODA
1985

As told to me

This year alone over fifty
head of cattle were found
dead of strange mutilations.
Locals fear an invasion
from space.
—Kansas City Star

She banked the pickup nose to nose
with another half-grey hulk but
did not get out, just set the lights

low and yellow, just smiled.
Her hair stood from her head as
well-turned as a Texas cheerleader

but she kissed as if her cups cut.
Back at the cafe, he'd wondered
what they did in these towns.

Could take you on a tour,
she'd purred. Now, heaving him
off her, she slid out the door

into the ring of pickups. A peacock
advanced; she screamed with it.
Other women arrived, bending

in unison, looking like fungus
in their downfilled jackets,
leading a big animal. *What*

the hell? He thought he'd leave
but she had the keys. He could
only pop the locks down when

he saw her take something long and wet
into her lap, staining herself
as if from some overturned meal.

KAREN SWENSON
1983

I Have Lost the Address of My Country

"I have lost the address of my country,"
my friend says, her voice soft in her mouth
as barefoot dust on the streets of Persepolis and Bam—
dust baked to the hard bricks of old mosques.

In a bar in Indiana I watch
the square guarded by lupin spires of minarets
boil with a mass like krill before the jaws of a whale.
"I have lost the address of my country."

The night after the women strike,
burn their chadors, their black winding clothes,
we talk half the night our voices hard
as dust baked to the bricks of old mosques.

I've had no address for a year but car and suitcase
knowing only road, a typewriter ribbon
spilled out over mountain and plain,
trying to find the address of my self's country.

And I've felt my life blown, tumbleweed
before headlights in Wyoming or dust off the Colorado flats
and I have feared that I will be
dust baked to the hard bricks of old mosques.

I come home to hear her voice gentle
as the eroded profiles of Persepolis whose 6,000 years of
dust is baked to the hard bricks of old mosques,
"I have lost the address of my country."

RICHARD TAYSON
1995

First Sex

When we found your father's *Playboys,*
we went into your room and touched
the glossy tanned breasts of the naked
woman on the beach, you pressed
her unblemished skin against the milk-
white flesh of your twelve-year-old
body, I kissed my virginal
lips to your lips, and your father
walked in. I don't remember, now,
who had his pants down or who was
lying like a seed in the center
of the photos leafed around him,
all I remember is your father
stood in the doorway, shapely
as God, bearded, big-stomached, right
fist clenched, he wanted to eat us.
Yes, I tell you, fathers eat their sons.
I closed my eyes and waited for him to
tear away my best friend's leg or
carve a rib bone from his
untouched chest, I heard
the voice of my father:
Are you a girl? Do you know what evil
is? Are you a girl?
Are you? But my body proved I was
not a girl, if God
was about to send the flood
waters up over us, I must be
Satan, the spermatozoa hatching like
polliwogs in the twin fishbowls

of my testicles, and the kiss
I wanted even then, the work of Satan.
Your father began yelling in his deep
male voice, the earth of your room
shook, I
opened my eyes and thought he would
hit us with the bed or
bury us beneath a wall or two,
but he gave us one final look
which branded us for life and slammed
the door behind him: we were forever
separate from God, father, son, holy
spirit, we faced each other
in the dark and entered manhood.

CHASE TWICHELL
1980

Three Dreams of Disaster

A bank of cumulonimbus,
strangely colored, above trees.
A mountain in semi-darkness,
stony, through binoculars.
Someone said,
"Look up, where the dogs are looking."
The dogs ran ahead, diminutive in the lenses,
into a place without oxygen,
void of life and perfectly beautiful.

The sea sucked all its water away,
forsaking its billion shuddering fish
and the hopeless octopus heaving
in unnatural gravity.
Shellfish colonies dried, losing their colors.
The sea betrayed its mysteries,
and gave up its favors to anyone.
On the cliffs, a liar told the crowds
a convincing theory of physics.

It was the season for falling stars.
Even so, too many cars with open doors
were stopped on a back road, on a clear night.
Stars were falling. But why such silence,
why quiet the children? Then we drowned
in the cold thrill of science fiction.
It was exquisite, the white dust blown
from a whole portion of the sky
while we felt nothing, and nothing else changed.

REETIKA VAZIRANI
1996

Star Reader—Palm Reader

At Central Library in Bombay, my eldest cousin
Shyam was sifting through a stack of post-
colonial books on manufacturing, the best
technique for polishing plastic beads
(ongoing research for the Geeta Gem Factory).
But he was dying to read the astrology guides;
and, fixing his eyes on a chart, some dim star,
he began speaking to me of a family curse.
Every eldest daughter's eldest daughter
suffered from it: Nani Kadam, Savatri,
now Harmeen: not one could retain her husband.
There was polio, suicide, now divorce.

But I was the *second* daughter of an eldest one,
I was not pursuing marriage. "Don't mind it,"
he said. "Give the day and minute you were born.
Quick, the birth certificate."
                                    It was abroad.
So he hit my hand and said, "Show me—"

"Good," he said, "you'll be celibate, disease
will be fairly minor and you'll be rich
for several years. This is not bad fate."
Then he put away the books and led me through
the city's glittering streets to celebrate.

REETIKA VAZIRANI
1996

White Elephants

New to us: White Elephant Sale ads
and friends who'd never seen an elephant
except at the zoo, never seen one dance
at the market or loiter in a field.
They didn't know that if a boy tells a girl
she walks like an elephant, it means she
lured him with her sophisticated gait.
Now, when asked about India, I show
the garlanded creatures on the record stand,
an array of sandalwood carved by hand
in Mysore, a whole tusk in a chip of ivory,
the mother with her thick trunk raised
and the calves running after as if they
lead a pilgrimage or a parade.

KAREN VOLKMAN
1992

The Pregnant Lady Playing Tennis

The pregnant lady playing tennis
bobs on her toes at the court's left side,
raises the green ball high, and sets it

spinning. Then moving in circles
of deliberate size, she returns the lob
with the same giddy grace. In the quiet glide

of the lady playing tennis,
there's a knowledge of speeds and angles,
arcs and aims. From the other courts,

the players watch, dismayed, half-fearing
for the safety of the lady playing tennis,
half-wishing this odd distraction shut away.

Tennis, they notice, is a dangerous game.
But the ovals close
on the lady playing tennis, as if

the tight-knit mesh of her racket
were a magnet, with the ball
a perfect pole veering home. Watching

each hard-shot lob clear the net,
the pregnant lady playing tennis
braces in the pure sensation of her game,

in her body's stretch and haul, and plants
a crazy slam past the net: past the lines,
past the out zone, past the court's steel network wall.

DAVID WAGONER
1983

Peacock Display

He approaches her, trailing his whole fortune,
Perfectly cocksure, and suddenly spreads
The huge fan of his tail for her amazement.

Each turquoise and purple, black-horned, walleyed quill
Comes quivering forward, an amphitheatric shell
For his most fortunate audience: her alone.

He plumes himself. He shakes his brassily gold
Wings and rump in a dance, lifting his claws
Stiff-legged under the great bulge of his breast.

And she strolls calmly away, pecking and pausing,
Not watching him, astonished to discover
All these seeds spread just for her in the dirt.

DIANE WAKOSKI
1987

Sailor's Daughter

for Edward Abbey

Each summer morning in Michigan
in my cool air-conditioned apartment
I pad around closing curtains
against heat and light,
then check each plant for moisture
            —the ferns always have a drink—
then, go out on my tiny balcony where the sun
is beating on my tomatoes
and the sweet basil is pungently thrusting its fat leaves into the light.
I fill my watering cans several times. Drop
by drop, I water the babies just sprouting or the repotted anthuriums,
then deluge the sweet peas and marigolds.
The pansies (pensees) blink at me;
the Colorado Spruce,
a poor ragged thing, always slurps up a gallon or two.

And the first thing I drink (friends will tell you this)
                              each morning
is a goblet of icy tap water
with a golden slice of lemon floating
in it
and a sprig of fresh mint from
the porch garden.

This Westerner who loves the desert
loves water more. Yet, I too, Mr. Abbey,
appreciate those stoney, bare

waterless islands,
and the miles and miles of alkalai wastes.
Perhaps that is where I learned the preciousness of language,
each word, a drop, refreshing silence;

I, daughter of a pillar of salt,
lamenting a past I never had;
I, sailor's daughter, afraid of water, parched,
burnishing her salty, salty tongue.

RONALD WALLACE
1988

The Hell Mural

Iri and Toshi Maruki are painting the bomb.
Their painting, they say, will comfort the souls of the dead
in Hiroshima, Nagasaki, Belsen, Dachau, and Vietnam.

Because Hitler and Truman and Nixon with such aplomb
could order the deaths of millions, then go to bed,
Iri and Toshi Maruki are painting the bomb.

They draw in bees and maggots, and then go on—
a nipple here, a finger there, a head—
to Hiroshima, Nagasaki, Belsen, Dachau, and Vietnam.

Birds, cats, naked men and women spawn
on the floor in their mural, burning—the beautiful dead
of Iri and Toshi Maruki's painting, the bomb.

They paint with kindness and beauty, as if that song
must be sung, that corpse embraced, those right words said:
Hiroshima, Nagasaki, Belsen, Dachau, and Vietnam.

All history's heroes are here to be walked upon,
and *we* are here, beneath their brushstrokes' tread.
In Iri and Toshi Maruki's painting, the bomb
is Hiroshima, Nagasaki, Belsen, Dachau, and Vietnam.

BRUCE WEIGL
1988

The Way of Tet

Year of the monkey, year of the human wave,
the people smuggled weapons in caskets through the city
in long processions undisturbed
and buried them in Saigon graveyards.
At the feet of their small Buddhas
weary bargirls burned incense
before the boy soldiers arrived
to buy them tea and touch them
where they pleased. Twenty years
and the feel of a girl's body
so young there's no hair
is like a dream, but living is a darker thing,
the iron burning bee who drains the honey,
and he remembers her
twisting in what evening
light broke into the small room in the shack
in the labyrinth of shacks
in the alley where the lost and corrupted kept house.
He undressed her for the last time,
each piece of clothing
a sacrifice she surrendered to the war
the way of the world had become.
Tomorrow the blood would run in every province;
tomorrow the people would rise from tunnels everywhere
and resurrect something ancient from inside them,
and the boy who came ten thousand miles to touch her
small self lies beside the girl whose words he can't understand,

their song a veil between them.
She is a white bird in the bamboo, fluttering.

She is so small he imagines
he could hold all of her
in his hands and lift her to the black
sky beyond the illumination round's white light
where she would fly away from her life
and the wounds from the lovers would heal,
the broken skin grown back.
Bue he need only touch her, only
lift the blanket from her shoulders
and the automatic shape of love unfolds,
the flare's light burning down on them, lost
in a wave that arrives
after a thousand years of grief
at their hearts.

JAMES L. WHITE
1982

The Deaf Crone

I live alone like a fable, and
deaf as a two-by-four. The only thing
I ever hear is the constant rush of a waterfall
which is the working in my head.

When I was young they taught me to sign
at the state school and got me a job in the bakery.
I showed the girls words I liked: "beard", "angel",
"mother to this child", and "love". They nick-named me
Dummy. Signing fell away when I got older. For
me my life was more than a sleight of hand.

Now I love to watch T.V. and make up
my own stories. My favorite is a dead
movie star who wears a flight jacket and a white scarf
high in the mountains or people who kiss on the screen
late at night. This is when I kneel and join them.

You call this lonely, but I tell you it's
times like these I hear something nearly like music
above the rushing water. An "O" sound very high and out
of reach. This is my way of pushing through the night,
more harmless than what others may choose. Then I
sleep more quietly in the rushing water, the high singing "O"
and creaking bones of my mind.

PETER WILD
1984

Lies Between Fires

These cottonwoods strung out in winter
are what save nobody's wild horses
Al tells me. They approach carefully,
step by step across the snow,
rejected lovers turned buliminous
    who finding wilder lovers
rush in to sink their teeth deep into the trunks—
are what saved his own people once
    rushing in behind them, men and women
  feasting on the crumbs,
And so they dance now in thanks,
    a miracle of leaves growing from their ears,
        from their brown inappropriate thumbs,
or so he tells me as we jump over the tailgate,
    one race covered with soot, after the hour
  of gesturing through an obscene story about a fox
    to his enemy the laughing Navajo
    who won't speak English,
    knowing I'm as much a liar as he is,

Knowing what I really want, his kachina.
  So night after night waiting between fires
    he's got to tell me the whole story,
story after story, how covering himself with pollen
  he hacked this chunk from a riverbed with an axe,
    as if I were some hungry anthropologist,
  his back turned, hiding the work,
    then one day down at the toolshed
  performing some trick, flashes
  the little god at me in his open palm,

grinning at the universe with its wooden teeth,
a tuft of real Hopi hair
in its ear, he winks.
Take it, he says, understanding
everything. Think the right thoughts.
Make it walk.

ELEANOR WILNER
1995

Facing into It

for Larry Levis

So it is here, then, after so long, and after all—
as the light turns in the leaves in the old golden
way of fall,
        as the small beasts dig to the place
at the roots where survival waits, cowardly crouching
in the dark,
        as the branches begin to stretch into winter,
freed of their cheerful burden of green, then

        it comes home, the flea-ridden bitch of desolation,
a thin dog with its ribs exposed like a lesson
in mathematics, in subtraction; it comes home, to find its bowl
empty—then the numberless
things for which to be grateful dissolve
like the steam from a fire just doused with water
on a day of overcast grays, a wash
of colors dull to begin with, then thinned
by a cold slanting rain—
        it is October, that season when Death
goes public, costumed, when the talking heads
on the TV screen float up smiling at the terrible
news, their skin alight with the same strange glow
fish give off when they have been dead a week or more,
as the gas company adds odor for warning
that the lines may be leaking, the smell of disaster
hanging, invisible, in the air, a moment
before you strike the match—

it is then, brother, that I think of you, of your Caravaggio,
of the head of Goliath swung by its hair,
wearing the artist's own weary expression;
his head, exhausted of everything but its desire
for that beautiful David he used to be; and I think
of all the boys walking the streets
each carrying the severed head of the man
he will become—and the way I bear it is
to think of you, grinning, riding high in the cart leaving
the scene, a pair of huge horses hauling the wagon,
a fine mist rising from their damp shoulders,
unconcerned with what hangs, nailed
to the museum walls—luckily
the fall of Icarus has nothing to do with them,
nor the ruined Goliath who fell like a forest,
nor the wretched Salomes with their blood-splattered
platters, nor the huge stone griffins sobbing
at the gates of Valhalla as the litters are carried past . . .

the dark eyes of the horses are opaque with wisdom,
their hoofs strike the pavements with such a musical decision,
the derisive curl of their lips is so like the mysterious
smile on the angel at Chartres, on Kuan Yin, on the dolphin,
as they pull the cart safe through the blizzards
of Main St., the snow slowly swallowing the signs
though the crossing light beckons—
a soft glowing green like some spectral Eden
in the blank white swirl of the storm.

The stallion neighs once, sends a warm cloud
of breath into the snow-filled air,
and the mare isn't scared yet—at least
she's still pulling. There's a barn out there
somewhere, as they plow through the light's
yellow aura of caution, its warm glow
foretelling what hides in the storm:
a stall full of gold, where the soul—
that magician—can wallow
and winter in straw.

DAVID WOJAHN
1987

After

(Hurricane Gloria)

Below the hotel cocktail lounge TV
    the power crew in yellow Sou'westers
        sip Kamikazees under potted ferns beside him,
screen bristling static—sea water charging

through a condo window, a table
    set with daisies, breakfast dishes,
        suddenly upturned and floating,
destruction so voluptuous

it's broadcast twice. When he goes upstairs
    to their room, window taped with gray
        colossal xs, she's finally asleep
and he finds his place in Book Ten,

the speech, triumphant, of Satan to his minions,
    who with him transform into a vast
        arena of snakes, seething across
the plains of Pandemonium, a blind man's vision,

creation as opera. And the first sad couple
    averting their eyes from the burning
        sword. From sleep she speaks in prose,
and after this week of arguing separation,

he does not wake her to make love.
    After the frieze of wedding photos,
        her brother, anorexic, and his plumb bride
smearing icing in each other's face,

the country club and its guttering
    cathedral of candles, she told him that
        she wept because she now saw marriage
in all its stammering clarity. Beyond

the picture window, a powerline dangled
    broken white light on the roadside.
        On the beach, a pair of red sneakers
lodged in the bough of an elm. They walked there

scarcely talking, she holding up
    her blue satin hem; he, a little drunk,
        barefoot in evening clothes,
two wax figures, shabby in the damaged

evening light. Nothing epic here—this couple
    vaguely comic, already dividing the silver,
        the furniture, wading in a stream sluicing
brackish to the Sound. *I still don't know,*

she's saying, *what it is I have to do.*

Contributors

PROSE

Tony Ardizzone's most recent book is the novel *In the Garden of Papa Santuzzu* (Picador-St Martin's, 1999).

Tony Cade Bambara published the short-story collections *Gorilla, My Love* (1972) and *The Sea Birds Are Still Alive* (1977), as well as the novels *The Salt Eaters* (1980) and *If Blessing Comes* (1987). She edited and contributed to *The Black Woman: An Anthology* (1970) and to *Tales and Stories for Black Folks* (1971). She also collaborated on several television documentaries.

Lan Samantha Chang's story "The Eve of the Spirit Festival" was published in *Hunger: A Novella and Stories* (Norton, 1998) which won a California Book Award and the BABRA Award in addition to being a finalist for the *Los Angeles Times* Art Seidenbaum Award. Chang is an Alfred Hodder Fellow in the Humanities at Princeton University.

Ron Hansen is the author of the novels *Atticus, Mariette in Ecstasy, The Assassination of Jesse James by the Coward Robert Ford,* and *Desperadoes,* and of the short story collection *Nebraska* for which he received an Award in Literature from the American Academy and Institute of Arts and Letters. His novel, *Hitler's Niece,* was published in September 1999. He lives in northern California where he is the Gerard Manley Hopkins S. J. Professor in the Arts and Humanities at Santa Clara University.

Ivan Klíma, born in 1931 in Prague, was editor of the journal of the Czech Writers' Union during the Prague Spring. He has written plays, stories, and novels, though none of these was published in Czechoslovakia until after the fall of the communist regime. After the Velvet Revolution of November 1989 he became the chairman of the revived Czech PEN Center.

Joyce Carol Oates has been nominated two times for the Nobel Prize in Literature and her writing has earned much praise and many awards, including the PEN/Malamud Award for Excellence in short fiction, the

Ronsenthal Award from the American Academy-Institute of Arts and Letters, a Guggenheim Fellowship, the O'Henry Prize for Continued Achievement in the Short Story, and the National Book Award for her novel, *Them*. Her novel *Blonde* was published in April 2000. Other recent publications include *Broken Heart Blues*, *My Heart Laid Bare*, *The Collector of Hearts* (a collection of short stories), and a children's book, *Come Meet Muffin*.

Marlene Nourbese Philip is a poet and writer. She is the author of *Frontiers: Essays and Writings in Racism and Culture* and *She Tries Her Tongue; Her Silence Softly Breaks* for which she received the Casa de las Americas prize. Other prizes include both Guggenheim and MacDowell Fellowships.

Susan Power is the author of *Strong Heart Society* (Penguin Putnam, 1998) and *The Grass Dancer* (Penguin Putnam, 1994).

Reynolds Price has published thirty-three volumes of fiction, poetry, plays, essays, and translations. He is a member of the American Academy of Arts and Letters.

Richard Russo, novelist and screenwriter, is the author of *Mohawk*, *The Risk Pool*, *Nobody's Fool* and *Straight Man*. He wrote the film *Twilight* with Robert Benton. He is currently at work on a new novel and a screenplay.

Susan Fromberg Schaeffer is the author of the novels *Anya*, *The Madness of a Seduced Woman*, *Buffalo Afternoon*, and *The Autobiography of Foudini M. Cat*. Her poetry collection *Granite Lady* was nominated for a National Book Award. Two of her short stories have won O. Henry Awards, including "The Old Farmhouse and the Dog-wife" and "The Exact Nature of Plot."

Lynne Sharon Schwartz's novels include *In the Family Way: An Urban Comedy*, *Leaving Brooklyn*, *The Fatigue Artist*, and *Disturbances in the Field*. She is also the author of *Only Connect?*, a collection of essays, and *Ruined by Books: A Life in Books*.

POETRY

Elizabeth Alexander has published poems in *American Poetry Review*, *Callaloo*, *The American Voice*, *Southern Review*, and other literary journals. She is the author of a number of books, among them the poetry collection *Body of Life* (Tia Chucha, 1996).

Sherman Alexie is the author of several books of poetry, including *The Business of Fancydancing*, *Old Shirts & New Skins*, *First Indian on the Moon*, *The Summer of Black Widows*, and the chapbook *The Man*

Who Loves Salmon. He is also the author of the short story collection *The Lone Ranger and Tonto Fistfight in Heaven* which won a PEN/Hemingway Award for Best First Book of Fiction. This collection served as the basis for his first screenplay *Smoke Signals.* His novel, *Reservation* was the subject of his most recent screenplay.

A. R. Ammons most recent books of poetry include *Glare* (1997), *Brink Road* (1996), *Garbage* (1993), *The Selected Poems* (1987), and *Collected Poems, 1951–71* (1972), all published by Norton.

David Baker is the author of five books of poetry, most recently *The Truth about Small Towns* (1998), as well as *Heresy and the Ideal: On Contemporary Poetry* (2000) and *Meter in English: A Critical Engagement* (1996), all from the University of Arkansas Press. He is poetry editor of *The Kenyon Review* and teaches at Denison University.

Charles Baxter is the author of the novels *The Feast of Love* (Pantheon), *First Light* and *Shadow Play* (both from Penguin); the story collections *Believers* (Vintage) and *Relative Stranger* (Penguin); a collection of poetry *Imaginary Paintings* (Paris Review Editions) and a book of essays *Burning Down the House.*

Robin Becker's most recent collection of poetry is *The Horse Fair* (Pitt Poetry Series, 2000). Her book *All-American Girl* (U of Pittsburgh P, 1996) won the 1996 Lambda Literary Award in Lesbian Poetry. Becker teaches in the MFA Program at Penn State and serves as poetry editor for *The Women's Review of Books.*

Ruth Behar is the author of *Translated Woman: Crossing the Border with Esperanza's Story* (Beacon, 1993) and *The Vulnerable Observer: Anthropology That Breaks Your Heart* (Beacon, 1996), and editor of the anthology *Bridges to Cuba/Puentes a Cuba* (U of Michigan P, 1995). She lives in Ann Arbor and is a professor of Anthropology at the University of Michigan.

Sandra Berris is the editor of *Whetstone.* The recipient of the Hugh J. Luke Award from *Prairie Schooner,* she was also a finalist for the 1996 Randall Jarrell Poetry Prize.

Michael J. Bugeja's recent collections of poetry are *Millennium's End* (Archer) and *Talk* (U of Arkansas P). His poetry has appeared in *Harper's, Poetry,* and *TriQuarterly* among others.

Charles Bukowski was the author of numerous volumes of poetry, beginning with *Flower, Fist and Bestial Wail* (1959), that appeared almost annually. As early as 1963, the year he published *It Catches My Heart in Its Hands*—a collection of poetry about alcoholics, prostitutes, losing gamblers, and down-and-out people—Bukowski had a loyal following.

Scott Cairns's books include *The Theology of Doubt* (1985), *The Translation of Babel* (1990), *Figures for the Ghost* (1994), and *Recovered Body* (1998).

Rafael Campo is the author of *The Other Man Was Me* (Arte Publico, 1994), which won the National Poetry Series award, *What the Body Told* (Duke UP, 1996), which won a Lambda Literary Award for poetry, and a collection of essays *The Poetry of Healing: A Doctor's Education in Empathy, Identity, and Desire* (Norton, 1997), which also won a Lambda Literary Award, for memoir. His newest collection of poems is *Diva* (Duke UP, 1999). He practices and teaches internal medicine at Harvard Medical School and the Beth Israel Deaconess Medical Center in Boston.

Amy Clampitt was the author of many collections of poetry, the most recent *Westward* (Knopf, 1990) and *Predecessor, et Cetera* (U of Michigan P, 1991). *The Collected Poems of Amy Clampitt* was published posthumously by Knopf in 1999.

Judith Ortiz Cofer is the author of a novel *The Line of the Sun*, two collections of essays and poetry: *Silent Dancing* and *The Latin Deli: Prose and Poetry*, and of two books of poetry: *Terms of Survival* and *Reaching for the Mainland*. The recipient of numerous awards, her work has appeared widely in journals and prize series.

Martha Collins's fourth book of poems, *Some Things Words Can Do*, was published by Sheep Meadow in 1998. She is codirector of creative writing at Oberlin College where she also serves as an editor of *Field*.

Peter Cooley has published six books of poetry, the most recent *Sacred Conversations* (Carnegie Mellon).

Jim Daniels is the author of a collection of short stories, *No Pets* (Bottom Dog, 1999) and *Blue Jesus*, a collection of poems (Carnegie Mellon UP, 2000).

Helene Davis is the author of *Chemo-Poet* (Alice James Books). Her poems have appeared in *Southern Poetry Review*, *Black Warrior Review*, and other literary journals.

Toi Derricotte has published four books of poetry. Her latest book, *Tender*, received the Paterson Poetry Prize for 1998. Her memoir, *The Black Notebooks*, chosen by *The New York Times* as a Notable Book of the Year, also received the Black Caucus of the American Library Association Literary Award in Non-Fiction. Her second book, *Natural Birth*, was republished by Firebrand Press in 2000.

Tom Disch is the author of *Clara Reeve* published by Knopf under the pseudonym Leonie Hargrave. An article appeared in *Prairie Schooner* after that book was published trying to prove that Gore Vidal was the author of the book. Now, some twenty-five years later, we offer a correction.

Rita Dove served as Poet Laureate of the United States and Consultant in Poetry to the Library of Congress from 1993 to 1995. She has received numerous literary and academic honors, among them the 1987 Pulitzer Prize in Poetry and the 1996 National Humanities Medal. Her latest poetry collection, *On the Bus with Rosa Parks*, was published by Norton in 1999, and her play *The Darker Face of the Earth*, first produced by the Oregon Shakespeare Festival in 1996, opened at the Royal National Theatre in London in August 1999.

Denise Duhamel is the author of ten books and chapbooks, the most recent of which is *The Star-Spangled Banner* (Crab Orchard, 1999). Her work with Maureen Seaton includes the chapbook *Oyl* (Pearl Street Editions, 1999) and *Exquisite Politics* (Tia Chucha, 1997).

Stephen Dunn is the author of twelve books, ten of which are collections of poems, the newest being *Different Hours* (Norton, 2000).

Cornelius Eady is the author of *The Autobiography of a Jukebox* (Carnegie Mellon UP, 1997), *Victims of the Latest Dance Craze* (Ommation, 1986; Carnegie Mellon UP, 1997), and *You Don't Miss Your Water* (Henry Holt, 1995) among others.

Lynn Emanuel is the author of three books of poetry: *Hotel Fiesta*, *The Dig*, which received the National Poetry Series Award, and *Then, Suddenly*. Her work has been featured in the Pushcart Prize anthology and *Best American Poetry* in 1994, 1995, 1998. She is a professor of English at the University of Pittsburgh where she directs the writing program.

John Engman, recipient of the first Larry Levis Prize for Poetry from *Prairie Schooner* for poems published in the Spring issue 1996, was an adjunct faculty member in the writing program at the University of Minnesota at the time of his death.

Louise Erdrich's most recent books are *Last Report on the Miracles at Little No Horse* (Harper Collins, 2000) and the children's book *The Birchbark House* (Hyperion, 1999).

Jane Flanders has published three books of poetry, most recently *Timepiece* (U of Pittsburgh P). She teaches in The Writing Institute at Sarah Lawrence College.

Carol Frost is the author of several collections, including *Love & Scorn: New & Selected Poems* (TriQuarterly, Northwestern UP, 2000), *Venus & Don Juan* (NUP, 1996), *Pure* (NUP, 1994), and *Chimera* (Peregrine Smith, 1990).

Patricia Goedicke's most recent books include *The Tongues We Speak* (Milkweed, 1989), *Paul Bunyan's Bearskin* (where the poem "Cathay" also appeared, Milkweed, 1992), and *Invisible Horses* (Milkweed, 1996). Her most recent book is *As Earth Begins to End* (Copper Canyon, 1999).

Albert Goldbarth is a recipient of the National Book Critics Circle Award in poetry for *Heaven and Earth*. His recent titles are *Troubled Lovers in History* (Ohio State UP) and a collection of essays, *Dark Waves and Light Matter* (U of Georgia P).

Marilyn Hacker is the author of nine books, including *Presentation Piece*, which received the National Book Award in 1975, *Winter Numbers*, which received a Lambda Literary Award and the Lenore Marshall Award both in 1995, and the verse novel, *Love, Death and the Changing of the Seasons*. *Edge*, her translations of Claire Malroux's work appeared in 1996; *A Long-Gone Sun*, a new book of translations, was published by Sheep Meadow in 2000. Her most recent book *Squares and Courtyards* was published by Norton in 2000. She is the director of the M.A. program in English and creative writing at City College.

Rachel Hadas's most recent book is *Halfway Down the Hall: New & Selected Poems* (Wesleyan, 1998).

Linda Hogan is the author of many books, the most recent being *Intimate Nature* (Fawcett, 1999), *Power* (1998), and *Solar Storms* (Simon & Schuster, 1996).

Jonathan Holden's latest book, *Guns and Boyhood in America: A Memoir of Growing Up in the Fifties* was published in 1997 in the University of Michigan's Poets-on-Poetry Series. His critical text *The Old Formalism: Character in Contemporary American Poetry* was published by the University of Arkansas Press in 1999.

David Ignatow's twentieth and last collection of poetry *Living Is What I Wanted: Last Poems* was published by BOA Editions in 1999.

Richard Jackson is the author of *Heartwall* (U of Mass P, 1999) which was the winner of the Juniper Prize. He is also author of the chapbook *The Half Life of Dreams* (1998) and *Heart's Bridge* (U of Toledo P, 1999).

Phyllis Janowitz is a professor of English at Cornell University. Her first book of poetry, *Rites of Strangers*, was chosen as the first selection in the Associated Writing Program's book competition judged by Elizabeth Bishop in 1978. Her second, selected by Maxine Kumin for Princeton University in 1982, was nominated for the National Book Critics Circle Award. Her most recent book of poems is *Temporary Dwellings* (U of Pittsburgh P, 1988).

Mark Jarman's collection *Questions for Ecclesiastes* won the 1998 Lenore Marshall Poetry Prize. His most recent collection is *Unholy Sonnets* (Story Line, 2000).

Allison Joseph is the author of *What Keeps Us Here* (Ampersand, 1992), *Soul Train* (Carnegie Mellon, 1997), and *In Every Seam* (Pitt Poetry Series, 1997).

Ted Kooser is a retired insurance executive who lives on an acreage near Garland, Nebraska. His latest book of poems, *Winter Morning Walks: One Hundred Postcards to Jim Harrison* is from Carnegie Mellon UP.

Maxine Kumin was awarded the Ruth Lilly Poetry Prize in 1999. She is the author of numerous collections of poetry. Her most recent books are a novel, *Quit Monks or Die* (Story Line, 1999) and a memoir, *Inside the Halo and Beyond: The Anatomy of a Recovery* (Norton, 2000).

Alice Lee has published in many anthologies and literary magazines.

David Lehman, critic, editor, and poet has edited books of essays on John Ashberry and James Merrill (both from Cornell UP). His own recent books are *The Daily Mirror: A Journal in Poetry* (Scribner, 2000) and *Operation Memory* (Princeton UP, 1990). He is the series editor for *The Best American Poetry* (Scribner) and *Poets on Poetry* (U Michigan P).

Cynthia Macdonald has published six books of poetry and teaches at the University of Houston's creative writing program where she is a founder of the program and a former director. She has won many awards including those from the Guggenheim and Rockefeller Foundations, two NEAS for poetry, and a grant from the National Academy of Arts and Letters.

Walt McDonald is a former Air Force pilot and past director of creative writing at Texas Tech. He is the author of seventeen collections of poems, including *Blessings the Body Gave*; *The Flying Dutchman* (Ohio State UP), *Counting Survivors* (Pittsburgh), *Night Landings* (Harper & Row), and *After the Noise of Saigon* (Massachusetts).

Judson Mitchum's collection *Somewhere in Ecclesiastes* (U Missouri P, 1991) won the Devins Award and his novel *The Sweet Everlasting* (U Georgia P, 1996) won the Townsend Prize.

Judith Moffett is the author of nine books in several genres: poetry, Swedish translation, science fiction, literary criticism, and creative nonfiction. Her tenth book, *The North! To the North!/Five Poets of 19th Century Sweden* was published recently by Southern Illinois UP.

Pat Mora is the author of *Tomas & the Library Lady* (Random House, 1997), *Rainbow Tulips* (Viking Penguin, 1999), and *This Big Sky* (Scholastic, 1998).

Les A. Murray is the author of *Collected Poems: The Rabbiter's Bounty* (1991), a poem-novel, *Freddy Neptune* (1999), and *Learning Human: New Selected Poems* (1999) (all from Farrar, Straus & Giroux).

Leonard Nathan's recent books include *The Potato Eaters* (Orchises, 1999) and *Diary of a Left-Handed Bird Watcher* (Graywolf, 1996).

Howard Nemerov held the position of Edward Mallinckrodt Distinguished University Professor of English at Washington University until his death in 1991. Nemerov was a member of the American Academy of Arts and Letters and a fellow of the Academy of American Poets and of the American Academy of Arts and Sciences. Among the dozens of awards he received are the National Book Award, the Pulitzer Prize for poetry, the Bollingen Prize for Poetry, and the National Medal for the Arts in Poetry. He was the author of over three dozen works of fiction, poetry and criticism.

Kathleen Norris's most recent book of poems is *Little Girls in Church* (Pittsburgh). She is also the author of three books of nonfiction: *Dakota*, *The Cloister Walk*, and *Amazing Grace*, all of which were *New York Times* Notable Books of the Year.

Naomi Shihab Nye's most recent books of poems are *Fuel* and *Suitcase* both from BOA Editions. She has edited various anthologies of poems for young readers, the most recent being *What Have You Lost?* (Greenwillow Books).

Ed Ochester's latest books are *Cooking in Key West* (Adastra, 1999), *Snow White Horses: Selected Poems, 1973–1988* (Autumn House, 2000), and *The Land of Cockaigne* (Story Line, 2001).

Sharon Olds's volumes of poetry include *Blood, Tin, Straw* (Knopf, 1999), *The Wellspring* (Knopf, 1996), *What Silence Equals* (Persea, 1993), *The Dead and the Living* (Knopf, 1984), and *Satan Says* (U of Pittsburgh P, 1980).

Carole Simmons Oles is a professor of English at California State University, Chico and coordinator of the California State University MFA Consortium. Her sixth book of poems is *Sympathetic Systems* (2000).

Mary Oliver is the author of *Winter Hours* (Houghton Mifflin, 1999), *American Primitive*(Little, Brown, 1998), *Twelve Moons* (Little, Brown, 1998), and *A Poetry Handbook* (Houghton Mifflin, 1994) among others.

Alicia Ostriker has been twice a finalist for the National Book Award in Poetry. Her most recent volume is *The Little Space: Poems Selected and New* (1998). As a critic, she is the author of *The Emergence of Women's Poetry in America*. She has received awards from the Guggenheim Foundation, the Rockefeller Foundation, the National Endowment for the Arts, the Poetry Society of America, and *Prairie Schooner*.

Eric Pankey is the author of *For the New Year* and *Heartwood*.

Linda Pastan's tenth book, *Carnival Evening: New and Selected Poems 1968–1998* was a finalist for the National Book Award.

Michael Pettit is the author of *American Light; Cardinal Points; Writing Path 1* and *Writing Path 2*.

Alberto Ríos is the author of seven books and chapbooks of poetry, including *Teodoro Luna's Two Kisses* (Norton, 1992), and two collections of short stories, including *Pig Cookies* (Chronicle, 1997) and *Capirotada: A Nogales Memoir* (U New Mexico P, 1999). He is the recipient of numerous awards and fellowships, including those from the Guggenheim Foundation and the NEA.

Pattiann Rogers is the author of nine books and has received a Guggenheim Fellowship, a Lannan Poetry Fellowship, five Pushcart Prizes, two Strousse Awards from *Prairie Schooner*, and three prizes from *Poetry*. Her book, *Firekeeper, New & Selected Poems* was named one of the Best Books Published in 1994 by *Publishers Weekly*.

Liz Rosenberg's poem "Crushed: Chapter Nine" appears in her book of prose poems *These Happy Eyes* published by Mammoth Press.

Hillel Schwartz's most recent book is *The Culture of the Copy* (Zone, 1996). He was reprinted in *Best American Poetry* in 1997 and was the winner of the Richard Hugo Prize from *Poetry Northwest*.

Maureen Seaton is the author of three books of poetry, *Furious Cooking* (U of Iowa P), *The Sea Among the Cupboards* (New Rivers), and *Fear of Subways* (The Eighth Mountain Press). She is the recipient of an Illinois Art's grant and an NEA Fellowship. With Denise Duhamel, she is the author of *Exquisite Politics* (Tia Chucha, 1997) and *Oyl* (Pearl).

Dave Smith is the author of numerous volumes of poetry, including *The Wick of Memory: New and Selected Poems, 1970–2000, Floating on Solitude* (U of Illinois P, 1996), and *Fate's Kite* (Louisiana State UP, 1995) and criticism, including *Local Assays: On Contemporary American Poetry* (U Illinois P).

Gary Soto is the author of numerous children's books, including *Buried Onions* (Harcourt, 1997; HarperCollins, 2000), volumes of poetry, and the memoir *Living Up the Street* (Dell, 1992). He has received many awards and honors including a Guggenheim Fellowship.

Marcia Southwick's most recent poetry book is the winner of the Field Poetry Prize, *A Saturday Night at the Flying Dog* (Oberlin, 1999). Her work was reprinted in *Best American Poetry* in 1999 and in 1998 she won a Pushcart Prize.

Ruth Stone teaches at the State University of New York at Binghamton in the English Department. She is the author of *Ordinary Voices*

(Paris, 1999), *Simplicity* (Paris, 1995), and *Second Hand Coat Who is the Widow's Muse* (Yellow Moon, 1987).

Stephanie Strickland's book of poems, *True North*, won the Poetry Society of America's Di Castagnola Prize and appeared as the Sandeen Prize volume from the University of Notre Dame Press. Her other books include *The Red Virgin: A Poem of Simone Weil* (U of Wisconsin P, winner of the Brittingham Prize) and *Give the Body Back* (U of Missouri P).

Terese Svoboda is the author of *Mere Mortals* (U of Georgia P, 1995), *Laughing Africa* (U of Iowa P, 1990), and *All Aberration* (U of Georgia 1985).

Karen Swenson's poetry volume *The Landlady in Bangkok* was a National Poetry Series winner. *A Daughter's Latitude*, her new and selected, was published by Copper Canyon in 1999.

Richard Tayson's first book of poetry, *The Apprentice of Fever*, won the 1997 Wick Poetry Prize and was published by the Kent State University Press in 1998. Other awards include a Pushcart Prize and a *Prairie Schooner* Bernice Slote Award. His coauthored book of nonfiction, *Look Up for Yes*, has appeared on the bestseller lists in Germany. Tayson teaches on-line writing workshops for the New School for Social Research in New York City.

Chase Twitchell's most recent books include *The Snow Watcher* (1998) and *The Ghost of Eden* (1995, both from Ontario Review P).

Reetika Vazirani is the author of *White Elephants* (Beacon, 1996). She is the Banister Writer-in-Residence at Sweet Briar College and a contributing editor for *Shenandoah*. The recipient of a Pushcart Prize, she has earned fellowships from Bread Loaf and the Sewanee Writers conferences and a Discovery/*The Nation* award.

Karen Volkman is the author of the poetry collection *Crash's Law* (Norton, 1996).

David Wagoner is a poet, novelist, and professor. His most recent book is *Traveling Light: Collected and New Poems* (U Illinois P, 1999).

Diane Wakoski is a writer-in-residence at Michigan State University. Her book *Emerald Ice: Selected Poems 1962–1987* was the winner of the William Carlos William's Prize. Her most recent book is *Argonaut Rose* (Black Sparrow, 1999).

Ronald Wallace's recent books include the story collection *Quick Bright Things* (Mid-List, 2000), collected poems *The Uses of Adversity* (U of Pittsburgh P, 1998), and *Time's Fancy* (U of Pittsburgh, 1994). He is Felix Pollak Professor of Poetry at the University of Wisconsin-Madison.

Bruce Weigl is the author of ten collections of poetry, most recent *Song of Napalm* (Atlantic Monthly, 1988), *What Saves Us* (TriQuarterly Books, 1999), and *Archeology of the Circle: New and Selected Poems* (Grove/Atlantic, 1999). For his work, he has been awarded the Paterson Poetry Prize, the Pushcart Prize twice, and a prize from the Academy of American Poets.

James L. White published four books of poetry before his death, the last being *The Salt Ecstasies* (Graywolf).

Peter Wild is the author of *The Opal Desert: Explorations of Fantasy and Reality in the American Southwest* (U of Texas P, 1999).

Eleanor Wilner's most recent books are *Reversing the Spell: New & Selected Poems* (Copper Canyon, 1998) and a translation of Euripides' *Medea* (Penn Greek Series, U of Pennsylvania P, 1998).

David Wojahn is the author of five collections of poetry, most recently *The Falling Hour* (U of Pittsburgh P, 1997). He is director of the program in creative writing at Indiana University and also teaches in the MFA writing program at Vermont College.